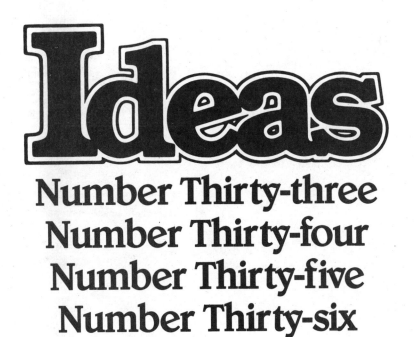

# Ideas

## Number Thirty-three
## Number Thirty-four
## Number Thirty-five
## Number Thirty-six

Four Complete Volumes of Ideas in One

Edited by
Wayne Rice

Previously published as four separate books

# Your Idea May Be Worth $100

It's worth at least $15 if we publish it in a future volume of **Ideas**. And it's worth $100 if it's chosen as the outstanding idea of the book it appears in.

It's not really a contest, though—just our way of saying thanks for sharing your creativity with us. If you have a good idea that worked well with your group, send it in. We'll look it over and decide whether or not we can include it in a future **Ideas** book. If we do, we'll send you at least 15 bucks!

In addition to that, our **Ideas** editor will select one especially creative idea from each new book as the outstanding idea of that particular book—and send a check for $100 to its contributor.

So don't let your good ideas go to waste. Write them down and send them to us, accompanied by this card. Explain your ideas completely (without getting ridiculous) and include illustrations, diagrams, photos, samples, or any other materials you think are helpful.

## FILL OUT BELOW

Name _____

Address _____

City _____ State _____ Zip _____

I hereby submit the attached idea(s) to Youth Specialties for publication in **Ideas** and guarantee that, to my knowledge, the publication of these ideas by Youth Specialties does not violate any copyright belonging to another party. I also understand that I will receive payment for these ideas, the exact amount to be determined by Youth Specialties, payable upon publication in **Ideas**.

Signature _____

Write or type your idea(s) (one idea per sheet) and attach to this form or to a copy of this form. Include your name and address with each idea you send. Mail to Youth Specialties, 1224 Greenfield Drive, El Cajon, CA 92021. Ideas submitted to Youth Specialties cannot be returned.

ISBN 0-910125-33-3 (Ideas Combo 33-36)
ISBN 0-910125-00-7 (Ideas Complete Library, Volumes 1-52)

Ideas in this book have been voluntarily submitted by individuals and groups who claim to have used them in one form or another with their youth groups. You will need to evaluate each idea on its own merit for its appropriateness to the needs and personality of your group, potential risk, safety precautions that must be taken, advance preparation that might be required, and possible results before you use it. Youth Specialties, Inc., is not responsible for, nor has it any control over, the use or misuse of any of the ideas published in this book.

# Ideas Combo 33-36

# CONTENTS

# CROWD BREAKERS

## Balloon Surprise

Here's a crazy stunt that is a lot of fun. Before your meeting, carefully insert a small amount of shaving cream into four or five balloons. Then, blow them up and tie them as usual. Next, blow up a number of "regular" balloons.

Announce to your group that you need some volunteers for a balloon-popping race. The trick is that they have to pop the balloons by biting them. For every "popper" have a "helper" who will quickly pass the balloons. Clue in the helpers to save the loaded balloons for last.

Begin the race as usual, with helpers and poppers frantically at work, keeping a tally of the number of balloons popped. Just before the time is up, signal the helpers to pass on the joke balloons and watch the fun.

As a safety precaution, tell the kids to keep their eyes closed when they are popping the balloons. Or, if you want to be a little nicer, substitute whipped cream for the shaving cream. (Contributed by John Stumbo, Monticello, MN)

1

# Bible "Crazy Clues"

Here's a word game that involves names and books of the Bible. Each kid is given the list of "clues" on the next page and asked to write in the biblical name that fits each clue. While it's only a game, it can help kids remember names and places in the Bible.

Thinking up clues like these can be just as much fun as solving them. Have the kids divide into teams and allow each group to come up with ten of their own clues. Here's how to do it:

First, think of the word or name you will be using as the answer. Second, imagine what that word or name immediately brings to your mind by association, sound, or spelling. Then, write a sentence that describes it

and—presto!—you have a crazy clue.

Collect the clues from all the teams. If you have time, make a master list of clues, make copies, and distribute them for everyone to solve. Otherwise, read clues aloud one at a time and have each team record its answer privately. Then go through the answers together and score: Each team gets one point for solving a clue from any other team, and one point for every clue they have written which stumps the rest of the group. If the total group (by consensus) agrees that the unsolvable clue is misleading or poorly written, however, then no points are awarded. (Contributed by Bill Gnegy, Hanover, IN)

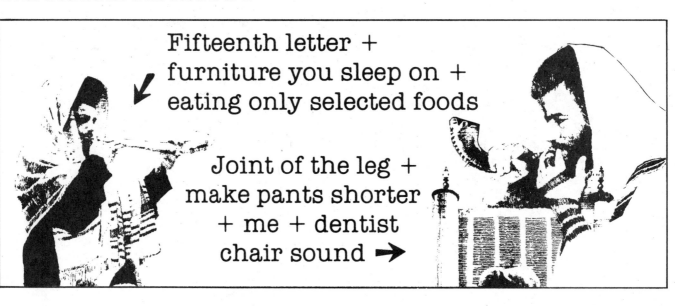

Fifteenth letter + furniture you sleep on + eating only selected foods

Joint of the leg + make pants shorter + me + dentist chair sound →

Answers:
1. Song of Solomon
2. Daniel (Dan-yell)
3. Proverbs (pro-verbs)
4. Ezra
5. Luke
6. Corinthians (core-in-the-hands)
7. Galatians (Gail-Asians)
8. Titus (tight-us)
9. Genesis (Jenny's sis)
10. Joel (Joe-will)
11. Obadiah (O-bed-diet)
12. Mark
13. Jonah
14. Jude ("Hey Jude")
15. Timothy (timid-Thee)
16. Ruth (Babe Ruth)
17. Leviticus (levy-to-kiss)
18. Chronicles
19. Ezekiel (easy-kill)
20. Nahum (neigh-hum)
21. Matthew (book of New Testament)
22. Hosea (hose-ea)
23. James (Jimmy Carter)
24. Hebrews
25. Deuteronomy (due-to-Ron-and-me)
26. Esther
27. Lamentations (lamb-men-day-shuns)
28. Zechariah and Zephaniah (disease = "the z's")
29. Acts (ax)
30. Thessalonians (the-saloonians)
31. Kings
32. Job
33. Jeremiah
34. Revelation
35. Peter (he denied Christ)
36. Exodus (exit-us)
37. Psalms (in middle of Bible)
38. Isaiah (I-say-ah)
39. Samuel (Sam-mule)
40. Micah (my-cah)
41. John (Johnny Bench)
42. Malachi (mail-a-chi)
43. Romans (Rome-ants) or (Romance)
44. Philemon (file-lemon)
45. Joshua (walls of Jericho)
46. Ecclesiastes (Ekkly's siestas)
47. Habakkuk (a-bad-cook)
48. Amos (a-miss)
49. Numbers
50. Judges (give jail sentences)
51. Ephesians (a-fee-shun)
52. Nehemiah (knee-hem-I-AH)
53. Philippians (Flippians)
54. Haggai (Hey guy!)

## BOOKS OF THE BIBLE "CRAZY CLUES"

1. A wise king's tune
2. If little Danny lets out a scream, it is a...
3. If you are not opposed to words denoting action, you are...
4. A "captive speaker" for the Jews
5. Not actually hot, just _____ warm
6. If you are holding the middle of an apple in your palms
7. Two Asian women named Gail
8. Ballerinas wear these on their leg-us
9. Sister to Jennifer
10. Joseph agrees to do something. You could say that...
11. Fifteenth letter + furniture you sleep on + eating only selected foods
12. Right on! You really hit the...
13. A "whale" of a good book
14. Word in the title of a famous Beatles song
15. If a man named "Thee" was shy, he would be a...
16. Famous baseball player's last name given to him when he was just a babe
17. A tax on smooching
18. Newspapers
19. A murder that is not difficult
20. The sound of a horse that forgot the words to a song
21. The first of the Bible's new writers
22. You water your grass-ea with a...
23. Formal first name of the U.S. president in 1978
24. The Jews, the Israelites, the...
25. Ronny and I are collecting an inheritance. We're getting what is...
26. A famous swimmer named Williams
27. A young sheep + males + not night + avoids
28. Two answers: Disease of the Old Testament
29. You get this when you're fired
30. The persons born in the old western saloons
31. Higher than Queens
32. An employment
33. A famous bullfrog in a Three Dog Night Tune
34. A confusing look at what lies ahead
35. You can't deny this Bible writer
36. When we leave
37. The "central" book of the Bible
38. The way a shy person might greet a stranger
39. A donkey named Sammy
40. How a person from Brooklyn would introduce his auto. "This is..."
41. Formal first name of a Cincinnati Red who rarely sat on the bench
42. If you wanted to ship a Greek letter to someone you might...
43. What insects at picnics are called in Italy's chief city
44. What file would you classify a sour yellow fruit in?
45. A successful demolition man
46. When George Ekkly takes naps in Spain
47. Not a good chef
48. Not a hit
49. 6 12 18 43 55 76
50. People who must pronounce their sentences well
51. Refusing to pay a doctor's bill
52. Joint of the leg + make pants shorter + me + dentist chair sound
53. Two people born in Flippy, Montana
54. If you're yelling at a strange man from across the room, you might scream...

---

# Color Your Neighbor

Give your group an assortment of **watercolor** markers, and allow them to paint and draw on each other's faces, arms, hands and feet for about a half hour. Then have a "beauty contest" and award prizes to the winners. Kids will love it.

Afterwards, provide soap and water so that the kids can wash the artwork off before they go home, or you may be getting some interesting phone calls from parents. Most water-based markers will come off easily, although some colors (black, purple) are rather stubborn. (Contributed by Dave Barr, Cincinnati, OH)

# Compliment Contest

If some of your kids have trouble saying nice things to each other, try this. It makes a competitive contest out of giving compliments.

Have the group sit in a circle, and put one person in a chair in the middle of the circle. The person in the middle gets to choose two people: one will be complimented, and the other will compete with him or her in complimenting the first person.

Both give their compliments, and the person who is the object of the compliments decides which compliment he or she likes the best. Of course, they may have trouble deciding, but they must choose one over the other. The person whose compliment was not chosen must then take the center chair.

A variation is to have the person in the middle be the recipient of compliments from two people he or she chooses. Then the winning compliment-er takes that person's place in the center and gets to receive compliments next. A game like this can help kids get used to the idea of building each other up. (Contributed by Paul Mason, Colorado Springs, CO)

# Fuzzy Fotos

Collect a number of 35mm slides which contain recognizable objects, places, or people on them. Then show them to your group, but begin by showing them terribly out of focus. Slowly bring each picture into focus and see who can be first to identify correctly the person, place, or thing on the slide.

The secret is in your previewing the slides, carefully choosing those which give odd effects and misleading shapes when out of focus. Cartoons make good choices, as well as pictures from magazine ads. You will also need to practice s-l-o-w-l-y bringing slides into focus in a smooth motion. It's great fun. (Contributed by Carlita Hunter, Harrisburg, NC)

# Guess Whoo

For an easy get-acquainted activity, ask each young person to write down something about themselves that probably no one else knows. If they have trouble coming up with a unique contribution, suggest an unusual pet they might have, or a weird snack or sandwich they like. If you get really desperate, ask for their mother's middle name. Collect all the responses.

Next, instruct the group to listen to the clues as you read them and try to guess the person they think the clue identifies. Give 1,000 points for each correct guess, everyone keeping his own score. For a prize, give away a copy of the church directory or an address book to write in things they learned about people in the group. (Contributed by Jim Bourne, Douglas, GA)

# Ice Breaker

Here's a mixer that takes the idea of an "icebreaker" literally. Kids sit in a circle (on the floor or around a table) with a bucket of square ice cubes close by. As each person around the circle gives his or her name, he or she must place an ice cube on the ground or on the table. Each cube must go on top of the previous cube, with players attempting to stack them as high as possible. The object is to see who can achieve the highest stack of ice cubes before they all fall over.

The name sharing can be done a variety of ways. One good way is for each person to give his or her name, described by an adjective beginning with the same initial (e.g., "Goofy Gary"). Then, as each person gives a name in succession, they must repeat all those

previously given in order without making a mistake. (Contributed by Keith Curran, Huntingdon, PA)

---

# Mangled Mother Goose

Below are a number of "newspaper headlines" which correspond to familiar Mother Goose rhymes. See how many of them your young people can recognize. Print them up on a sheet of paper and distribute to the group, giving them about five minutes to identify all 30. Give a prize (a Mother Goose book?) to the winner. (Contributed by Doug Newhouse, Florence, KY)

1. "Mother Disciplines Daughter Astraddle Cinders"
2. "Pumpkin Shell Solves Marital Problems"
3. "Farmer's Spouse Attacked by Rodents"
4. "Girl Terrified by Spider"
5. "Married Couple Eat Heartily"
6. "Men and Mounts Fail To Revive Crash Victim"
7. "Wool Supply Sufficient, Inquiry Reveals"
8. "Unique Pie Served Royalty"
9. "Dogs Herald Pauper's Appearance"
10. "Pig Thief Punished"
11. "Command Performance By Violinists"
12. "Poverty Strikes Home: Dog Starves"
13. "Pupil Queried About Tardiness"
14. "Appreciation of Porridge Varies"
15. "Tart Thief Repents"
16. "Scoundrels Bathe Together"
17. "Swine Sale"
18. "Animals Display Human Actions"
19. "Accident Occurs at Well"
20. "Girl Grows Garden"
21. "High Jump Skills Displayed"
22. "Amorous Advances Rejected"
23. "Lost Lambs Distressing"
24. "Lamb Incites School Riot"
25. "Bugler Sleeps on Job"
26. "Cat Tours London"
27. "Christmas Pie Reveals Character"
28. "Multi-Colored Hamper Appealing"
29. "Directions to London Given"
30. "Swine Tour, Eat, and Weep"

Answers:

1. Little Polly Flinders
2. Peter, Peter, Pumpkin-Eater
3. Three Blind Mice
4. Little Miss Muffet
5. Jack Sprat
6. Humpty Dumpty
7. Baa, Baa, Black Sheep
8. Sing a Song of Sixpence
9. Hark, Hark! The Dogs Do Bark!
10. Tom, Tom, the Piper's Son
11. Old King Cole
12. Old Mother Hubbard
13. A Diller, a Dollar, a Ten O'Clock Scholar
14. Pease Porridge Hot
15. Queen of Hearts
16. Rub-A-Dub-Dub
17. To Market, To Market
18. Hey, Diddle, Diddle!
19. Jack and Jill or Ding Dong Bell
20. Mary, Mary, Quite Contrary
21. Jack Be Nimble
22. Georgy Porgy
23. Little Bo-Peep
24. Mary Had a Little Lamb
25. Little Boy Blue
26. Pussy-Cat, Pussy-Cat
27. Little Jack Horner
28. A Tisket, A Tasket
29. See, Saw, Sacradown
30. This Little Piggy

## More What's the Meaning?

Here are a few more "What's the Meaning?" riddles to try on your kids. These can be done individually or in teams. The object is to decipher each word picture. Print up copies to distribute to each person. Give a prize to whoever comes up with the most correct answers.

**1.** STANDARD STANDARD

**2.** *TOP* SHAPE

**3.** X

**4.** TAKE
TAKE

**5.** BAN ANA

**6.** EDGE

**7.** OPTIONS
OPTIONS
OPTIONS

**8.** PIERRE

**9.** LOREJOICERD

**10.** BULL
HE SPOKE TO THEM
BULL

**11.** MOSES

**12.** MWHOSOEVER BELIEVESE

**13.** BELIEVE
LORD JESUS CHRIST

**14.** VICTORY
——————
SIN DEATH

**15.** JUSTIFICATION/FAITH

**16.** WAY

**17.** E

(Contributed by Sr. Diane Burgess, Corpus Christi, TX and Herbert Saunders, Milton, WI)

1. Double Standard
2. Tip-Top Shape
3. Crossed Eyes
4. Double Take
5. Banana Split
6. Rough Edge
7. Several Options
8. French Curve
9. Rejoice in the Lord
10. He Spoke to them in parables
11. Go Down Moses
12. Whosoever Believes in Me
13. Believe on the Lord Jesus Christ
14. Victory over sin and death
15. Justification by Faith
16. Narrow Way
17. Sunny

6

# Name That Place

This game is great for a small group divided into two teams, or for a group split into several teams. Find a book that has pictures of a number of recognizable spots in your city, or go on a photo spree and take some yourself. Once the group is divided into teams, hold up a picture for them to see. The group that is first to correctly identify the spot wins a point. The team with the most points wins.

If it is too hard for everyone to see the photos, you could photocopy the pictures, or use slides and put them up on a large screen. The team that correctly identifies the most pictures in a given amount of time wins.

Make sure that you include a wide variety of photos—some that are easy to identify like the city hall or the high school, and some that are difficult, like a pond in a certain park or a tree on a street near the church. (Contributed by Jan Bartley, Cincinnati, OH)

# Number Nonsense

Here are several "tricks" that are easy and fun to do, seem baffling to the kids in your youth group and make you appear to be a genius. Try 'em sometime just for fun. It's best to memorize each procedure, and pull them out like you do it all the time.

**1. CHOOSE A NUMBER:** Suggest that someone in your group (or the entire group secretly) choose a number between 10 and 100. This number is not to be told to the leader. He proceeds to find out what the number is. Let's say that the number is 44.

| | |
|---|---|
| **Number selected** | **44** |
| **Double it** | **88** |
| **Add 1** | **89** |
| **Multiply by 5** | **445** |
| **Add 5** | **450** |
| **Multiply by 10** | **4500** |

The leader now subtracts 100 from the result without saying anything. Thus 100 from 4500 is 4400. Strike off the last two digits and announce the number is 44.

**2. THE AGE OF YOUR POCKET CHANGE:** Have someone in your

group think of their age (without telling anyone). Have them double it, and then add five, and then multiply by 50. Now add to that number the amount of pocket change someone else has in their pocket. Now have them subtract the number of days in a year—365—from that number. At this point the number can be disclosed to the entire group. To this number you (the leader) secretly add 115. The age of the person will be the first two digits. The amount of change will be indicated by the last two digits.

The person's age . . . . . . . . 15
Double the person's age. . . 30
Add 5. . . . . . . . . . . . . . . . 35
Multiply by 50 . . . . . . . 1750
Add pocket change
(37¢). . . . . . . . . . . . . . 1787
Subtract 365 days in the
year . . . . . . . . . . . . . . . 1422
(this number is given to
group)
Secretly add 115 . . . . . . . 1537

You announce that the age is 15 and the amount of change in the pocket is 37 cents.

**3. WHEN WAS I BORN?** The leader announces that he can guess the age and the month of birth of anybody in the group. He gives the volunteer the following instructions:

Write down the number of the month you were born (August). . . . . . . . . . . . . . . . 8
Double it . . . . . . . . . . . . . 16
Add 5. . . . . . . . . . . . . . . . 21
Multiply by 50 . . . . . . . 1050
Add your age (16). . . . . . 1066
Subtract the number of days in a year (365) . . . . . . . . . 701

The leader then calls for the result; he secretly adds 115, making the total 816. He immediately announces August as the month of birth and 16 as the age. The first one or two digits indicate the month and the last two indicate the age.

**4. SECRET NUMBER:** This simple trick furnishes fun as the kids try to figure it out. Ask someone to select a number, keeping it a secret. Now ask them to double it, then to multiply by five, and then to tell you the total. Immediately you are able to tell them the secret number. All you have to do is to knock off the final digit, for what you have really done is to get the number multiplied by 10. Example: the number selected is 13. Multiplied by 2 it is 26. Multiplied by 5 it is 130. Knock off the last digit and it is 13, the secret number. This may be worked on a crowd, the teller staying outside the room while the group decides on the secret number.

(Contributed by Russ Matzke, Colorado Springs, Colorado)

---

# Oh, No!

Here's a fun mixer for your next meeting or social event. Give everyone a few "tokens," such as marbles, poker chips, clothespins, or whatever. Everyone should begin with the same number of tokens. Then allow the group to mingle and talk to each other.

Whenever someone says either a word "no" or "know," that person must give one of his or her tokens to the person with whom he or she is talking. It's difficult to avoid saying those two words in normal conversation, so this game produces lots of good laughs. Give a prize to the one who collects the most tokens. (Contributed by Charles V. Boucher, Ocean Park, ME)

## Puzzling Proverbs

Here's another "brain teaser" that can be used a variety of ways. Below are 40 proverbs in abbreviated form. Each line represents a saying in which the key words have been replaced by initials. For example, "The R. to H. is P. with G.I." stands for "The road to hell is paved with good intentions."

You can print up this list in its entirety and pass it out to your group to see who can solve the most proverbs. Or divide into teams and have each group pool their problem-solving abilities. Another approach is to write the abbreviated proverbs on the blackboard one at a time. Teams then try to see who can be first to yell out the correct solution. To adjust the level of difficulty to your group, use more or fewer full words in the clues. For example, "The proof of the pudding is in the eating" could be "The P. of the P. is in the E."; "The P. O. the P. I. I. the E."; or "T. P. O. T. P. I. I. T. E."

This game could be tied in with some positive learning by discussing some of these proverbs in light of scripture and personal experiences. (Contributed by Doug Newhouse and Tommy Baker, Florence, KY)

1. Y. Can L. a H. to W., but Y. can't M. H. D.
2. A R. S. G. no M.
3. O. and W. don't M.
4. A P. S. is a P. E.
5. N. V., N. G.
6. E. to B., E. to R., M. a M. H., W. and W.
7. The L. of M. is the R. of all E.
8. A S. in T. S. 9.
9. A W. P. never B.
10. If at F. Y. don't S., T., T. A.
11. The S. W. gets the O.
12. S. the R. and S. the C.
13. S. and Y. shall F.
14. H. who H. is L.
15. B. is only S. D.
16. M. H. while the S. S.
17. I. too L. to C. the B. D. after the H. E.
18. A C. S. on a H. cannot be H.
19. N. is the M. of I.
20. A F. in N. is a F. I.
21. A B. in the H. is W. 2 in the B.
22. S. is G.
23. C. should be S. and not H.
24. Don't C. Y. P. before S.
25. W. G. for the G. is G. for the G.
26. A F. and H. M. are S. P.
27. Y. C. J. a B. by its C.
28. P. is as P. D.
29. Don't C. Y. C. before T. H.
30. C. is N. to G.
31. W. there's S. there's F.
32. P. is a V.
33. T. and T. W. for no M.
34. Don't C. over S. M.
35. S. W. R. D.
36. A. is no R. of P.
37. Don't P.O. till T. W. Y. can D. T.
38. I. an I. W. that B. N. G.
39. P. who L. in G. H. shouldn't T. S.

ANSWERS:
1. You can lead a horse to water, but you can't make him drink.
2. A rolling stone gathers no moss.
3. Oil and water don't mix.
4. A penny saved is a penny earned.
5. Nothing ventured, nothing gained.
6. Eary to bed, early to rise, makes a man healthy, wealthy and wise.
7. The love of money is the root of all evil.
8. A stitch in time saves nine.
9. A watched pot never boils.
10. If at first you don't succeed, try, try again.
11. The squeaky wheel gets the oil.
12. Spare the rod and spoil the child.
13. Seek and ye shall find.
14. He who hesitates is lost.
15. Beauty is only skin deep.
16. Make hay while the sun shines.
17. It's too late to close the barn door after the horse escapes.

18. A city set on a hill cannot be hidden.
19. Necessity is the mother of invention.
20. A friend in need is a friend indeed.
21. A bird in the hand is worth two in the bush.
22. Silence is golden.
23. Children should be seen and not heard.
24. Don't cast your pearls before swine.
25. What's good for the goose is good for the gander.
26. A fool and his money are soon parted.
27. You can't judge a book by its cover.
28. Pretty is as pretty does.
29. Don't count your chickens before they hatch.
30. Cleanliness is next to godliness.
31. Where there's smoke there's fire.
32. Patience is a virtue.
33. Time and tide wait for no man.
34. Don't cry over spilt milk.
35. Still water runs deep.
36. Age is no respecter of persons.
37. Don't put off till tomorrow what you can do today.
38. It's an ill wind that blows no good.
39. People who live in glass houses shouldn't throw stones.

# Story-Song Skits

Remember the records we listened to as children? Over and over we played them until we knew every word. Here is a way to use all of those old familiar story-songs and get a good laugh with your youth group.

Divide your group into several smaller groups and give each group a cassette recording of one of these children's songs. (Check local record stores in the children's sections for songs if necessary. The cornier, the better!) Each group should also get a cassette player.

Each group must pantomime the entire song—music, speaking parts, narration, movements—and dress accordingly. Give them enough time to prepare their outfits and practice a little. Then take turns presenting the story-songs. The result is great! And to insure plenty of long-lasting laughs, tape it all on video! (Contributed by Doug Newhouse, Florence, KY)

# The Twelve Days of Class

Using the tune to "The Twelve Days of Christmas," here's a song to sing just after Christmas vacation, during finals week, or any time your kids feel overwhelmed by school:

**On the _____ day of school, my teacher gave to me: _____**
(Insert the words below in the blanks for the 12 verses.)

1st a headache when the final bell rang
2nd two study halls
3rd three pop quizzes
4th four research projects
5th five themes to write
6th six math problems
7th seven book reports
8th eight Home Ec projects
9th nine lab experiments
10th ten biology dissections
11th eleven art assignments
12th twelve history books to read

Another way to enjoy this song is to write the verses on pieces of paper and have each person draw one out of a hat or bowl. Give them five minutes to find others with that same verse. Then sing the song together on the first line, with each group singing their assigned part as it comes up in the song. (Contributed by Allen Johnson, Hannibal, MO)

## Wake-Up Calls

Here's an idea that can be lots of fun, but it takes a little work. Get a group of youth sponsors together who are willing to get up early on Saturday mornings. Then go to several of your young people's homes before they wake up (with parents' permission, of course) and wake the kids in their bedrooms. Take a camera along, and photograph them as they crawl out of bed, bleary-eyed in their pajamas. Then simply leave.

After collecting a good number of these pictures, use them for a hilarious slide show at one of your youth meetings. Kids will love to see each other looking half-asleep. This could be used as a fund-raiser by asking kids to pay a certain amount to **not** have their picture shown. The money can then be donated to one of the group's mission projects. (Contributed by David C. Wright, Vienna, VA)

# CHAPTER TWO

# GAMES

## Ambitions

This game is fun for all ages. Two groups sit in a circle or along the walls. Ask them each in turn to mime an ambition or occupation. The player that guesses the answer should raise his hand, but let the mime continue until everyone gets it. Some ambitions can be really fun to act out, such as rock singer, actor, Miss Universe, astronaut and others. (Contributed by F.W. Swallow, Auckland, New Zealand)

## Aquatic Baseball

The swimming pool game can be a lot of fun without being too hectic. You will need a rubber ball, or volley ball, and a medium-sized pool. Divide the group into two equal teams. The team that is up sits along the side and provides the pitcher. The other team is distributed throughout the pool.

The batter gets only one pitch and must hit the ball with his or her hand. Anywhere inside the pool is a fair ball. The batter must then swim to the bases using any course he chooses to avoid an out. Outs are counted if the ball goes out of the pool, if the ball is

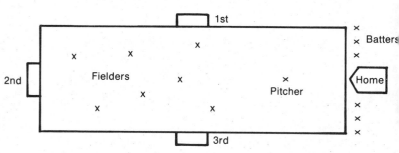

caught in the air, if the player is tagged with the ball before reaching the base, or if the ball is thrown to first base before he reaches it. The other rules are the same as regular baseball—or you may agree to some additional rules of your own. (Contributed by Russell Saito, Haleiwa, HI)

## Balloon Burst

Divide your group into two teams and pick a captain for each. Arrange them as diagrammed below. Each team tries to hit the balloon in the

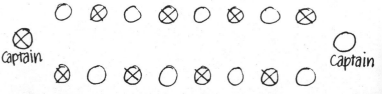

direction of its captain, who will then burst the balloon with a pin. One point is scored for each balloon burst.

Players must stay seated and use only one hand. (Contributed by Kathie Taylor, Carpentersville, IL)

# Basket Brawl

Here's a co-ed basketball game that can be played with both junior and senior highers together. Divide your youth group into two teams. Try to distribute boys, girls, tall kids, short kids, junior highers, and senior highers, equally among the teams to make the competition as fair as possible. Each team should also have an adult captain to help everyone get organized. It doesn't matter how many are on the team, and even the adults can play.

Give each team identifying armbands. There should also be a scorekeeper, a time keeper, a referee, and any other officials you desire.

The game is a continously-played, seven-period, 21-minute game. Each period is three minutes long and involves players from a particular category or mix of categories such as:

1. **Mixed players** (boys, girls, junior highers, senior highers)—five players per team on the floor. Only girls can score.
2. **Junior highers only.**
3. **Senior highers only.**
4. **Girls only.**
5. **Guys only.**
6. **Mixed guys and girls.** Only guys can shoot, and only girls can carry the ball. Girls must move the ball to the boys who shoot. Five players per team on the floor.
7. **Everybody!** The entire team plays in the grand finale. If you have "ball hogs" who tend to dominate the

game, you can insert an alternating rule: a guy shoots, then a girl, then a guy, and so on.

The clock never stops. A period is indicated by banging a pan lid with a wooden spoon at the end of three minutes. The team captains should have a period order sheet so that they can have their teams ready to change. If a team scores while the other team is getting organized, the point counts.

The referee needs a whistle, but he can only stop the game for an injury. The ref can call fouls if they are serious and continuous. Keep in mind that many younger kids may not know how to play basketball, so fouls may be unavoidable. But if flagrant fouls are being committed, just award free points to the other team rather than stopping to shoot free throws.

Each basket can be worth any number of points you choose, or a different number of points in different periods. The winner of the game can be the team with the most points or the team that wins the most periods.

You can adjust other rules as needed to deal with dribbling, boundaries, rotating players, and so on. The object of the game is to allow everyone to play and have a great time. Anything you can do to make that happen is good. (Contributed by Mark Simone, Ravenna, OH)

# Bedlam Ball

This is a game that would be good to kick off a camp or retreat, since it can accommodate a couple hundred kids divided into four teams. It is really a combination of several games. You play football, soccer, basketball, frisbee, and giant pushball. The catch is all four teams play all five games at the same time, in the same place.

You will need four soccer-type goals. They can be made out of P.V.C. pipe if you want to build your own.

Place these goals on the playing field equally distant from the center. With some field chalk, line a defensive zone. This zone is five yards wide on each side of goal, and ten yards in front. In the center of the field, place the giant pushball, ten footballs, ten basketballs, twenty frisbees, and ten soccer balls. (You could add more or less depending on the size of your group.)

The objective of Bedlam Ball is two-fold. One is to protect your goal. The final winner is the team

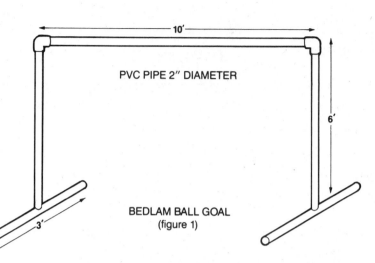

PVC PIPE 2" DIAMETER

10'

6'

3'

BEDLAM BALL GOAL
(figure 1)

with the fewest points scored through its goal. So each team will want to have a defensive unit to guard its goal. Second, you want to score as many points in the other three goals as possible.

Since the playing area is chaotic there must be something to designate teams. Try ten-inch balloons and rubber bands. The balloons (each team should have a different color) are distributed before the game begins. Each person has to blow up his balloon, attach the rubber band, and place the balloon on his head so that it stands up straight. (This looks hilarious.) Popping balloons is not allowed. They are for team designation only.

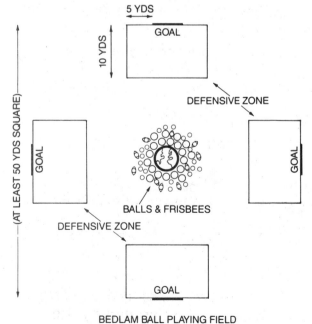

5 YDS

GOAL

10 YDS

DEFENSIVE ZONE

(AT LEAST 50 YDS SQUARE)

GOAL

GOAL

BALLS & FRISBEES

DEFENSIVE ZONE

GOAL

BEDLAM BALL PLAYING FIELD
(AERIAL VIEW)
(figure 2)

BEDLAM BALL
PLAYING OUTFIT
(figure 3)

To keep score, place several sponsors at each goal with pad and pencils. They keep up with the points and also watch for infractions of the rules. They are also armed with whistles and flashlights.

The game is played in four quarters of five minutes each. To begin each quarter, the teams gather around their own goal. On the signal they rush out to the balls and begin play. Between quarters the teams regroup, rest, and plan strategy. All the balls are placed back in the center of the field. If played at night, the last quarter can be played with the lights out. Running is not allowed during lights out. Have two spotlights sweeping the field looking for runners.

Special Note: During the game, play "The Ride of the Valkries" from **Apocalypse Now** over some very loud speakers. Any wild music would be a good substitute.

**Additional Rules:**
1. You must keep your balloon on. (Have extras on hand.)
2. **Football:** You may pass or run with it. The only way to score is to run it through the goal. You get seven points. If you are tackled, you must give up the ball.
3. **Basketball:** You may dribble or pass, but not run. The only way to score is to throw it through the goal from outside the defensive zone. It scores two points.
4. **Soccer:** You may only kick the ball. This is the only way to advance or score. Again the scoring kick must come from outside the defensive zone. It scores one point.
5. **Frisbee:** You may pass or run with the frisbee. You score by throwing it through the goal from outside the defensive zone. It scores one point.
6. **Pushball:** It can be advanced any way possible. It must go through the goal. You receive ten points.
7. Only your five defensive specialists are allowed to stand in your team's defensive zone.
8. Offensively, only someone with a football trying to score, or a group pushing the pushball are allowed in the defensive zone of other teams. All other scoring must be done from outside the defensive zone.

It helps to have an extra-loud PA system to control the game once it starts. Bedlam Ball is fantastically received by youth because it can be fun for the more timid players, and still have some tough competition for the aggressive kids. (Contributed by Joey Womble, Lubbock, TX)

# Billiard Fling

If your group has access to an older billiard table and some old balls, here is a game that combines the excitement of pinball and the speed of video games. Be sure to give lots of protection (with mattresses or cardboard) to any windows or lamps in the room.

Set up thirteen balls in random spots on one-half of the table. Designate the cue ball and the eight ball (or any two balls) as the "Fling Balls" that can be handled by the

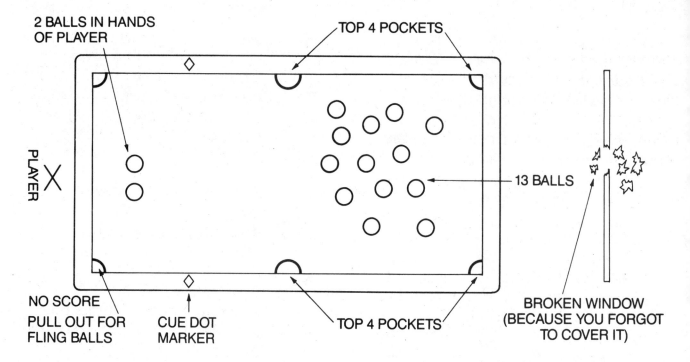

2 BALLS IN HANDS OF PLAYER

TOP 4 POCKETS

PLAYER X

13 BALLS

BROKEN WINDOW (BECAUSE YOU FORGOT TO COVER IT)

NO SCORE
PULL OUT FOR FLING BALLS

CUE DOT MARKER

TOP 4 POCKETS

players. Once the game begins, the player may not reach across the cue dot marker on the table to retrieve a Fling Ball.

When the timer starts, the first ball is flung across the cue dot marker at the other balls. The object is to knock all the balls into the top four pockets in the shortest time possible. Any ball rolling back across the cue dot toward the player may be used as a Fling Ball. Balls that pocket on the players half of the table may be retrieved and used as Fling Balls and do not count as scores.

Scoring is as follows: When all the balls have been knocked into the top four pockets, including the Fling

Balls, the score is what shows on the timer less 30 seconds. When no Fling Balls roll back to the player's half of the table, the game stops and the score is the clock time plus 10 seconds for every ball left on the table. When a Fling Ball drops into the top pocket without touching another ball, the game stops and the score is the time on the clock plus 10 seconds for each ball left on the table.

Give everyone in the group at least one turn, and then you might have some eliminations to determine one winner. (Contributed by Alan Hamilton and Dick Moore, Long Beach, CA)

## Bite The Bag

Stand a grocery bag in the middle of the floor and ask everyone to sit in a wide circle around it. One at a time each person must come to the bag and try to pick it up with just his or her teeth, then return to a standing position. Nothing but the bottoms of their feet are ever

allowed to touch the floor. As you go around the circle you will observe that almost everyone can do this. After everyone has a turn, cut off or fold down an inch or two of the bag. Go around again. With each round, shorten the bag more. When a person is no longer able to pick up the bag and stand again, he or she is out. The winner is the one who can pick it up without falling when no one else can. (Contributed by Jim Walton, Rochester, NY)

## Blind Wheelbarrow Race

This game is as much fun to watch as it is to play. Needed are two large wheelbarrows, two identical obstacle courses, and three people on each team. One person rides inside the wheelbarrow and is the navigator. The other two are the motors and are blindfolded. Each of the blindfolded motors takes one handle of the wheelbarrow and pushes the wheelbarrow through the obstacle course, following the directions of the navigator. Be ready for some crashes and spills! You can run heats to determine the winner, or you can use a stopwatch to determine the best time. Be sure to play this game on a soft surface like a grass field. (Contributed by Dan Scholten, Oak Park, IL)

## Bread and Butter Clumps

Here is a new variation of a great old game, "Clumps" (see **Ideas #1-4**). Divide the group into equal halves, giving one group the name "Bread" and the other group the name "Butter." Instruct everyone to mingle around the room, saying only their group name — "Bread" or "Butter". When the whistle is blown, the leader calls out a number, and the players must form a clump of that number — but only with members of their team. Anyone left out of a group, or in a group that accidently mixes the two teams, is eliminated. The last person left is the winner.

More variations can be made using different team names, such as "Peas and Carrots," or "Peanut Butter and Jelly." It's a lot of fun to play. (Contributed by Glenn T. Serino, La Grangeville, NY)

# Bubble Head

For this simple game, have two people stand facing each other about four feet apart. Blow up a round balloon and have one player bump the balloon off his or her head to the other player. The second player bounces the balloon off his or her head back to the first player, and so on, back and forth. See how many times they can bounce it without dropping it.

The balloon must be hit with the head only. The distance can be varied for greater or lesser difficulty. Each player can move only the left foot while reaching to hit the balloon. The right foot must remain planted. Each player may pivot on the ball of the right foot, but no jumping is allowed.

A variation of this game is to have teams line up, with players about four feet apart. Each team must bounce a balloon all the way down the team line, from one head to the other. Again, right feet must remain planted. If a balloon is dropped, the team must start over again. The first team to succeed is the winner. (Contributed by Scott Rokely, Hemet, CA)

# Cannonball Run

Here is a game which combines creativity with athletic ability. Begin by dividing the group into teams. Each team gets a pile of car parts, one large appliance box, tape, streamers, balloons, magic markers, tin cans and anything else they can scrounge up on their own. They then have 45 minutes to an hour to build themselves a "car."

In the race itself, there are two people per car—a driver and a passenger—who provide the legpower. There is also one person—the "tow truck"—who must run

alongside the car all the way. If any piece of the car falls off, the tow truck must pick it up, carry it, and—from that point on—must hang onto the shoulder or arm of one of the people in the car.

Every so often in the course—whether it's a long grand-prix-type course or a circular race track—each team must make a pit stop and change crews. It is a good idea to require a boy/girl team in the car each leg of the race. For an added surprise, place an unannounced "toll booth" along the way and require exact change to pass. Delay each team one minute for every penny they are short of the seven cents needed to pass. Doorways to buildings and narrow points on the path make great toll booths.

There are two winners when the race is completed: the team which finishes the course first and the team with the slickest looking and best-designed car, or what's left of it, when the race is over. (Contributed by Dan LeRoy, Hertford, NC)

# Cotton Ball Race

This is a good indoor relay game. Divide into teams and provide each team with a number of cotton balls in a container such as a dish or pan. Each team also gets a spatula and an egg carton.

On a signal, the first person on each team picks up a cotton ball with the spatula, then tries to keep it balanced on the spatula while running to a goal and back. Of course, if they go too fast, they will lose the cotton ball and must start over. When they return to their team with the cotton ball, they must place it in the egg carton in one of the unoccupied spaces. The first team to fill their egg carton wins. Obviously, this works out evenly if you have teams of four, six or twelve. (Contributed by Stan Lindstadt, Burlington, IA)

# Cup-It

Here is a "field" game that can be played indoors in a large room without carpeting. Break the group into two equal teams. Team A is at "bat" first and sits behind home plate. Team B is in the "field" and is scattered about the room.

A player from Team A must throw a ping-pong ball into the field from no lower than shoulder height. Team B players must attempt to catch the ball with a paper cup in as few bounces as possible. Team A receives a point for each time the ball bounces on the floor before being cupped. (Set a maximum at 15, due to the dribble effect of the ball just before it rolls.) Use a couple of referees to keep track of the bounces. Each member of the team gets one throw, and then the other team comes to bat. Total the points scored every inning. Play as many innings as time will allow.

**Additional rules are:**

1. **Out of bounds:** A line drawn from left to right through home plate and open doorways. Ball must not be thrown behind the plate or through doorways. Low hanging lights that might obstruct a ball may also be considered out.
2. **Throwing ("Batting"):** May be done in any direction, but when the ball is released, the hand must be above the plane of the batter's shoulder. Fielders may not stand directly in front of the batter, or hinder the batter in any way.

(Contributed by Phil Blackwell, West Columbia, SC)

# Dice Grab

To play this game, you will need to buy some oversized dice at a game or stationery store. Or, if you want to make your own, cut two small blocks of wood into 1¼" cubes. Sand and paint them if you wish, then mark them with dots similar to a pair of dice.

Mark a 2' diameter circle with chalk on the floor, or a rug, or on the top of a card table. One person starts the game by rolling the dice toward the center and simultaneously calling out any single number between 2 and 12. If the dots total the number called, all may grab for them. Each die is worth one point on the grab and the scramble may continue out of the circle or off the table.

The game becomes more exciting as the time between throws is cut down. The roller continues until the number he calls is thrown, then he passes the dice to an adjacent player. A game is usually won when someone earns 11 points. (Contributed by Bud Moon, Collegedale, TN)

## Dragon Dodge Ball

Have the entire group make a circle. Pick four to five people for each team. The first team goes into the center of the circle and forms a line by attaching their hands to the waist of the person in front of them. The people who make up the circle throw the ball at the "dragon," trying to hit the last person below the waist. Once hit, the last person returns to the outside circle and players continue to hit the new person at the end of the dragon until there is only one person left and they too are hit. A new team then goes into the middle. Time each team to see which one can last the longest. (Contributed by Kathie Taylor, Carpentersville, IL)

## Electric Fence

For this game you need two poles and a piece of rope or string. The rope is tied between the two poles, about two feet off the floor to begin.

Divide into teams. The object of the game is for the entire team to get over the "electric fence" (the rope) without getting "electrocuted" (touching the rope). Each team takes a turn, with team members going one at a time.

After each successful try, the rope is raised a little higher, as in regular high jump competition. Eventually, teams will be eliminated as they find the rope too high to get over.

What makes this game interesting is that even though one player goes over the rope at a time, the other team members can help any way they want. Once a person is over the fence, however, he or she must stay over the fence and not come back around to help anyone. So the last person each time must somehow get over the fence without help on one side. This game requires lots of teamwork and cooperation.

Teams can be eliminated entirely if one person touches the fence, or you can eliminate individual members only as the rope gets higher and higher. Make sure your teams are evenly divided according to height, age, and sex. (Contributed by Jim Bowes, Lakeside, CA)

## Flamingos

This game works best outdoors with two contestants at a time. The winners can compete in play-offs until there is a champion. Each player is given a filled water pistol. They must hold one foot off of the ground and hop while squirting the other person, making them lose their balance. The round is over when someone drops their other foot to the ground, or when both contestants are out of water. In the event neither person loses their balance, you should appoint a judge to determine the winner by who is the driest. (Contributed by Kathie Taylor, Carpentersville, IL)

## Floating Rocks

Here is a challenging game that can be used in a swimming pool or in a lake, to take a break from the heavy splashing and frantic swimming. Have each person find a flat, smooth rock and bring it back to the water. Then tell each person to get in a floating position and place the flat rock on his or her forehead. Each person must float as long as possible with the rock on their forehead without bumping into someone, or the rock falling off. Have an official, or the audience, time them by counting out seconds. Whoever lasts the longest is the winner. (Contributed by Mary Kent, Tyler, Texas)

## Four-Team Soccer

The object of this game is to have the fewest goals scored against your team. The playing field is a large square. Have each sideline clearly marked. Goals can be scored over any part of the sideline.

Divide the group into four equal teams. Distribute team members

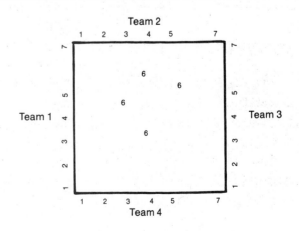

evenly along their sideline. Each member is given a different number, starting with one and numbering consecutively. In case a team has one less player, assign two numbers to one player so that each of the four teams has the same set of numbers.

Each round begins with the referee calling out a number or set of numbers. These players run to the ball in the middle and attempt to kick the ball over one of the three other sidelines. Soccer rules are used to advance or stop the ball. Play continues until a score. If over a long period of time no score is made, new numbers can be added, or play can be stopped and completely new numbers can start over. A score is made when the ball is kicked through any team's line. The ball must be shoulder height or lower to be good. If a kick is high, there is no score, and the ball is returned to play by a two-handed overhead toss. Team members protecting the sidelines can use their hands and catch the ball. The ball is returned to play by a two-handed overhead toss.

Have one official keep track of which numbers have been called so that each number is called an equal number of times. Officials should periodically announce the scores. Teams can then gang up on the leading team. The game will stay amazingly close. (Contributed by Dan Scholten, Oak Park, IL)

## Free Throw Up

This is an exciting game if your young people have the guts (literally) to do it. Have one basketball and one basketball goal per team, and at least 12 ounces of root beer per player. The teams should have an equal number of players. The root beer can be either warm or cold, but should be put in pitchers, an equal amount given to each team. The teams line up and take turns shooting free throws, keeping strict order in taking turns. All players must shoot the same number of free throws, give or take one. The object of the game is to be the first team to empty their pitcher by drinking its contents. This is done by appointing someone to drink a six-ounce dose whenever a free throw is hit. Obviously, the same person does not do the drinking; this duty should be shared by as many players as have a tolerance for the brown foamy fluid.

The game can also be played with darts, spitballs, snowballs, or anything else aimed at a target. The important features are 1) emptying the pitcher(s) of root beer rather than hitting the target a certain number of times; and 2) each player shoots at the target in the designated order.

If you are concerned about the massive mess that could develop by trying to pour root beer rapidly, have it ready dispensed into little cups. Also, depending upon the group's degree of ''microbe-phobia,'' a separate cup may be available to each player. (Contributed by Lew Worthington, East Canton, OH)

# Frisbasketball

Next time your group wants to play basketball, why not try this one. Instead of a basketball, use a frisbee and as many players as you wish on a regular basketball court. Of course, you can't dribble a frisbee, so you must advance it by passing. The refs should call penalties such as fouls, traveling, and out of bounds just as they normally would in a basketball game.

Points should be awarded as follows: one point for hitting the backboard, two for hitting the square on the backboard, and three for making a goal (including foul shots). Double the scores for any shot made from behind half-court. Make sure you are in shape before you try this one out! (Contributed by Kim Hall, Shreveport, LA)

# Frisbee Miniature Golf

This game is a takeoff on the classic game of "Frisbee Golf," in which Frisbees are tossed from the "tee" to the "hole" some distance away, in the fewest number of tosses possible. If you play indoors, such as in a church, Frisbees can do some serious property damage, so you need an alternative: Try using those small plastic caps which come on tennis ball cans. If you have a few tennis players in your church, it shouldn't take long to build up an adequate supply.

Next, set up an intricate course throughout the church building. You can "dogleg" around corridors, go up and down stairs, and make it as tough as you choose. The "holes" can be shoeboxes, or just 8$\frac{1}{2}$" by 11" sheets of paper taped to the wall with the number of the hole on it. The object is to hit the paper with your little Frisbee or land it in the box. With some creativity kids will love it. (Contributed by Lew Worthington, East Canton, OH)

# Frisbee On The Run

Here's a relay game that involves Frisbee throwing and hard running. Divide your group into two teams and then divide each team in half. Line them up opposite each other across the playing area. The first player for both teams will throw a Frisbee to a teammate at the other end of the playing area. After throwing it, he must run and tag the person to whom the Frisbee was thrown. The receiving player cannot be tagged unless he or she is behind the team line on their side of the field. So if

the first player throws the Frisbee inaccurately, the receiving player must go get the Frisbee and run back to his or her original position before being tagged. After being tagged, that person can throw the Frisbee back the other way and repeat the process. The object of the game is to have the two halves of the team switch ends of the field. The first team to do so wins. You can lengthen or shorten the playing area depending on the skill of group members. (Contributed by Brian Fullerton, Wenatchee, WA)

# Giant Pin Ball Machine

Here's an outdoor game that is best played on a grassy slope. At the bottom of the slope, place a few large inner tubes or tires. Stake them to the ground, if possible, and assign each of them a point value. You will also need one or more large, round balls.

Players stand at the top of the slope. Each player aims the ball and gives it a push to roll in the direction of the inner tubes or tires. Points are awarded for each tube or tire that it hits before coming to rest at the bottom. The player must follow the ball to the bottom of the

hill without touching it, and return the ball to the top.

You can make this even more like a pinball machine by dividing up into teams. When each player takes his or her turn, fellow team members stand among the tubes in various places. If the ball comes close enough to them (they must remain in the same place), they can kick the ball to score more points (like the flippers on a pinball machine). Try it sometime. (Contributed by Ronald Allchin, Geigertown, PA)

# Guess the Menu

Copy the ingredients from a few common items from your pantry or refrigerator. Pass this list around to your kids and have them guess what each item is. Here are a couple of examples:

1. Soybean oil, eggs, vinegar,

water, salt, sugar, and lemon juice (Mayonnaise)
2. Tomatoes, vinegar, corn sweetener, salt, onion powder, and spice (Ketchup).

(Contributed by Kathie Taylor, Carpentersville, IL)

# Hand Over Hand

Divide your group into two or more teams of five or more participants. Each team forms a circle and everyone holds

his or her right hand in the middle of the circle. Have them stack their hands "basketball huddle style." Then have them place their left hands in the circle in the same manner so that left hands are stacked on top of the right hand stack. At the signal, the person whose hand is on the bottom should take that hand and place it on top of the stack. The next person should do the same, and so on until the person who began the process is again on the bottom. The first team to complete this process is winner of round #1. For the next round try three "laps." Then try five. After everyone is getting the hang of it, try going backwards. (Contributed by Ben Sharpton, Kissimmee, FL)

## Hat and Go Seek

Here's a game that combines the best of "tag" and "hide-and-go-seek." One person wears an old hat, hides his eyes and gives the rest of the group one minute to run and hide. Then, the hat-wearer begins to search. (The hat must be worn, not carried.)

When someone is found and tagged, that person must wear the hat, cover his eyes for 20 counts and continue the search. Each person should keep track of how many times he or she wears the hat. The one who wears it the least number of times wins. (Contributed by Rusty Zeigler, Midway, KY)

## Hired Gun

This game would be good for camps or outdoor events where you have lots of room to run and hide.

Each person needs a squirt gun or a rubber-tipped toy dart gun. To begin the game, each person writes his or her name on a piece of paper cut into a "tombstone" shape, with "R.I.P." at the top. All these "tombstones" are then put into a hat, and everyone draws the name of the person he or she has been hired to "kill."

The players are then released to go out alone and plan their strategy, hide, or whatever. When the whistle is blown, the hunting begins. Each player tries to find the person he or she has been hired to gun down, and to shoot him or her with the squirt or dart gun. For a shot to be "legal," no one else may be present at the time. (It must be done secretly, so that only the victim knows that he or she has

been knocked off.)

You must carry your tombstone with you at all times (the one you drew at the beginning of the game.) When you successfully "kill" your victim, he or she must sign your tombstone (with his or her name on it). The victim is then eliminated from the game. Then that tombstone is posted so everyone can see who is still in the game.

When players are eliminated, they give their tombstones (the name of the person they were trying to "kill") to the players who shot them. Those names become the successful killers' next targets.

If you want the game to have a less violent theme, call it "KISSER." When a person is shot with the squirt gun (or hit with a water balloon), he or she has been "kissed" rather than "killed." Your choice. (Contributed by Dan Gray, Lafayette, IN)

# I Never

This is a living room game which is fun and also fosters communication and openness among your youth. Each person is given ten tokens of some kind, such as marbles, matches, pennies, etc. The point of the game is to collect other people's tokens by telling everyone "how life has passed you by." Players take turns relating some life experience that almost everyone has had but they haven't—ridden a roller coaster, been to Disneyland, eaten at Taco Bell, etc.

Then everyone who **has** done this thing must give a token to that player.

The one rule is that everyone must tell the truth. You may also want to make some rules about good taste. For the most part, this will challenge the kids to do creative thinking and will show that everyone has missed out on something in one way or another. Not only that, but the person who has missed out the most in this game will end up taking home the most. (Contributed by Brad Braley, Ida Grove, IA)

# Indoor Putt-Putt

This game is as good as you are creative. Most churches have short-pile commercial grade carpet, which is an excellent surface for putting. Design a nine-hole or 18-hole course throughout the building, using obstacles, pews, downstairs, or whatever. With masking tape, make each "hole" at least a square foot. (The bigger the hole, the easier it is.) A strip of tape will designate the "tee." Use real golf clubs and balls.

Here are a few simple rules:

1. The ball **must** be "teed" from behind the strip of tape and not outside the length of tape.
2. The ball **must** stop completely inside the taped "hole" in order to be declared finished. No part of the ball may be touching the tape.
3. Balls that rest against or near any object or wall may be placed one club head length from object or wall, but **not closer** to the hole. (No penalty.)
4. Any ball that is unplayable may be moved one club length from where it lies, but not closer to the hole; or it may be returned to the position of the original shot. (Penalty: one stroke.)

Have scorecards ready for groups of two, three, or four depending on the total number of players involved. If you want to do it up big, have a tournament with a leader board, closest-to-hole contests, and prizes for winners. All ages may play this game, but the younger the ages the more supervision is needed to avoid damage by club or ball. (Excellent game for adults tool) (Contributed by Thomas Hopewell, Springfield, OH)

# Inversion

This game requires a great deal of teamwork. It can be played as a competitive game (teams compete against each other), or as a cooperative game (everyone is on the same team).

Draw two parallel lines on the floor, about 18 inches apart. The team lines up inside those two lines. They number off 1, 2, 3, 4, and so on from one end of the line to the other.

On a signal, they must reverse their order without stepping outside those two parallel lines. If there are 20 people on the team, then player number 1 must change places with player number 20, and so on. Only the person in the middle stays in the same place.

Let the teams practice this once and come up with a strategy for doing it quickly and accurately. Then compete against the clock (try to set a "world record"), or see which team can do it in the quickest time. It's a lot of fun to watch. Referees can penalize a team (in seconds lost) any time a person steps outside one of the two lines.

$\uparrow$
18" ① ② ③ ④ ⑤ ⑥ ⑦ ⑧ ⑨ ⑩ ⑪ ⑫ ⑬ ⑭
$\downarrow$

(Contributed by James Bowes, Lakeside, CA)

# Irongut

If you have some daring kids in your group, try this contest. Prepare a concoction using ingredients found in any kitchen, and carefully list ALL the ingredients you use. (Fifteen to twenty-five are needed.) At your meeting, call for some volunteers to be the "Irongut." If teams are already formed, choose one or two from each team.

Those who are brave enough to accept the challenge take turns tasting the potion, which is usually a yucky brown color and thick. The winner is the person who can write down the most correctly-identified ingredients in the brew. Some suggested ingredients are:

Catsup
Mustard
Horseradish
Cinnamon
Nutmeg
Garlic
Milk
Salad Dressing
Pickle Juice
Onion Salt
Vinegar
Orange Juice
Tartar Sauce
Paprika
Oregano
Soda
Salt
Hot Sauce
Pepper
Worcestershire Sauce

Keep a careful watch on the kid who asks for seconds! (Contributed by Byron Harvey, Roanoke, VA)

# The Jail Game

The Jail Game is played in and surrounding a good-sized room, preferably one with at least two exits. A jail is constructed in the room by making a square with chairs, tables or benches. Team A tries to capture all of the members of Team B by tagging them and sending them to jail. Team B, while avoiding being tagged, attempts to free their teammates who are in jail. To free the prisoners, they must simply touch the jail. No more than three guards can be in the jail room at any time — if there are more than three, all of those in the jail are set free. Have the teams switch when everyone has been caught or after a certain time period has elapsed. To make it easier, players who have just been freed should have a ten-second count before they can be caught again. (Contributed by Andy Brown, Los Angeles, CA)

# Kooky Kickball

This game can be played on either a baseball diamond or on an open field. Like regular kickball or baseball, one team is up and the other in the field.

The first batter kicks the ball as it is rolled to him by a teammate. A miss, foul, or ball caught in the air is an out. There are three outs per team per inning. If no outs are made, everyone on the team may go up once during the inning. When the ball is kicked, the fielding team lines up behind the fielder who retrieves the ball. The ball is passed between the legs of all the players from front to rear. The last team member then takes the ball and tags the runner.

Meanwhile, the batters (or kickers) do not run around the bases. Instead, the team which is up lines up single file behind the batter, who runs around the team as many times as possible. One run is scored for every complete revolution before the batter is tagged with the ball. Play as many innings as you wish. (Contributed by James Alderson, Poteet, TX)

# Kubic Kids

This one is simple, yet lots of fun. Draw a square on the floor (as large or small as you choose), and see how many kids each team can get inside the square. Anything is legal, as long as no part of the body is touching the floor outside the square. Set a time limit and have team competition. (Contributed by Jim Bowes, Lakeside, CA)

# Line Soccer

Here's a variation of soccer that is simple and a lot of fun. Divide your group into two equal teams. Each team numbers off successively (1,2,3, etc . . . ) and lines up opposite each other on two sides of a playing area, about 30 feet apart. A gym floor will work fine. A line can be drawn in front of each team to designate the scoring area.

A ball is placed in the middle of the field and a referee calls out a number. The players on each team with that number run out to the ball and try to kick it through the opposite team (across their line). It cannot go over their heads. It must go between them, below the heads — or below the waist

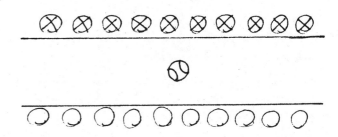

if you prefer — in order to count as a goal. The defenders can catch the ball and toss it back in to their own player, or kick it back when it comes to them. After a minute or two, the referee can call out a new number. It really gets wild when you call out several numbers at once. (Contributed by Christine Rollins, Turtle Creek, PA)

# Mad Hatter

Here's a free-for-all type game which is really wild. Everybody should have a cap or hat of some kind. If you want the game to last longer, use ski caps. Then give everybody a "club" which is a sock stuffed full of cloth or something soft. When the signal to begin is given, everybody tries to knock off everybody else's cap while keeping their own on. No hands may be used to protect yourself or your cap, and you may not knock off anyone's cap with anything except the sock club. When your cap is gone, you are out of the game. See who can last the longest. (Contributed by Ed Laremore, Lynchburg, VA)

## Marshmallow Golf

Here is a game which puts to good use your leftover stale marshmallows from the last beach party. Get some of those plastic putting cups from a sporting goods store, and a few golf putters. Then lay out a course around the church, using steps, corridors, barriers, and the like. You can even create a few water hazards and traps.

Players may "tee up" their marshmallow on its side when starting, but once it has been hit, it must be played where and as it is. The marshmallow cannot be rotated or moved to its side, which creates some interesting rolls. It's challenging and fun! (Contributed by Doug Newhouse, Florence, KY)

## Mini Grand Prix

If someone in your group has one or two of those radio-controlled toy cars, see if you can borrow them for this game. Set up a Grand Prix course around the room (be creative) and have the kids take turns to see who can maneuver the car around the track in the fastest time. Have a stopwatch handy and deduct seconds for knocking over objects, leaving the course, etc. Some kids will really get into this. (Contributed by Jim Walton, Rochester, NY)

## Musical Costumes

Here is a funny game that allows everyone to look a little silly. Before you start, have a laundry bag or pillow case filled with various articles of clothing—funny hats, baggy pants, gloves, belts, or anything that can be worn. (The leader can use his or her own discretion as to how embarrassing the items are.) Keep the bag tied shut so the clothing will not spill out.

Have your group make a circle and start passing the bag around as music is played. If you don't use music, use some other random signal like an egg timer or toaster to stop the action. When the music stops, the person holding the bag must reach in and take out an article without looking. Then he or she must put it on and wear it for the remainder of the game. Try to have enough so that each person gets three or four funny articles of clothing. This can lend itself to seasonal clothing (Santa's bag, Easter Parade, etc.). It may also be a fun way to create an instant costume for a Halloween party. After the game you can have a fashion show or take pictures to hang up on the group bulletin board. (Contributed by Paul L. Fuqua, Nashville, TN)

## Name That Scripture!

This game is a spin-off from the old TV show **Name That Tune**. It can be used at a youth meeting or at a youth group social to test your group's knowledge of familiar Bible passages.

Divide into two teams. The two teams position themselves on opposite sides of the room. The leader stands in the middle. The leader needs to have a list of well-known verses from the Bible that aren't too long—10 or 12 words.

Next, the two teams send out one person from their team to compete in the first round. One of the players is given the opportunity to "bid" on the first verse. He or she would say something like "I can name that Scripture in six words!" The other player then can say "I can name that Scripture in five words!"—if they think they can. This goes back and forth until someone stops. The idea is to stop at some point where you think the other player—if he or she wins the bid—will be unable to complete the verse. Or you want to stop at a point where you will be able to say the verse if you win the bidding.

If the winning bid is two words, for example, then the leader gives the first two words of the verse and the player must finish the verse correctly. If he or she is successful, the team gets a point. If unsuccessful, the opposing player gets an additional word and the opportunity to complete the verse. If successful, he or she gets the point. In other words, whoever wins the bidding gets first crack at winning the point. If the second player doesn't complete the verse correctly, then it goes back to the first player again with an additional word, and so on.

However, to make the game a bit more risky, the following rule could be used. If you win the bid and cannot complete the verse correctly, the opposing player gets **two** points instead of just one for quoting the correct verse. To make it even more risky, the second player may consult with his or her team before answering. What this does is make sure that the bidding is taken seriously. It's a lot of fun, and educational, too! (Contributed by Christopher Davis, Los Osos, CA)

## Old Testament—New Testament

Here's a good Bible game for younger teens which is a lot of fun to play. Seat everyone in a circle. The person who is "it" tosses a rag to someone in the circle and calls out either "Old Testament" or "New Testament." The person receiving the rag must respond appropriately with either the name of an Old or New Testament book before the person who is it can count to ten. If they respond correctly, the person who is it must try again. But if the person with the rag responds incorrectly or is too slow in giving the correct answer, they become the person who is it. The game becomes more difficult as it goes along as each book of the Bible may be used only once.

For another version of this game, the person who is it tosses the rag to someone and calls out the name of a book of the Bible. The person receiving the rag must then correctly respond either "New Testament" or "Old Testament" before the person who is it can count to ten. The person who is it can also call out the name of a non-existent book of the Bible (e.g., First Peaches), at which time the person with the rag should respond by saying "No Testament." (Contributed by Richard L. Starcher, Sumner, NE)

## Paper Badminton

Here's a variation of badminton which can be played indoors. The racquet is made of a sheet of ordinary 8¹/₂″ by 11″ paper. Old church bulletins work fine. The sheet is folded in half and stapled along two edges. Naturally, the thicker the paper, the stronger the racquet. Each player's hand goes inside the paper, sort of like a glove.

The net is a real one, and the "birdie" is a regular shuttlecock (or you can use a wad of paper). Play by whatever rules you wish: badminton, volleyball, or all-out war.

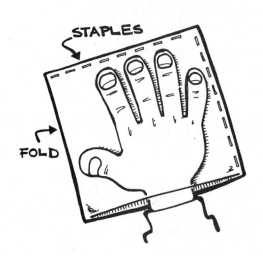

(Contributed by Keith Curran, Huntingdon, PA)

## Paper Route

This game is an adaptation of the "Chariot Race" game in which kids are pulled around a track on a blanket. In "Paper Route" the rider on the blanket is given an armload of "newspapers" to deliver as he or she is being pulled around the room. Cardboard boxes or

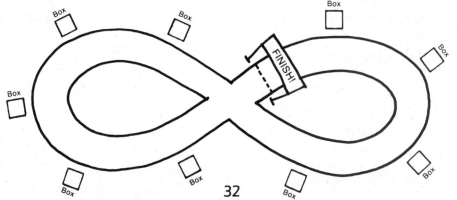

32

trash cans can be used as houses along the way, and the papers must be tossed accurately into them for points.

Another way to do this would be to have teammates seated in chairs along the route, but far enough away that the paper would have to be tossed a good distance. The person in the chair must catch the paper without leaving the chair, or the paper deliverer on the blanket must make another pass and try again. For added excitement, have several teams going at once with their courses criss-crossing, going in opposite directions, and the like. (Contributed by David Washburn, Brockport, NY)

## Penguin Football

Give each person a rag about four inches wide and two feet long (sheets torn into strips work well). Each person then ties the rag securely around his or her knees so that running is impossible. Players can move only by shuffling their feet along the floor.

Now, divide into teams and play football using a Nerf football. The game takes on a hilarious dimension when players must hike, run, throw, and kick with their knees tied together. Of course, this opens up the possibility of playing PENGUIN BASEBALL, PENGUIN VOLLEYBALL, PENGUIN SOCCER, and countless other games! (Contributed by Susan DeWyngaert, Charlotte, NC)

## Piggyback Balloon Poke

Here is a relay-type race that's fun to watch. Mark off several lanes on the ground, using flour or lime. At even intervals along each lane, locate a balloon on the ground, fastened securely with a stake of some kind. (If done indoors, you could just tape the balloons to the floor.)

Players should pair off, with one person designated as carrier and the other as rider, piggyback style. The rider gets a long, pointed (not too sharp) stick, like a broom handle. The carrier is blindfolded.

On a signal, they start down their lane. The object is for the rider to break the balloons with the stick by poking them as they walk by. The rider will have to give the carrier directions. After each round, replace the balloons and do it again with new contestants. Be sure kids avoid stabbing each other in the feet. (Contributed by David Washburn, Brockport, NY)

# Psychiatrist

Here's a fun indoor game for a small group that calls for creativity and encourages kids to get to know one another. Sit the group in a circle and choose someone to be the "psychiatrist." The psychiatrist has to leave the room while the game is explained.

Tell the group that their job is to take on the personality of the person to their left. All questions must be answered as if they were that person. You might want to take one minute and have everyone tell as much as they can about themselves to the person who will be them.

Bring in the psychiatrist. He is free to ask any question he wants, and must try to figure out what is ailing these patients. If he begins to notice the pattern, the leader may yell

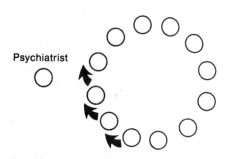

"Psychiatrist!", and everyone will have to scatter and regroup, taking the identity of the new person on his left. When the psychiatrist can guess what the pattern is, the game is over.

One good variation of this would be to have three or four kids leave the room, bring them in one at a time, and see how quickly they figure out the game. Time each one with a stopwatch. The one who figures it out in the least amount of time is the winner. (Contributed by Scott McLain, Akron, OH)

# Rainbow Soccer

Here's an active game played with two teams and 60 balloons (30 each of two colors). The balloons are mixed together and placed in the center circle of a regulation basketball court. The two teams line up on the end lines facing each other. One person from each team is the "goalie" and stands at the opposite end of the floor from his team, in front of a large container.

At the whistle, each team tries to kick (using soccer rules) their balloons to their goalie, who then puts them into the container behind him. To play defense, a team stomps and pops as many of the other team's balloons as possible. Play continues until all the balloons are scored or popped. The team with the most goals wins. (Contributed by Byron Harvey, Roanoke, VA)

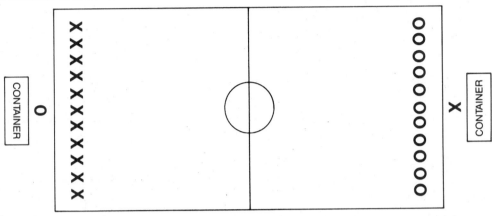

# Revival!

Here are some games that can be used to promote church attendance with your kids. Tell them that in order for them to know how to attend a church service, they need to practice certain church-going skills. Then play games like these (you may be able to make up a few of your own):

1. **Find a Seat:** Just in case there is a standing-room-only crowd at the next church service, they had better practice getting a seat. Play "musical chairs."
2. **Pass the Plate:** It takes skill to pass the offering plate! Play any relay game here (like the "Banana Relay" in **Ideas #5–8**), but use an offering plate to pass along.
3. **Grab the Hymnal:** There aren't always enough hymnals to go around, so you've got to be quick! Play "Steal the Bacon," only use a hymnbook. Make sure it's an old one you don't mind getting damaged.
4. **Name That Hymn:** It's time to sing! Play charades with titles of hymns. As soon as the guessing team knows the name of the hymn, they must sing a few bars.
5. **Memory Verse:** This is practice for listening to the reading of the scripture for the day. Play the "Gossip" game, using a verse of scripture. Kids line up, and the verse is whispered in the ear of the first person, who whispers it to the second, and so on down the line. The last person must quote the verse correctly.
6. **Sermon Cheers:** Kids need to practice responding to good points in the sermon, right? Distribute on slips of paper words and phrases like "Amen!", "Hallelujah!", "Preach it,

Brother!", "Glory!", and other enthusiastic responses, with several slips for each expression. On signal, players must find everyone else in the room who is yelling out the same thing they are. The first group to get together wins. (Contributed by Alan C. Wilder, Jacksonville, FL)

## River Raid

This game would be best played in a big church with lots of corridors, staircases, and the like. Divide into two teams. Both teams are armed with rubber bands and a few paper "bullets," as illustrated below.

One team begins the game at one end of the church, and the other team begins at the other end. The object of the game is for the two teams to change positions— but they must follow the same trail to get there. This is a lot like "Chinese checkers." On the way they can eliminate opposing team members by "shooting" them with their rubber band slingshots.

You can add to the excitement of the game by having more than one route, playing in the dark, and so on. There will be lots of skulking, some huge "shoot-out" scenes, and strategies for penetration and avoidance, offense and defense.

Make sure kids don't shoot each other in the face. Although these rubber band paper-shooters are reasonably safe, there is a slight chance of getting shot in the eye. If you prefer not to take that risk, you can substitute simple "tagging" for shooting. (Contributed by Jim Walton, Rochester, NY)

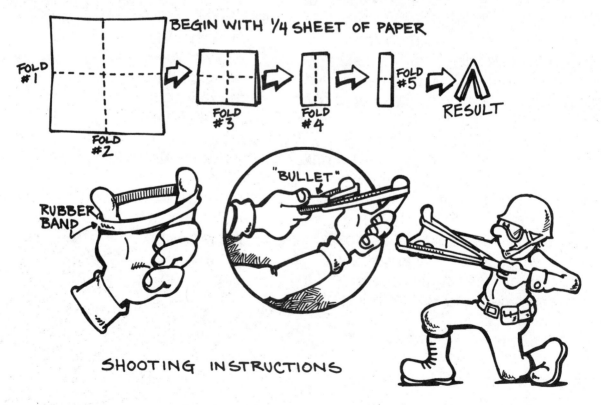

BEGIN WITH ¼ SHEET OF PAPER

FOLD #1 FOLD #2 FOLD #3 FOLD #4 FOLD #5 RESULT

RUBBER BAND "BULLET"

SHOOTING INSTRUCTIONS

# Sanctuary Soccer

This version of soccer allows you to play indoors and has a built-in equalizer to keep one team from dominating the game.

Play in a large room with all the chairs removed. You will need a Nerf (or some other soft) soccer ball, and eight folding chairs. Line up four chairs at each end of the playing area for goals. Play regular soccer, with as many players as you wish. A goal is scored when the soccer ball hits one of the other team's chairs.

When points are scored, the chair that is hit is removed from the goal of the team that was scored upon, and added to the chairs of the team who scored. Before the first goal, for example, the setup would look like this:

Team "A" Goal  Team "B" Goal

After team "B" scores a goal, the setup would look like this:

Team "A" Goal  Team "B" Goal

This way, the team that was just scored on will have an easier, larger target when the ball is back in play, while the other team has a smaller, more difficult target. Each team can have one goalie, as in regular soccer. (Contributed by Larry Bong, Moline, IL)

# Sculpture Machine

This is a fun charades-type game that involves everyone in the group. Put everyone in a circle and have them pass an object "hot potato" around hand-to-hand until the music stops. The last one to touch the object must come to the front and choose a number. This number corresponds to a machine on the group leader's list. Some might be:

1. Telephone
2. Stereo
3. Video Game
4. Motorcycle
5. Can Opener

Once the number is chosen, that person picks four assistants to help him "sculpture" the machine. They are given 60 seconds to prepare their sculpture, using all four people. When time is called, the rest of the group (or a panel of judges) must rate the sculpture on a scale of 1 to 10 (10 is best). The remaining players resume the "hot potato" and repeat the process until everyone has been a part of a sculpture. Then, the scores are compared and the one with the most points wins. (Contributed by Phil Blackwell, West Columbia, SC)

## Shoe The Donkey

This game can be played indoors or outdoors. The only equipment needed is two chairs, eight shoes, and two blindfolds. Two chairs are set up in the middle of the area. These are the "donkeys." Then two kids are blindfolded and seated on the "donkeys." At least four kids donate their shoes and scatter them around the chairs. The object of the game is for the two players to locate and place a shoe on each leg of their "donkeys." The first one to shoe his or her donkey successfully is the winner.

To add excitement to the game, the players may be allowed to "steal" the shoes already placed on each other's donkeys. This game guarantees squeals of laughter! (Contributed by Cheri Brent, Mansfield, OH)

## Simple Soccer

Here's a fantastic game that any number of kids can play. Mark a court in a large rectangle with the backcourt lines and center line clearly visible. Divide the players into two teams, one on each side of the court. Each team should then establish an offense and a defense—the offense stands on their side of the center line, the defense at the backcourt line.

The object is to kick the ball past, over, or through the opposing team's backcourt line. However, no player may use hands or arms. The official puts the ball into play by throwing it into the court at the center line. Each successful score earns one point. The

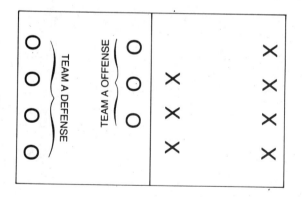

team with the most points in a certain time period wins. (Contributed by Brett Wilson, Florence, KY)

# Singing Circles

If your group likes to sing, this game will be an instant winner. If your group doesn't like to sing, then maybe this game will cure them. Here's how it works.

Divide into small groups of about five or six each. If your group is already quite small, then just divide into two teams. In advance, think up a number of common words like:

| | | |
|---|---|---|
| Jesus | Peace | Prayer |
| Abide | Fellowship | Love |
| Comfort | Glory | King |

These words can be written on cards, or you can just write them on the blackboard when you are ready for them. Choose some easy words, and a few that are not so easy.

The game can be played several different ways. One way is to hold up one of the words, and each group tries to be the first group to stand and sing a song that has that word in it. Judges can determine which group wins each round.

Another way to play is to give each group a stack of cards with all the words. The groups then get five minutes to get organized and come up with the songs they want to sing. Again, the idea is to sing a song that has each word in it (a different song for each word). Then, each team stands and sings their songs, holding up the appropriate word for each song. Judges determine the winner. This game can be used with secular music as well as with hymns and gospel songs. (Contributed by Pam George, Lancaster, OH)

# Soccerfriz

Here is an active field game that can involve any number of kids. Divide your group into 3 to 7 teams of 5 to 15 people each. Each team should have some kind of identifying mark, such as a colored wristband or tie. Next have each team mark a goal—a circle on the ground about 3 yards across. Each goal should be 20 yards or so from the center of the field and equidistant from the others.

The object of the game is for each team to get as many Frisbees as possible into their own goal and to prevent Frisbees from going into other goals. The referee starts the action by throwing a Frisbee into the group, and they take it from there. More Frisbees can be added when the players get the hang of the game. The more the better. Once a Frisbee is in a goal, it is dead and stays there until all of the Frisbees are down and that round is over.

Here are the rules:
1. Frisbees may only be thrown, kicked, or rolled. They cannot be carried—you may move only one step when you throw.
2. People who have Frisbees in their possession cannot be touched, only guarded.
3. Frisbees may not be grabbed from anyone.
4. If two people catch one at once, the boy must give it up to the girl and the larger person must give it up to the smaller person.
5. Players who break the rules must sit out of the game for three minutes.

(Contributed by Alan C. Wilder, Lakeland, FL)

# Solo Soccer

When you don't have enough people for a regular soccer game, or even when you do, you might want to try this challenging variation. Arrange the players spread apart in a large circle. Mark a goal by each player by putting two stakes in the ground about six feet apart. The object is to protect your own goal while trying to score through someone else's. The last person to touch the ball before it goes through the goal receives one point. The person who is scored upon receives a negative point. Goals should not be allowed that are kicked

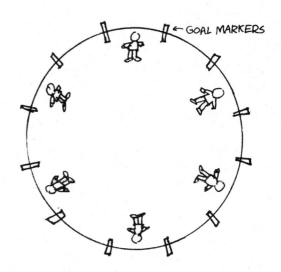

above the goalie's head. (Contributed by Kathie Taylor, Carpentersville, IL)

# Square Volley Ball

Here is a great idea for volleyball if you have a large group with a few "superstars" that make regular volleyball difficult. It may not only humble those few, but demonstrate how cooperation is mandatory for the Christian life.

Create your playing area by setting up four portable nets in a square. Have the "superstars" be one team, inside the square. Divide the rest of the group into four teams, one on

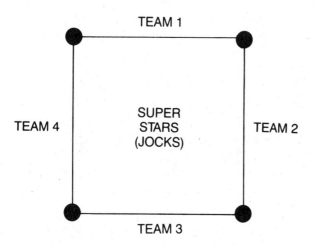

each side of the square. Each of these outside teams is given a ball with a distinctive marking of some kind.

The outside teams always serve, and the "superstars" must return the correct ball to the correct team. Outside teams should serve all at once, or two at a time. When a point is scored or a ball is dead, that team must wait for another ball to be available, so that the two can be served at once. The outside teams keep score with double points.

Each team will need a referee and scorer who can watch closely for correct returns and keep track of points. Play continues until a time limit, when all of the scores are compared and the winning team is discovered. (Contributed by Ron Tipton, Grove City, OH)

## Straw Contest

Here's another contest which looks easier than it really is. Each contestant receives two straws and a cup filled with water. One straw is to be put in the cup of water, the other is not. However, both straws are to be inserted in the contestants' mouths. As the contestants race to empty their cups, they won't realize that they will be slowed down by the straw which is only sucking air. (Contributed by Kathie Taylor, Carpentersville, IL)

## Strength Test

Here's a good stunt you could use on contest night. All you need is a flat, ordinary bathroom scale. Each person holds the scale with two hands and squeezes it, pressing as hard as possible to register the highest weight on the scale. Or, you could have two people, one holding the scale and the other pushing, attempt to register their highest score. (Contributed by Kathie Taylor, Carpentersville, IL)

## Strike Force

If you have a number of kids who make airplanes out of your Sunday School papers, here's a game that puts their expertise to good use! You need a gym or a large room, marked into a court.

Divide the group into two teams, each having a "home front" (safe) zone, with a "battle zone" in the middle. Each person makes a paper airplane and a paper wad "grenade." The object of the game is similar to dodge ball, using planes and grenades to hit opponents. If a player is hit with a plane, he hands over his plane and is out of the game. If a player is hit with a grenade, he forfeits his plane and can only throw grenades. He must also remain in the battle zone at all times and any planes that he picks up must be HANDED to a teammate.

**Additional Rules:**
1. Airplanes and grenades MUST BE thrown. Simply touching your opponent with your airplane or grenade is

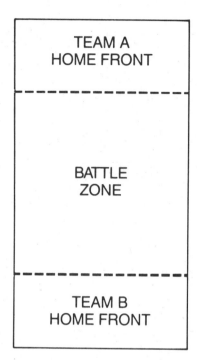

TEAM A
HOME FRONT

BATTLE
ZONE

TEAM B
HOME FRONT

considered a "self-destruct" and you are out of the game, forfeiting your planes and grenades to your opponent.

2. Players may not cross over into the opponents home front except during "air raids" which the referee will grant at certain times. However, players may stand at the line and throw planes and grenades into the opponents' home front.

3. A hit on the head or face of an opponent while he is standing (not ducking) is a self-destruct and the thrower is out of the game.

4. "Grounder" grenades and airplanes that slide or roll count the same as airborn ones if they touch you. Airplanes and grenades cannot be picked up until they STOP moving. (They can't be stopped with your foot, either.) Grenades and airplanes that bounce off the wall are dead and don't count as hits.

5. Hand-to-hand combat is not permitted and is sudden death to the player who starts it.

**Signals:**
1. One long whistle = 15 seconds retreat to home front by both teams.
2. Two short whistles = air raid.
3. One short whistle = attack—all players must go to battle zone.

(Contributed by Allen Johnson, Hannibal, MO)

# Tangle

This game allows for lots of close contact and cooperation among the group members.

Using an even number of people (between 6 and 20), have them get into a close circle. Have all players put their right hands into the circle and grab someone else's right hand, though not the person's next to them.

Now have them put their left hands into the circle and take someone else's left hand, though not the person next to them or the person with whom they've joined right hands.

Now, without letting go of hands, everyone must maneuver into one large circle by twisting, turning, going under, and going over each other. It can be done and it's a lot of fun to try. You might want to have two groups going at once to see who can finish first. (Contributed by Murray Wilding, Bicton, Western Australia)

# Touch Telephone

This game is based on the old telephone game but involves touch rather than hearing. No talking is allowed. Divide the group into teams of about six each. Each team sits in a line, one behind the other. The last person is shown a simple hand drawn picture of an object such as a house, a cat, or a Christmas tree, for example. The person who is shown the drawing then tries to draw an exact copy of it, using their fingers on the back of the person in front of them. This continues until it gets to the person at the front of the line, who then must draw what he or she felt on a piece of paper. The team whose picture most resembles the original wins that round. (Contributed by Kathie Taylor, Carpentersville, IL)

# The True-False Scramble

Here's a good quiz game that can test how sharp your kids are when it comes to the Bible. Two numbered teams sit in opposite rows of chairs. At either end of the rows are the "True" and "False" chairs. The leader makes a Bible-based statement, such as a false one like, "The lunch Jesus used to feed 5,000 plus was five hamburgers and two cokes," or a true one like, "Jesus said, 'I am the Way, the Truth and the Life.'" After the statement, the leader calls out some numbers. The players with those numbers race for the correct chair. The first one there wins a point for his team. When the players return to their seats, the leader goes over the correct answer. The team that answers the most questions with the right answer wins.

TEAM A

① ② ③ ④ ⑤ ⑥ ⑦ ⑧

TRUE CHAIR Ⓣ          Ⓕ FALSE CHAIR

① ② ③ ④ ⑤ ⑥ ⑦ ⑧

TEAM B

(Contributed by F.W. Swallow, Auckland, New Zealand)

# Tube Mania

Here's a physically exhausting game that can be lots of fun, but might be best if played boys against boys and girls against girls.

Mark a large square in the field, and place a stack of seven to ten inner tubes in the center of the square. Divide the group into four equal teams, each one lining up on their side

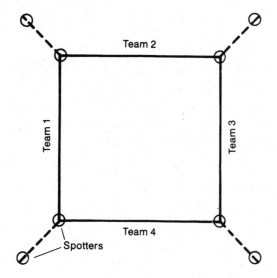

of the square. Number the players on each team from one to however many players are on each team.

The object of the game is to get as many inner tubes as possible across your team's line. Call out several numbers. The players with those numbers run to the center and start dragging the inner tubes to their lines. There may be several players tugging on the same tube. Each tube successfully pulled across a team's line scores one point for that team.

Once the kids get the hang of it, add a soccer ball to the game. Each team gets a point deducted from their score if the ball is kicked over their line. Team members along the team line act as goalies. Once the ball touches the ground in their territory the point is scored against them.

To further complicate the game, add a cage ball four to eight feet in diameter. The team that gets this ball across their own line gets three additional points. (Contributed by Rob Yonan, Oak Park, IL)

## Tug of War Times Two

By tying two ropes in the middle so that you have four ends of equal length, you can have a tug of war with four teams instead of two. Draw a circle on the ground so that each team is outside the circle when the war begins.

When one team is pulled across the circle line, it is eliminated from the game, leaving the other three teams to tug against each other. Then those three play until another is eliminated, and finally two teams play to determine the winner. Each time, the tug of war is conducted across the circle.

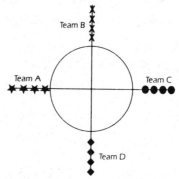

For a TUG OF WAR TIMES THREE, just get three ropes and begin with six teams. It works! The primary advantage to this version of tug of war is that the least strong teams can gang up on the stronger teams and eliminate them from the game early. (Contributed by Lew Worthington, East Canton, OH)

## Valentine's Day Scavenger Hunt

Since it's too cold in most parts of the country to go outside on February 14th, this scavenger hunt takes place indoors with magazines. Each team sits in a circle with a pile of magazines and the following list. The first team to find and tear out all ten items is the winner.

44

1. A picture of a person that you would like for a valentine.
2. A picture of something people give for a Valentine's Day gift.
3. A word "love."
4. A picture of something that rhymes with the word "valentine."
5. A picture of a romantic looking couple.
6. A picture of a piece of clothing that is red.
7. A word or picture that describes your valentine.
8. A picture of a red food.
9. A picture of anything that begins with the letter V.
10. A picture of a box of chocolates.

(Contributed by Kathie Taylor, Carpentersville, IL)

## Volley Tennis

Volley Tennis is played on a tennis court with a volleyball. It is a great game for as many as want to play, and it requires no great athletic ability. The serve is just like regular volleyball, from behind the back line. But the receiving team must allow the ball to **hit the court** before touching the ball. They have up to three volleys to get the ball back across the net, but the ball must touch the court between each volley. The game is played to 15 points, and only the serving team can score. Line hits are in play. This is most fun when at least a dozen people are on each team. (Contributed by Ralph Bryant, Alvin, TX)

## Water Balloon Boppers

Here's a new way to have a water balloon war. Have everyone bring a regular sock to use—long tube socks work best. Then give each person a water balloon, which goes inside the sock.

Now have a water balloon fight in which kids try to ''tag'' each other with their ''Water Balloon Boppers.'' If your water balloon breaks, you are out of the game, but if you can hit someone without breaking your water balloon, then you can remain in the game to hit someone else. The winner is the last person left with a water balloon still intact.

A variation of this game would be to eliminate anyone who gets ''tagged'' as well as anyone whose water balloon breaks. Either way, it's lots of fun.

(Contributed by Jim Ruberg, Burlington, !A)

# Water Bronco

This game is played on a lake, pond, or swimming pool. Tie a long rope to a "snow saucer," or any other flat-bottomed object you can ride on with a handle of some kind attached to it. Next, get several kids on the end of the rope (out of the water) and one person to ride the saucer while it is being pulled by the group across the pool or lake. The object is for the rider to hang on. It's a lot like water skiing. Teams can compete for best time, or you can do it just for fun. (Contributed by Paul Mason, Colorado Springs, CO)

# CHAPTER THREE

# CREATIVE COMMUNICATION

## Anger

Here's a powerful way to get your group hooked into a session on anger. First recruit one young person beforehand to play the role of photographer. From the beginning of the meeting time, the photographer shoots flash pictures of the games, singing, and announcements. You then gently ask him to please stop taking pictures, and repeat this with increasing intensity as he continues to go ahead and take more pictures anyway.

As the serious time of the meeting approaches, you give the photographer one last ultimatum. Then just as you start to speak, he takes one last picture. You react with fury, walk over to the young person, grab the camera and pull out the film, shouting about the previous warnings. The kids will react in a variety of ways, and the atmosphere will be highly charged. The situation turns around when you walk back to the front and say, "Tonight we are going to discuss handling our emotions. Let's start with anger." Debrief the episode by pointing out the tremendous power of one angry person and the various reactions of the group to the anger that you demonstrated.

Possible questions for discussion:
1. What makes you angry?
2. What do you do when you get angry?
3. How do you deal with anger?
4. Anger is listed as one of the "Seven Deadly Sins." Is anger a sin? Or is it a normal human emotion?
5. What does the Bible teach about anger?
6. Do Christians express anger differently than non-Christians?

(Contributed by David C. Wright, Vienna, VA)

## Appendices, Unite!

Here is a game that would be great for kicking off a discussion on the Body of Christ or Christian unity. When the group arrives, give everyone a slip of paper with a part of the body on it, like ear, nose, foot, kneecap, hand, eye, etc. You should try to distribute these so that there will be enough "parts" to make up two or more complete bodies. In other words, if you have thirty kids, you might want to have three bodies, each with ten parts.

When the signal to go is given, the kids try to form complete "bodies" as quickly as possible by getting into groups. The "body" that gets together first is the winner. A complete body has, of course, only one hand, two arms, two legs, and so on. If a "body" has three legs, then obviously something is wrong.

Once the bodies are formed, you can then proceed with some small group discussions or other activities which require those bodies to work together as a team. This simulates how the Body of Christ works. An experience like this can help kids to understand passages of Scripture like 1 Corinthians 12 much better.

(Contributed by Larry Michael, Rockville, MD)

## The Ballad of Luke Warm

One of the best ways to get young people involved in learning is to allow them to create a drama, film, or slide show. The following script was used by one youth group for a "silent film" which they produced and showed to the entire congregation of the church with excellent results. It could be adapted to include sound (for video or sound super-8), or it could be done using slides. It could even be acted out as a play. It might also serve as a model for another of your own design or another topic altogether. Use your own creativity. Something like this would be excellent for use at a camp or retreat. You will probably need to allow several weeks for the production and final completion of the project. (Contributed by Dick Gibson, St. Petersburg, Florida)

THE BALLAD OF LUKE WARM
a three scene movie script

CAST:   Luke Warm
Church congregation      Bandits
Deacon #1      The Judge
Deacon #2      The Bailiff
The Preacher      Witness #2, Church Member
The Sheriff      Jury

DIRECTION:   The Major Roles of Luke Warm, the Sheriff and the Preacher must remain consistent throughout the film. Other parts can be assigned by scene and actors may play multiple roles.

Each Scene Director should choose the location for their scene, bring any necessary props and explain the action to the cast.

SCENE ONE: *The Church Scene*
*Signboard:*   "As our story opens, we look in on the Sunday services of the Town Church."

| | |
|---|---|
| *Action:* | Congregation is singing, sincerely but timidly, except for Luke Warm, who is bellowing full voice. Everyone quiets as Luke finishes the song. All applaud Luke. |
| *Signboard:* | "Next the offering is passed." |
| *Action:* | Everyone puts their money in the plate as it is passed to them. When the offering comes to Luke, he puts in so much that the Deacon needs help to carry it off. Everyone stares in awe. |
| *Signboard:* | "The Sunday sermon." |
| *Action:* | The Preacher is speaking. All are listening politely while Luke furiously takes notes. Camera pans back to Preacher who mouths a sentence forcefully. |
| *Signboard:* | "Yes, only one is perfect and we should all try to be like him. And that man is . . ." |
| *Action:* | Everyone points to Luke. |
| *Signboard:* | "Luke Warm!" |
| *Action:* | The Preacher looks confused. Camera zooms on Luke's face, who gives his most humble and angelic expression. |

### SCENE TWO: The Hold-Up

| | |
|---|---|
| *Signboard:* | "When Church is over, everyone greets the Preacher on their way home." |
| *Action:* | People walk out shaking the Preacher's hand. When Luke comes out, the Preacher pats him on the back. The Sheriff comes out behind Luke. |
| *Signboard:* | "Meanwhile, just down the road." |
| *Action:* | Bandits mount their "horses" and ride toward the Church shooting at everyone. The Preacher and several others fall to the ground. The Sheriff tries to return fire and is shot in the leg. Luke, who sees all of this, is asked to help but he walks away. Bandits ride off. |

### SCENE THREE: The Court Room

| | |
|---|---|
| *Signboard:* | "Several days later, Luke goes on trial for being a Christian." |
| *Action:* | The Judge calls the Court to order. Luke is brought in by the Bailiff. |
| *Signboard:* | "First Witness — the Sheriff." |
| *Action:* | The Sheriff, limping, is helped to the witness stand and pantomimes action of the shooting. |
| *Signboard:* | "Second Witness — a Church Member." |
| *Action:* | The Church Member pantomimes Luke's actions at Church. The Judge turns to Luke and asks if he has anything to say. |
| *Signboard:* | "Do you have anything to say?" |
| *Action:* | Luke hangs his head sorrowfully. The Judge asks the jury for their verdict. |
| *Signboard:* | "What is your verdict?" |
| *Action:* | The Jury turns thumbs down. |
| *Signboard:* | THE MORAL: You can't just talk the talk. You've got to walk the walk! |

# Biblical 60 Minutes

One of the most popular TV shows of recent times is the news program **60 Minutes**. It usually features good investigative reporting along with some exciting drama as well. Why not use the format of that program as a Bible-study exercise?

Divide the group into smaller units and have them do some investigative reporting (study) of a biblical text and then present their findings as if it were a **60 Minutes** program. The following example covers the events of Pentecost as described in the second chapter of Acts. Each group could take one section, act out the events, select a reporter who describes the action and so forth. Let the group's creativity run wild.

60 Minutes: Pentecost—What Really Happened

1. The Event (Acts 2:1-4)
2. Interviews with the Witnesses (Acts 2:5-13)
3. Peter's News Conference (Acts 2:14-41)
4. Follow-up Report (Acts 2:42-47)
5. Letterbag (Responses to the Story)

(Contributed by Bruce Schlenke, Wexford, Pennsylvania)

# Biblical Time Machine

The dilemmas people faced in the Bible can often seem remote to us today because they happened so long ago. This activity is aimed at making biblical dilemmas more immediate and understandable to contemporary young people.

Begin by selecting several passages of Scripture which describe people faced with a dilemma. Examples are: when God spoke to Abraham about offering up Isaac, when Ruth had to decide whether to return to her people or to stay with Naomi, when Jesus is asked why he hasn't paid taxes, when the disciples realize that there is a crowd of over five thousand which is hungry and needs to be fed, when the people of the Corinthian church are faced with a variety of leaders and are wondering who to follow.

Read one of these stories to the group. Ask them to describe the main truth to be learned from the story. Have them then describe a modern context where a similar type of dilemma might be found. Discuss how the truth learned from the Bible story might apply in this circumstance.

Ask the group to get in small groups of about 6 each. Give each group one of the biblical dilemmas you've selected or let them pick their own. They should read the passage where the dilemma is found, discuss its main point and then re-create it within a modern context. They should find a modern situation which parallels the same circumstances.

Each group should act out their dilemma for the other groups. Encourage discussion on complexities of the issues presented in the dilemmas, the gray areas they open up, and the questions that evolve. Aim at leading the group to make some discoveries as to how they might begin to deal with them in a realistic manner. End the discussion by asking them to think and share how the insight they have could, should, or will affect their lives. (Contributed by Anna Citrino, Santa Cruz, CA)

# Cryptoquip

Communicating Scripture to young people is often very difficult. Getting them to memorize it is next to impossible. But "cryptoquipping" them with it is the ultimate.

Cryptoquipping is a way to help young and old alike learn and memorize Scripture truths and promises. A "quip" can be used to introduce retreat topics, Bible studies or Sunday School Lessons. Here's how it works:

WIL AMTY WT ORM
BWIY ECI YR YCWY
ORM, YNCWY YOCE DI
YVC TWEC BWO.

**W = A**

This cryptoquip is a simple substitution cipher in which each letter stands for another. If you find that Y = T, it will be that way throughout the puzzle. The solution is accomplished by trial and error. Hint: short words can give you clues for locating the vowels. The age of your group will determine the number of "equal-to" clues that you give away.

Try the above example; then make up cryptoquips for your own verses. Be sure to double-check your letters for accuracy, because the kids will never let you forget it if you're wrong. By the way, this "quip" is found in Luke 6:31 NAS. (Contributed by William T. Bell, Sweetwater, TN)

# Dating Data

This idea provides a good opportunity for youth to express their values and opinions about dating in a relaxed and natural way. Place the following assignments around the room, providing blank paper, felt-tip markers, and resource materials at each station. Ask the youth to choose and complete as many assignments as possible in the time allowed. They may work together in small groups or individually. At the end of the period, call for reports and discuss the findings.

*Assignments* :

1. Write a plan for two people who like each other to get together.
2. Devise a fool-proof method for deciding the difference between love and infatuation.
3. List at least 20 fun things to do on a date. Each must cost less than $10.00 total.
4. List five guidelines for making a date successful.
5. What advice would you give a Christian who has a crush on a

non-Christian? Include the pros and cons of a dating a non-Christian.
6. Write a plan for breaking up in the least painful and most healthy way.
7. List the number of people you tell about your dates, and write out 10 pros and cons for talking about your dates.

*Questions for Discussion* :

1. Why do some people seem to date "below" themselves? (Put up with anger, being used, disrespect, etc.)
2. Why do some youth find romance earlier than others?
3. How can we be more comfortable on dates?
4. Should girls ask guys out?

(Contributed by Karen Dockrey, Burke, VA)

---

# Dating Round Robin

This exercise is a lot of fun and it introduces the subject of dating in a new and helpful way.

Have the group sit in a circle. Go around the circle, giving each person ten seconds to come up with an idea for a cheap date in their town. If they can't think of one, they are eliminated from the game and you go on to the next person. Continue playing until only one person is left, or until a specified time limit has been reached. In the church where this game was originated, twelve young people came up with 82 ideas! Here are some examples:

Go swimming
Go to the zoo
Go get a pizza
Work in a garden together
Make popcorn
Listen to a record
Walk a dog
Cook a meal together

Help an old person
Draw or paint
Talk
Run errands for someone
Play tennis
Play Risk
Have a pillow fight
Visit someone in a hospital
Go on a picnic
Wash the car
Go shopping
Take a train or bus ride
Go to a ball game
Go to a movie
Go to a museum

When the game is over, have the group choose the best ideas, or rank the list from most expensive to least expensive, or from best to worst. Follow up with a discussion on dating, and talk about what makes a good date. Your list of ideas can be duplicated and distributed to the group as a resource for future dating. (Contributed by Karen Dockrey, Burke, VA)

# Family Forum

If your church has a mid-week service that separates youth from the adults, why not try an inter-generational program that can bring about open and honest communication between the two groups? Here's one good way to do it.

As people enter the room, they are handed a mimeographed sheet inviting them to write out a question that they would like answered by a teen or adult, or by a male or female. For example, questions might be, "Why do teenagers always feel they should be able to stay out past their established curfews?" or "Why are parents so suspicious of everything we do away from home?" Collect these questions during the service and give them to the leader to organize into a logical progression.

Begin the service by singing choruses from youth song books, asking teens and adults to intersperse and share books. This breaks up clusters of teens or adults and allows for more intimate contact among them.

The leader then proceeds with the program by addressing the first question to the group, repeating it, then asking if anyone would like to respond. After the first few responses, most of the inhibitions will be gone and there will probably be some strong feelings expressed. Usually remarkably honest communication will occur, leading to a better understanding and closer relationship between the two groups.

The leader should field the questions quickly and keep the responses moving without any person (including himself!) taking too much time. Someone whose age is midway between the two perspectives might be best. (Contributed by Paul Flores, Pueblo, CO)

---

# The Friend at Midnight

One of the lesser known of Jesus' parables is the story of the Friend at Midnight in Luke 11:5-8. But here's a way to teach it to young people that will make it unforgettable.

Have one volunteer come forward and be the person who went to bed early. Tell that person: "It is approaching midnight in Jerusalem, and you are sound asleep. You are sleeping in a big bed with the rest of your family. To get up out of bed would be a tremendous inconvenience and would wake everybody up. There is nothing in the world that would get you up out of bed at this time of night."

Have a second volunteer come forward and be the first person's neighbor. Tell that person: "It is midnight and some out-of-town guests have just arrived at your house. They are very hungry. But, alas, you don't have a thing in the refrigerator; nothing in the pantry. There are no stores open. It would be a terrible disgrace to send your guests to bed hungry. So, you go next door to your neighbor's house, try to wake him (or her) and borrow some food. You won't take no for an answer. You try to get food no matter what."

And to the first person again, you say: "Remember . . . You aren't getting out of bed for anything!"

Now let the two people role-play the situation as you've described it to them. Chances are they will really get into it, with the second person trying every argument in the book to get the other out of bed and to lend some food. Let it go for a few minutes, or as long as you want. When finished, give the participants a hand, and then discuss what happened.

Ask the group what they think the lesson of this parable is. After everyone has shared, be sure that the kids understand that this was a lesson on prayer, taught by Jesus. His point was that we should pray with the same kind of persistance that the friend at midnight tried to get food out of his neighbor. We shouldn't just go through the motions and pray without feeling, but instead with a real sense of urgency.

## A Friend For All Time

Here is a poem written by a youth worker to one of his young people that you might find useful at a senior banquet, a year-end party, or some other way. It could be read, presented with music or slides, or used as an inscription in books and Bibles. (Contributed by Dan Engle, Tallahassee, FL)

## A Friend for All Time

There is no knowing how God puts it in the minds of certain people, to be in a certain place, at a certain time—to work, to live, to learn.

Yet, suddenly here *we* were. At first just faces—just acquaintances, but with so much in common—so much to share; a love for God, a zest for life, an interest in others.

In no time at all we were best of friends. Those once unfamiliar faces turned into the warm smile of a brother. That one time acquaintance became the encourager who helped you through exams, through a heartache, through a problem at home.

We had been full of foreboding, skeptical of being a part of so large a mass of unknowns, just a drop of water awash in a sea of people. But that place so foreign soon became home, and *we* became family.

We ate together, we traveled together, we endured awkward and tough times. And we laughed. And the bond between us grew and grew. Brothers, family, friends.

Then, in no time at all, a year had come and gone. For some there would be a time of parting—graduation, summer jobs, visits with parents, vacations— there might even be those we wouldn't see for a very long while.

But we knew we had something that would last, something that years could not take away, something that would even ripple into forever. We had A Friend For All Time.

# Grab-Bag Testimonies

This idea provides a good way to get your kids to reflect on their present spiritual condition and to share their thoughts with others. Prepare several slips of paper each containing a verse of Scripture and a sentence instructing them to read the statement and relate how they have or have not applied this verse to their own life in the past weeks or months. The following are several examples.

---

*Read this verse and tell how it has or has not been applied to your life this school year:*

"Be anxious for nothing, but in everything by prayer and supplication with thanksgiving, let your requests be made known to God. And the peace of God, which surpasses all comprehension, shall guard your hearts and your minds in Christ Jesus." — Philippians 4:6, 7

---

"A disciple is not above his teacher, nor a slave above his master. It is enough for the disciple that he become as his teacher . . ." —Matt. 10:24-25

*Looking at yourself objectively, in what ways are you growing to be like Jesus? In what ways not? What are some characteristics that Jesus had that you would like in your own?*

---

"Seek first His kingdom and His righteousness, and all those things shall be added to you." —Matt. 6:33

*Read this verse aloud and tell us how you have or have not put this into practice this month.*

---

"Now flee from youthful lusts, and pursue righteousness, faith, love, and peace, with those who call on the Lord from a pure heart." — 2 Tim. 2:22 ff.

*Read aloud, then share with us what this verse means to you in your life now and how you seek to apply (or how you can see you've failed to act on it).*

---

At the beginning of your youth group meeting, ask for volunteers—it is your choice whether or not to tell them what's going on. Have them reach into a paper bag and take one of the slips of paper. Give them enough time to look over the slip of paper and to collect their thoughts. Then, call them up one at a time, giving them the option not to participate if they feel "on the spot," and have them respond to the verse and the question. You should be prepared to ask a follow-up question to the person to be sure they talk about their life and not just say, "I think this verse means . . ." The activity doesn't take a lot of time—allow two to three minutes per person—and many others might share as well if you ask for final comments. (Contributed by Fred O. Pitts, Atlanta, GA)

---

# Guided Meditation

Here is a "guided meditation" that can be used with high school or college students to introduce a study of values, social concerns or Christian responsibility to others.

Instruct the group to completely relax, close their eyes, breathe deeply and clear their minds. Slowly and deliberately, read the following story, which takes them on a thought-provoking, imaginary journey. Afterward, discuss the issues and emotions raised by the experience. (Contributed by Terry Tippens, Durham, NC)

You're in a nice clothing store in a shopping mall near your home. Festive music playing over the P.A. system fills the mall with appropriate accompaniment to the sound of shuffling feet hustling and bustling about and the beautiful decorations that adorn the mall. After you buy a friend of yours a nice shirt for $25 and an even nicer sweater for $35, you step from the mall into the cold dusk air, get into your car and head home.

On your way home you stop at a traffic light in a slums section of the town. You're nervous. Your grip tightens on the steering wheel as you look around to make sure all the car doors are locked. On the bare ground in front of the shack on the right side of the street, five short-sleeved little black boys are playing with an old flat football. "How can they stand to be out there without a coat?" you ask yourself.

Your attention is diverted to the left of your car by the sound of barking dogs. Two of them are approaching a skinny, mange-covered hound that has just trotted out the front door of the house on the corner. The latter dog has something in his mouth, and he snarls at the other two. A second later, a middle-aged black woman comes running out of the house yelling expletives at the dog. The first two dogs flee as the woman yanks a ham bone out of the mangy dog's mouth and carries it back into the house.

The light turns green and you hit the accelerator. A wave of relief flows through your body as you exit the run-down section of town. You pull into the driveway of your suburban two-story house and walk across the lawn to the front door. It's dark outside by now.

Inside, your parents are having a party. Warm light radiates from the living room, and upon entering the house you're dazzled with a rich myriad of sights, sounds, and smells. Your mother has cleaned and decorated the house. Soft stereo music is barely audible over the din of cocktail conversation. Some of the wineglass-holding friends of your parents greet you as you wind your way through the crowded living room. On the dining room table are plenty of petite sand-wiches, hors d'oeuvres, and some luscious-looking desserts. The smell of freshly baked choco-late chip cookies tantalizes your nose, and you grab one off the plate as you walk by. The cookie is rich, warm, and moist in your mouth.

You enter the kitchen and find your mother cleaning off platefuls of leftovers from the party's turkey dinner into a trash bag. She smiles, says hello, and drops a sizable chunk of turkey into the smacking mouth of your eagerly waiting pet poodle. "I'm just trying to clean up a little here and there during the party so I don't have it all piled up on me in the morning," she explains.

You consider asking your Mom if she needs any help, then think better of it and head upstairs to your room to watch some TV. Before you close your door you recognize your father's boister-ous laugh over the party noise downstairs.

The next morning you are awakened by the familiar but nevertheless distressing sound of your parents arguing fiercely downstairs. They're yelling back and forth at each other—something about how much time your father spends away from home, intermingled with how much money your mother has been spending lately. Their fighting depresses you, and to escape it you pull the warm, soft covers closer to you and struggle back into sleep, and into a dream.

In your dream you find yourself floating in space, down toward the small blue planet of earth. You touch down in a tiny country in western Africa, and suddenly you're the parent of three children in an African bush tribe. It's unbearably hot, and your mouth is dry with thirst. Tears well up in your eyes as you cradle the dying body of your youngest child. Her bloated stom-ach makes her limp arms and legs look dwarf-like. You do your best to keep the flies away from her face.

Suddenly you're floating again, and this time you land in an Iranian town on the border of Iraq. You're deafened by the whistling and crashes of bombs and mortar shells exploding all around you. People on the street are screaming and running frantically in all directions. Your company

leader is shouting something to you about evacuating the building, but you can't really hear his orders. Suddenly you are knocked to the floor by the force of an explosion at the other end of the room. Your head is throbbing, and you taste blood. Ten feet to your left you see a civilian screaming in agony through clenched teeth, his hands gripping themselves white against the floor. You feel nauseous as your eyes meet the source of his pain. His right leg has been severed at the thigh by the explosion. Your vision dims as you lose consciousness.

You're floating again; this time to a nursing home in New York City, where you're working as an attendant. You enter the room of an old, frail widow to administer to her her twice-a-day drugs. You're used to the stuffy, medicinal smell of the nursing home, but the odor of decaying flesh and stale urine in the room still makes you cough. You try to get the woman's attention to change her bedpan and feed her the medicine, but she seems to ignore you, lying still in the bed, staring at the ceiling with gloomy eyes sunk into a wrinkled, weathered face.

Suddenly you're floating again, and you now find yourself in Belfast as a frightened British teenager fleeing with a friend from four other teens hurling curses as they chase you. Your friend trips and falls. In seconds, the other four are upon him, kicking him and beating him with sticks. You stop and turn around for only a second. You're crying, violently. You feel your heart in your throat as you turn and run in desperation for your own life.

Then you're floating again, to a state prison in Louisiana. You've been convinced of burglary, and you've been locked up for three years now. You stare out the bars of your "home," watching other inmates walk by on their way to supper as you wait for the guard to unlock your cell. After three years in prison, you still occasionally wish you could eat when and where you wanted to, but it's been so long since you were free that your desire for choice has been almost completely numbed. The loneliness is another story. You still haven't gotten used to the loneliness. You wonder if you ever will. The inmates you walk with to the cafeteria reek with body odor.

You're floating again, back across the ocean to Africa—South Africa this time. You're a black coal miner. Your sister has malaria, and her health is declining rapidly. You're standing at the front counter of the hospital emergency room, pleading with the attendant there. He repeats again, "For the last time, I'm sorry, but you **know** that this hospital doesn't take coloreds."

You're floating, once again; this time out of your dream and back into consciousness, as you slowly awaken from restless sleep. The house is silent. Your parents are gone.

That night you're walking down a street downtown with a group of friends. You've just been to a movie. You see a young woman leaning against the entrance of a basement bar. Her clothes, makeup, and posture are strange and gaudy, and your assumptions about why she's standing there like that are confirmed when she walks off with a man who comes up to her and flashes a bill from his pocket.

An hour or so later, as the group is heading back to your car to go home, you walk past a dark alley. Out of the corner of your eye you catch a glimpse of what you think is a scuffle. Briefly you hear muffled grunts and a thud and the faint clinking sound of coins striking the pavement. It may be a mugging but you're afraid to look. So you walk on, half hoping that someone else in the group saw what was happening and half hoping that none of them did.

Suddenly, someone grabs your shoulder from behind. You recognize the panic-stricken face as that of Cindy Rodriguez, the Puerto Rican girl who used to work as a maid for your next-door neighbor. "Please, come quickly," she stammers. "My sister . . . my mother throw her out . . . she having baby! Please help!"

You and your friends run to your car with her and drive to an old, abandoned service station on the outskirts of town where Cindy takes you.

The garage door is closed, but you can see through the glass at the top of the door that the light is on inside. Cindy lifts the rickety garage door and quickly assures the startled teenage boy and girl inside that everything's okay. Only after a moment does she notice the baby in the girl's arms. Her eyes widen and she gleefully squeals some Spanish exclamation.

You stare in astonishment. The frail, sweaty girl, clad in old jeans and a dirty T-shirt and jacket, reclines against a rusty cabinet with nothing but the boy's jacket between her and the cold, oil-stained cement floor. She smiles weakly at Cindy, but her eyes look apprehensive. The trembling boy kneels beside her, stroking her hair. He looks down at the baby, wrapped in rags and newspaper, as he wipes the bloody fluid away from the newborn's face and head.

John, one of the guys in your group, whispers, "What a dumb son-of-a-bitch! Not only does he get this girl pregnant, but then he's stupid enough to stick around to see the results!" Susan hushes him and approaches the mother. "Do you want us to take you to the hospital?" The exhausted girl shakes her head politely.

Just then the baby coos softly and opens his tiny eyes for a split second. The light from the ceiling makes his eyes seem to twinkle.

As the group turns to go, you silently wish there was **something** you could do for this small family. Susan verbalizes your wish. John shakes his head nonchalantly. "It wouldn't matter," he says. "The baby'll be dead in a few days anyway." Just as you turn your head to walk out of the garage, you think you see a slight smile grace the baby's face briefly.

After you've driven the others home you talk with Susan. It's hard for you to express what you're feeling. "I don't know," you say. "But there just seemed to be something different about that baby, something special. It's a miracle that it's even alive, being born out there in that old garage ... I felt so sorry for them. Lord, I hope that baby doesn't die."

"I thought I saw him smile," Susan replies softly.

The years pass by and time buries the garage incident in the obscure recesses of your mind. About thirty years later, you're on the downhill side of middle age, reading the morning paper, and a headline catches your eye: **Radical Cult Leader to Be Executed Today.** You recognize the name of the condemned, Juan Marcolez, from previous articles in the paper.

A few days later, you notice another, even more interesting headline: **Body of Executed Criminal Disappears from Coffin.** The subtitle reads: **Officials Claim Body-Snatchers Responsible.** You recognize the name again, but this time it disturbs you a bit. It seems that you remember having had some familiarity with the name "Marcolez" even before the many articles about his activities began to appear in the news three years ago. But the memory is way in the back of your mind—it seems to come from a long time ago.

Weeks later you read another article, a feature on the Juan Marcolez cult that still persists after his execution and has actually grown in numbers since Marcolez' body disappeared from his coffin. You are struck by the boldness of one of the followers of Marcolez who is quoted in the article. He claims that the body of Marcolez was **not** stolen. Rather, he says, Marcolez has risen from the dead, and is actually alive again. "Juan was not only our leader and friend—he was our teacher. He made us believe that we **can** make a difference in life ... that we actually **can** make the world a better place. He assured us that if we continue to struggle against the evil, injustice, suffering, and ignorance that plague our entire world, our work will not be in vain."

The quote in the article continued, "Because of Juan Marcolez there is hope for this world. He has saved us from death. We must **continue** the work of Juan. He has called us to minister to the poor, the hungry, the lonely, and the oppressed. He has commanded us to change the world through love.

"There is a new world yet to come. All will be well, if only we will follow Juan."

Something in what this Marcolez follower is saying triggers in your mind the sudden, cruel memory of a terrible dream you had back in your high school or college years. You hope out loud that what this radical follower of Juan Marcolez is saying is true.

# Handicapped Meeting

Here's a good way to sensitize your young people to the particular needs of handicapped persons. Conduct a regular youth meeting or banquet, but as the young people arrive, have them draw from a box the name of a handicap that will be theirs for the duration of the meeting. For example, one person might draw "poor eyesight" or "blindness"; another might be "hard of hearing," "unable to walk," and so on. The possibilities are, of course, many. As the meeting progresses, each person tries to act as if they actually had the handicap which they drew.

Later in the meeting, or following the meal, the young people may return to being their normal selves. A discussion can then be held regarding their feelings and observations during the experience. (Contributed by Rick Bell, Albuquerque, NM)

## Hands

This idea can be used as a crowd breaker or as an opening for a worship service and is most effective with a large group of participants.

Have everyone pair off with someone they do not know, and introduce themselves. Then blindfold all participants and explain that there can be no more talking during the course of the game.

The couples are then directed to face their partner and feel each others hands—memorizing the feel of them, size, distinguishing features, etc. Once they have had time to do this, mix all the participants around. Without making any noise, everyone must find their partner by feeling everyone's

hands.

Once all participants have paired up, they may remove the blindfolds to see if they found the correct partner. This game can open up a handful of discussions covering topics such as: handicaps, senses, cooperation, the hands of Christ, and others. (Contributed by Gaye Lynn Sharp, Fort Worth, TX)

## Hang-Man Lessons

Do you have a good idea for a lesson, but you aren't sure how to present it? For a little variety, play the simple game of "hang-man" to reveal your outline. For example, four points on a lesson about friendship might be: 1) Acquaintance; 2) Casual; 3) Special; 4) Intimate. Instead of just telling your group these points, have them guess each word a letter at a time. For every wrong guess, hang a part of the body from the noose. They will usually guess the word, and will be more involved in the lesson. (Contributed by John Stumbo, Monticello, MN)

## Lesson on Listening

It can often come as a shock how much of our energy in conversation is used for "ego-speaking" and self expression rather than for listening.

The following exercise is designed to help your kids become aware of how easy it is not to listen to the messages of others.

To begin, prepare four cards as follows:

| | |
|---|---|
| **Your Favorites:**<br>1. What do you like most about school?<br>2. What is your favorite time of year?<br>3. What is your favorite Bible verse? | **Exposing Weaknesses:**<br>1. What is your greatest personality weakness?<br>2. What is your most annoying habit?<br>3. What is your greatest spiritual weakness? |
| **The Pits:**<br>1. What bugs you the most about school?<br>2. What is your least favorite vegetable?<br>2. When were you last bummed out? | **Revealing Strengths:**<br>1. What is your most positive personality trait?<br>2. What is your greatest skill?<br>3. What is your best spiritual strength? |

Divide everyone into groups no larger than five people. Each group should be given one of the four cards. Everyone should then briefly answer the questions on the card for the whole group. After about five minutes the groups should exchange cards so that they have a new set of questions. As before, the group members should take turns answering them.

After all of the groups have been through every category of questions, each person is given a sheet of paper and is asked to list every fact they can remember from the answers given in their discussion group. Of course, those with the better memories are at a slight advantage, but those who really tuned in and listened to others in their group (rather than concentrating on their own responses) will be able to recall the most. A prize could be given for the person with the most correct recollections on their list. A discussion of the importance of listening would be a good way to wrap up this exercise. For some helpful verses, take a look at Proverbs 18:2,13; 22:17; and Ecc. 3:7. (Contributed by Lew Worthington, Anderson, IN)

# Light Over Darkness

The following is an effective way to present the metaphors of light and darkness found in Scripture. You will need one 18" by 11" cross, one medium-size candle which cannot be blown out (you can get this at a magic shop) and one regular candle for each youth present at the meeting. Begin by setting the cross on a table and by putting the candle—the one that won't blow out—in front of the cross.

Light the candle and turn off all of the lights to the room so that it is completely dark. As the youth enter the room, give each of them a regular candle and have them sit down facing the cross.

• Explain that light represents good (God) and darkness represents the evil forces of this world (Satan).

• Read Genesis 1:3,4.

• Light the first person's candle; they are to light the next person's candle until all the candles are lit.

• Read John 8:12.

• Explain that if you put your trust in Jesus, you will walk in the light, but if you put your trust in the world, you will walk in darkness.

• Read 1 John 1:6.

• Explain how if you merely say you are a Christian and go through the motions of walking in the light, you're only fooling yourself because God knows your heart.

• Have your youth blow out their candles and experience darkness. Ask the question, "Can you find the sin which is darkness in your life?" Think for a minute about the darkness Satan is putting in your pathway. Jesus was tempted by Satan to come into darkness also.

• Try to blow the main candle out 3 times.

• Explain how the attempts to extinguish the candle represent the sin Satan put in Jesus' way. He did not fall, and his light kept shining and is still shining today.

• Explain that in 1 John 1:5 God is light and in him there is no darkness.

• Ask the youth if they will let the eternal light of the world reignite their faith. (Have the youth come forward one at a time, relight their candles and return to their seats.)

• Challenge youth by asking them if they will commit themselves to the light of the world and to the work of sharing the light with those in darkness.

• Read Isaiah 2:5 and end with a prayer. (Contributed by Chip King, Rex, GA)

---

## Lights On, Lights Off

This idea can be used as a discussion starter with any topic, or it can be used simply as a fun way to test everyone's power of concentration. You will need some large drawings, photographs or slides.

Pass out a worksheet to each youth and explain that they will be seeing some pictures and they should respond to these three questions:

1. What is the first word that this picture brings to your mind?
2. What feeling did you experience when the picture was revealed?
3. What sentence could you write that would summarize what the picture was about?

Turn out the lights and put up the first picture. Flip the lights on for five or ten seconds and then off again. (If you are using slides, simply show the slide for a few seconds while the lights are off.) Next, remove the picture and put the lights back on just long enough for the kids to write down their responses. Repeat this for each picture.

After all of the pictures have been viewed, discuss their responses, pointing out the differences and the various points of view that arise concerning what they have seen. Hopefully, the group will learn to appreciate one anothers' viewpoints as well as have a better understanding of the content of each photo. (Contributed by John Peters, Louisville, KY)

## Love Programs

The following two program ideas deal with relationships in a creative way that is strong on personal application. They might be especially useful if there is evidence of cliques or snobbery building in your group.

### "LOVING THE UNLOVELY"

#### Part I – Role-play

This role-play uses three characters: Joe Director (leader of the youth group); Grungey Gertrude (dirty, unmatched clothing, out of style); Mod Mary (fashion-able, neat, pretty).

Joe is getting ready for the youth meeting to start when Grungey Gertrude walks in. Joe says hello, but then keeps busy setting up chairs, etc., ignoring Gertrude. She follows him around relentlessly, telling him about her day—she got a "D" in Home Ec, went to a worm wrestle after school, lost a chess tournament, got to buy lunch at school instead of taking a sack. Joe is cold.

Mod Mary arrives. Joe meets her with a big smile and handshake. He asks her questions and listens sympathetically. He invites her to have dinner with his family that week. Gertrude tries to join in the conversation, but is not acknowledged by Joe and Mary. Mary sits down. Gertrude looks for a seat, but they are all taken. Joe suggests that she sit on the floor on the far end of the circle. Joe and Mary enthusiastically start singing, "We are one in the Spirit." Gertrude sits with a dejected, puzzled look on her face.

#### Part II – Discussion

Lead the group in discussing their response to the role-play by asking these questions: How did they feel toward Joe, Gertrude and Mary? Did anyone identify with one of the characters? Should any of them have acted differently? How? What would Jesus have done? Have you seen this type of behavior in our group? What can you personally do to prevent it?

### Part III – Wrap-up

Turn to James 2:1-13 and I Samuel 16:7. Conclude the lesson with a brief explanation of the principles of love at work in these passages.

## "BEING KIND"

### Part I – Preliminaries

During the opening minutes of your youth group (games, announcements, singing), plan for a few leaders and a group of kids to make cruel remarks, critical comments, belittling cuts and to be generally sarcastic towards the activities. Hand out paper and pencils to the group after this and have them answer the following questions:

1. How do you feel about youth group today? Why?
2. Does anything seem unusual about youth group today?
3. Are you glad you're here or do you wish you had stayed home?

### Part II – Group Discussion

Go over the questions and expand on the subject of cutting and criticizing. Ask the kids to share an experience when they felt really cut down.

### Part III – Role-play

Using the story of the Good Samaritan as a model, act out the responses of three passers-by to a robbery and beating victim on the street. The first person to come along throws a Bible to the man and tells him to read it. The next one acts snobbish and turns away. Another kicks him and complains about drunks on the street. Finally, someone comes to the victim's aid.

### Part IV – Discussion

Review the various options of the characters and discuss how your kids might respond in similar situations.

### Part V – Wrap-up

Read Ephesians 4:31-32, I Peter 3:8-12, John 13:35. Suggest that the kids look for opportunities to be kind to others and have them keep track of the kindnesses done to them during the coming week. (Contributed by Vaughn Van Skiver, Corning, NY)

---

# Male Or Female?

For a simple discussion starter on the complicated subject of male/female roles and societal norms, print up a copy of the list below and pass it out to your group. Ask them to decide which of the tasks or roles on the list are "male" and which are "female" (they must choose one or the other). After each person has completed his or her list, have the group break into smaller groups and try to come up with a consensus in those groups. The small groups can then report their conclusion to the larger group. Chances are pretty good that there will be a lot of disagreement and heated discussion. Feel free to add your own items to the following list:

1. Cooking supper
2. Grocery shopping
3. Paying bills
4. Maintaining the car
5. Washing windows
6. Painting the house (outside)
7. Painting the house (inside)
8. Caring for children
9. "Making a living" (work)
10. Playing soccer
11. Mastering a musical instrument
12. Initiating a date
13. Paying for a date
14. Proposing marriage
15. Deciding which church to attend
16. Choosing a house or apartment
17. Talking openly about feelings
18. Getting drunk with the gang on weekends
19. Getting high with the gang on weekends
20. Being a good listener
21. Building furniture
22. Hanging pictures
23. Doing laundry
24. Driving a car on trips
25. Disciplining children
26. Saying grace at meals
27. Decorating home/room
28. Attending a concert
29. Watching TV
30. Going to a play
31. Going camping
32. Attending a sporting event
33. Doing dishes
34. Taking out the garbage
35. Crying
36. Choosing a form of birth control
37. Mowing lawn
38. Tending garden
39. Staying home from work with sick child
40. Cleaning house

You may want to expand this into a Bible study by finding Bible characters that exhibit these role distinctions, or by studying the teaching of Jesus and the Apostle Paul concerning male/female roles in society. (Contributed by Jeff L. Bunke, Maumee, Ohio)

## Midnight Picnic

Here's a Bible study idea that the kids will love. First, have the group look up information about star formations and planets visible from the earth. Then, on an evening when the moon is dim, have a picnic at midnight. Each person should pack a lunch, a lantern, and a blanket. After eating, look at the stars and try to identify the formations. You can even try to count the stars. Tie the evening together with some thoughts on how God created the stars (Genesis 1) and how God's handiwork is expressed through the heavens (Psalm 8, 19). This could be done anytime after dark, but there is more of a sense of drama for the kids if it is done at midnight. (Contributed by Alva Wiersma, Englewood, CO)

## Musical Blanks

Here's a fun way to use music in your youth meetings. It will not only help kids listen well, it will encourage them to evaluate the type of music they hear.

Choose some contemporary songs (Christian or secular) that have a meaningful message and which have lyrics that are reasonably easy to hear. Duplicate the words on a handout, leaving a blank in place of some key words in each phrase.

Pass out the lyric sheets and some pencils to the group. Play the music, instructing your kids to fill in the blanks with what they hear. When you are all through, go over the lyrics and give a prize for the one with the most correct write-ins. Then, discuss the message of the song. You might want to try and change the message by inserting your own lyrics in the blanks. Finally, play the songs again, for enjoyment and for a better understanding of the meaning. (Contributed by John Peters, Bedford, KY)

## My Life, Christ's Home

This activity is designed to help young people evaluate their lives in light of Christ's call to be totally committed to Him. A discussion of Matthew 19:16-30 or Luke 14:25-35 can start off the meeting, highlighting the radical and supreme commitment Jesus requires of His disciples.

Tell each young person to imagine his or her whole life as a huge mansion with many rooms. Each room represents a different part of our lives. Jesus wants to be allowed into every room to make some changes—redecorate, expand or close off some parts—and to oversee the use of each room. Without total commitment, we may want to control certain rooms ourselves and to shut Christ out of those rooms. Our goal is to examine our lives and to invite Christ into those areas we have kept to ourselves.

Ask each young person to draw a large diagram of his or her life as if it were a big house, with a number of rooms, and to put their name on the house. The rooms should be labeled according to areas of life that Jesus wants surrendered to Him. For example:

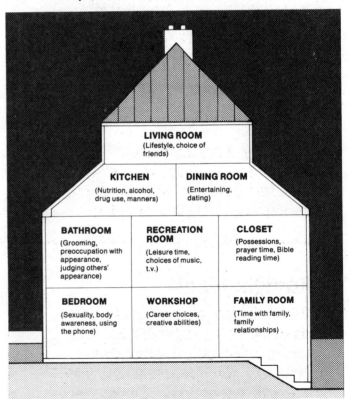

After the young people have done this, they can begin by rating each room from 1 to 10 depending on how much Christ occupies that particular room. For example, a room that is totally under Christ's control would be a 10, and a room that seriously lacks Christ's control would be a 1.

Finally, have the kids discuss the following questions (or others that come to mind) in small groups or to answer them in writing on the backs of their sheets.

1. Which rooms of your house are most occupied by Christ?

2. Which rooms are least occupied by Christ?
3. How does your "house-life" need to be remodeled?
4. What are some specific actions that you can take to make your house totally Christ's home?

(Contributed by Thomas Cairns, Rochester, NY)

## Paradoxes of Scripture

This program idea can be used to involve a number of students with Scripture. Plan a debate or series of debates using the paradoxes found in the Bible. Issues can include Law vs. License, God's Mercy vs. God's Justice, Forgiveness vs. Judgment, Strength vs. Weakness, Boldness vs. Gentleness, Old Covenant vs. New Covenant, etc. The debates should involve lots of research and should be conducted at the youth group meeting using regular debate format. It is an exciting and arousing way for youth to develop their communication skills and sharpen their reasoning abilities. (Contributed by Robert Crosby, Rochester, NY)

## Peer-Pressure Study

No youth group can afford to ignore the subject of peer pressure and conformity. The power that one's age group has to consciously or unconsciously force others to conform and act in harmony with the group can be a major obstacle in the spiritual development of your kids. The following study is helpful as a means of opening up discussion on the topic. It also presents some valuable tools which can be used by your kids to battle peer pressure.

---

**PART ONE — A QUIZ**

*Take this Peer Pressure Survey to see how you are affected and react to peer pressure:*

(1) When faced with a decision to act or not to act like others my age are acting, I usually:
   a) Flip a coin
   b) Freak out and hide under my bed
   c) Really think it over
   d) Pray and ask God to show me what to do
   e) Other _____

(2) I (often / sometimes / never) feel pressured to do something that others are doing in order to be accepted.

---

(3) There is a right and a wrong choice for each decision that I must make. (Yes / No)

(4) All peer pressure is bad. (Yes / No)

(5) There is peer pressure to act a certain way in our youth group. (Yes / No)

(6) The pressure I face most often is _____ .

(7) A Christian writer named Sören Kierkegaard once wrote, "There is a view of life which conceives that where the crowd is, there is also the truth. There is another view of life which conceives that wherever there is a crowd there is untruth." Which view do you agree with?

(8) In order of their importance to you, list five values or priorities in your life that you could use to guide you in making a decision:

    1.

    2.

    3.

    4.

    5.

## PART TWO — TWO BIBLICAL EXAMPLES

In the Old Testament we read how Daniel and his three friends were taken prisoner when the Babylonian army defeated Israel in 604 B.C. (Daniel 1). Daniel was probably about sixteen years of age at the time. He was taken from his country, his home, his school, and his parents and carried several hundred miles away to the Babylonian capital. He and his three friends were to be trained to serve the king.

They were suddenly faced with an intense test of their values. Would they continue to worship God or bow to the Babylonian idols? Would they break the Jewish dietary laws that they knew God had given them to keep them healthy and undefiled for His service? How would they react to the immoral practices of their captors?

They could easily have "gone along with the crowd" and compromised their values. But years before, they had decided to put God's values above the values of other people. Daniel and his three friends had already set their priorities; there was no further decision to make.

In the New Testament (John 7:1-7) Jesus was encouraged by His brothers to go on to visit the believers in Judea. No doubt, the argument presented by His brothers was a persuasive one. Jesus, however, was in touch with the larger plan and more perfect will of God the Father. Nothing, not even the pleas by His brothers, could veer Him from that plan.

## PART THREE — MAKING DECISIONS

Facing peer pressure comes down to one thing — Where are your priorities? What values do you place the most importance on? In Matthew 6:33, Jesus tells us to "Seek first the Kingdom of God and His rieghteousness." As Christians, we should put God and His will for our lives first, above everything else. There are three questions you can ask yourself about a choice:

    1. How does it affect me as an individual?

    2. What will be the effect it has on others?

    3. How will it affect the cause of Christ?

There are three tests to apply to each choice you face:

    1. *The Test of Secrecy.* Would you feel different if someone else you knew was aware of what you were doing?

    2. *The Test of Individuality.* Would you still do it even if all of your peers were not?

    3. *The Test of Prayer.* Can you ask God to go with you and bless you in this?

And finally, there are three sources of spiritual guidance for you:
1. From within — your conscience and the Holy Spirit.
2. From without — your parents (they do know something), Christian friends and church leaders.
3. From above — your relationship with Jesus Christ and your understanding of what the Bible has to say.

(Contributed by Greg Platt, Prattville, AL)

## Prayer Lab

Prayer is a subject which is often talked about but never carefully looked at. While there are many different styles and ways of praying, there are a few basic aspects to prayer worth examining. One way to get your kids to reflect on the subject is to set up a prayer lab. Simply prepare four posters like the ones below and

### SUPPLICATION

SUPPLICATION IS ASKING A SPECIFIC REQUEST OF GOD.

1. THINK OF WHAT IMPROVEMENTS GOD WANTS IN YOUR LIFE. ASK GOD TO HELP YOU ACCOMPLISH THESE.

2. MAKE A LIST OF TEN PEOPLE YOU KNOW WELL. LIST ONE SPIRITUAL NEED FOR EACH PERSON. PRAY THROUGH YOUR LIST.

3. PRAY FOR YOUR LEADERS, SUCH AS THOSE IN GOVERNMENT, PARENTS, YOUTH SPONSORS, AND TEACHERS.

4. PRAY THAT GOD WILL HAVE A GREATER INFLUENCE ON THE PEOPLE IN YOUR SCHOOL.

### CONFESSION

CONFESSION IS AGREEING WITH GOD THAT YOUR SIN IS IN FACT SIN AND THEN MAKING PLANS FOR HOW NOT TO REPEAT THAT SIN. SIN INVOLVES NOT DOING WHAT WE KNOW IS RIGHT ALONG WITH DOING WHAT IS CONTRARY TO GOD'S WORD.

1. MAKE A LIST OF THE ACTIONS AND ATTITUDES WHICH GOD WANTS IN YOUR LIFE BUT ARE NOT PRESENT.

2. CONFESS THESE AS SIN.

3. MAKE A PLAN BETWEEN YOU AND GOD FOR HOW NOT TO REPEAT THEM.

4. DESTROY YOUR LIST.

### SUBMISSION

SUBMISSION IS CONSCIOUSLY PUTTING YOUR WILL UNDER THE AUTHORITY OF GOD. ONE WHO SUBMITS HUMBLY WILL WANT WHAT GOD WANTS FOR THEM.

1. ASK GOD TO TAKE CONTROL OF THESE AREAS OF YOUR LIFE:

| | |
|---|---|
| FRIENDS | RELATIONSHIP WITH PARENTS |
| STUDIES | EMOTIONS |
| JOB | SPIRITUAL WALK |
| DATING | ATTITUDES |
| FINANCES | PRIDE |

### ADORATION AND THANKSGIVING

ADORATION IS TELLING GOD HOW MUCH YOU LOVE HIM BECAUSE OF WHO HE IS. THANKSGIVING IS TELLING GOD HOW MUCH YOU LOVE HIM BECAUSE OF WHAT HE HAS DONE.

1. PRAY THROUGH PSALM 103. THEN PRAY IT AND ADD YOUR NAME.

2. ADORE GOD FOR EACH OF HIS ATTRIBUTES. THEN THANK HIM FOR THE WAY THESE AFFECT YOUR LIFE:

| | | |
|---|---|---|
| LOVE | MERCIFUL | UNCHANGEABLE |
| WISDOM | CREATOR | TRUTH |
| HOLINESS | RIGHTEOUS | UNIFIED |
| SOVEREIGN | GRACIOUS | ALL-POWERFUL |
| KIND | SELF-EXISTENT | ALL-KNOWING |
| | | ALWAYS PRESENT |

place them in four separate areas or rooms of the church. Divide your kids into four groups and have them rotate from one lab to another. Each group should spend 10 to 15 minutes doing whatever is instructed on the poster. If the use of labs works well with your group, you may want to use it again only with different subjects.

(Contributed by Daniel Van Loon, Clear Lake, IA)

## Prayer Letter

One good way to care for your youth is to pray for them individually. If you do this, you might want to let them know with a personal letter similar to the one below. Each day, choose one or two youth for prayer and a special note. Here's a sample:

---

Dear Bob,
Hi! Hope you are having a great year in school! You know, you are special to me and our church. I don't tell you that enough, but I want you to know it. This morning you were the subject of my quiet time. I prayed that God would be especially close to you today and help you with your everyday problems and victories. God truly loves you and wants only the best for you. I do too.

In Christ,

Jim

---

(Contributed by James Bourne, Douglas, CA)

## The Pulpit Committee

Have your group learn about the Apostle Paul or discuss qualifications for spiritual leadership by using this simple strategy.

Divide the group into a number of small "pulpit committees" with the task of securing a new minister for your congregation. Have them compile a list of characteristics that they feel the candidates should have; then give them several "applications." Be sure to include this letter among them:

Gentlemen,

Understanding your pulpit is vacant, I should like to apply for the position. I have many qualifications . . . I have been a preacher with much success and also some success as a writer. Some say I'm a good organizer. I've been a leader most places I've been. I'm older than 50. I have never preached in one place for more than three years. In some places I have left town after my work has caused riots and disturbances. I must admit I have been in jail three or four times, but not because of any real wrongdoing. My health is not too good, though I still get a great deal done. The churches I have preached in have been small, though located in several large cities. I've not gotten along well with religious leaders in towns where I've preached. In fact, some have threatened me and even attacked me physically. I am not too good at keeping records. I have been known to forget whom I have baptized.

However, if you can use me, I shall do my best for you.

Go over the findings and reveal to the group that the letter above describes the Apostle Paul. Then, go on to study what true spiritual leadership requires. (Contributed by Dick Gibson, St. Petersburg, FL)

## R.O.T. Teams

Here's a good way to get your people involved in ministering to others. Divide your group into teams called "R.O.T." (Reach Out and Touch) teams. Each team should be composed of six to eight teens. Assign or elect a team captain and co-captain for each group. These captains are also to serve on the "R.O.T. Strategic Planning Committee" which plans the various ministry projects.

Let each team choose a different ministry project to work on. For example, you could have a Visitation Team to make calls on various fringe kids in your group and to visit church members in hospitals and nursing homes; a Work 'n' Witness Team to rake leaves, cut the grass, etc., for the elderly; a Prayer and Support Team to pray for needs within and without the congregation; and many other teams depending on the needs of your community. (Contributed by Mark Stone, Raytown, MO)

## Scripture's Common Denominators

The next time you are looking for a good way to get your kids into Scripture, why not give this idea a try. Divide everyone into groups of threes and give each group the following list—without the answers, of course. The object is simple: they are to look up each set of verses and decide on a common theme which is found in each of them. You can easily add other sets of verses as you like. Since there are no winners to this exercise—everybody benefits—you might want to close by having everyone share the verse that meant the most to them during the evening.

1. Matthew 9:13, Luke 6:36, I Timothy 1:12 ff. *(The Mercy of God)*
2. Acts 10:36, Romans 5:1, Philippians 4:7 *(Peace between God & Man)*
3. 1 Corinthians 12:27, Ephesians 1:22, Colossians 1:18 *(Christ as Head of the Church)*
4. 2 Corinthians 1:12, I Timothy 1:19, I John 3:21 *(Forming a Good Conscience)*
5. Matthew 7:15, Acts 19:9, James 4:4 *(Friendship)*
6. John 7:38, Romans 1:16 or 3:22, Galatians 3:8 *(Having a Visible Faith)*
7. I Corinthians 4:12, I Thessalonians 5:15, I Peter 3:9 *(Do Not Return Evil for Evil)*
8. Matthew 3:15, I Corinthians 5:6, James 3:5 *(Fidelity in Little Things)*
9. Galatians 5:20, Titus 1:7, Matthew 5:22 *(Anger)*
10. Mark 11:25, Luke 6:32, Colossians 3:13 *(Forgive Those Who Wrong You)*
11. I Timothy 1:5, I Peter 4:8, I John 4:16 *(Charity or Love)*
12. John 13:15, I Corinthians 15:49, Ephesians 5:17 *(We Should Imitate Christ)*
13. Matthew 17:26, Romans 14:1, 15, 2 Corinthians 6:3 *(Don't Give Bad Example)*
14. Matthew 4:22, Mark 7:10, Ephesians 6:1 ff *(Children & Parents)*
15. Philippians 3:13, Hebrews 12:28, Jude 1 *(Serving God)*
16. John 16:33, I Timothy 6:17, I John 3:21 *(Confidence and Trust in God)*
17. Luke 15:20, 27, 2 Corinthians 1:3, Ephesians 2:4 *(God's Goodness & Care Toward Us)*
18. Mark 7:6 ff., Acts 5:1 ff., 2 Timothy 3:5 *(Hypocrisy)*
19. 2 Thessalonians 1:4, 7; 2 Peter 1:6, James 5:7 *(Patience)*
20. John 13:17, Hebrews 4:2, James 1:22 ff. *(Word of God Must Be Lived)*
21. Matthew 5:29 ff., Acts 5:1 ff., Philippians 3:7 *(Self-Denial)*
22. 2 Timothy 2:14, 23, 23, Titus 3:1, 2, 9, James 4:1 *(Avoid Discord and Arguing)*
23. John 15:10 ff., James 2:10, I John 5:2 ff. *(Keeping God's Commandments)*
24. 2 Corinthians 6:14, 2 John 10, Revelation 18:4 *(Choose Friends Well)*
25. John 2:7, Acts 4:19, Romans 16:19 *(Obedience to God)*
26. 2 Thessalonians 3:13, 2 John 8, Jude 13 *(Perseverance)*
27. Romans 11:33, Colossians 2:3, James 3:15 *(Wisdom)*

(Contributed by Pat Andrews, Slidell, WA)

---

## Senior Snack

Here is a good method for breaking down the barriers between your young people and the elderly members of your church. Contact a number of elderly persons from your church and ask if they would be willing to visit with a small group of young people during your regularly scheduled youth meeting time. Invite them to include one or two of their friends to the visit, and ask if they will provide a drink of some kind if you bring a snack. Be sure to emphasize that the visit will not last more than 45 minutes.

When the youth arrive for the meeting, break them into groups of four or five, each with a sponsor. Explain what they will be doing, and have them go over a list of questions that would be appropriate to ask. These might include:

1. What were things like when you were our age?
2. What was one thing which really helped your growth in Christ?
3. Can you give us some suggestions or advice to help us in our faith?
4. What would you do differently if you had the chance?
5. Did you grow up in a Christian family?
6. When did you make a commitment to Christ?
7. What can we specifically pray for you about, or what concern can we help with?

Next, send each group out to visit with one of the elderly people you have contacted. Be sure they stick with your time limit and meet back at the church at the appropriate time. Discuss their impressions, new insights or unexpected outcomes of the visits, then pray for the specific concerns. (Contributed by Doug Van Essen, Grand Rapids, MI)

## Shopping Spree

For a creative look at money and how people spend it, here is a simple simulation to try with your young people. Buy or print several million dollars in play money. Then, divide it into random amounts ($3,000 to $450,000) placed in plain envelopes. Pass out these envelopes to your group.

Now for the shopping spree. Set up a table or bulletin board with a wide assortment of full-page advertisements for things like: cars, mansions, computers, vacations, food, savings accounts and Christian relief efforts. Each youth gets an order blank to "buy" any items they wish, as long as they can pay for it themselves or by pooling their money. Give them ten minutes to "shop" and five minutes to fill in their order blanks.

Gather all of the order blanks, or compile a blackboard list of everything ordered. Discuss the values expressed, their feelings about unequal distribution of the cash, and their responsibility to care for the needy. (Contributed by Bob King, Richardson, TX)

# Signposts to Life

Here's a good way to use the Ten Commandments as a discussion starter for your youth group. Read the following paraphrase of the Ten Commandments to the kids, or make a signpost of each one to hang on the wall:

1. I shall be the only God you will have.
2. I am the only image you shall worship.
3. My name shall always be taken seriously.
4. You shall receive My day as a holy one.
5. You shall act responsibly toward your parents.
6. You shall respect the sacredness of life.
7. You shall respect the possessions of others.
8. You shall be loyal to your family.
9. You shall always tell the truth.
10. You will be content and satisfied with what I give you.

After discussing each of these, ask the following questions:

1. Do the Ten Commandments apply to us today?
2. What is a covenant?
3. What are some modern day covenants we make?
4. What is the basis of God's covenant with Israel?
5. Why did this fail with Israel in the Old Testament?
6. Did Jesus change the Law?
7. How are the Ten Commandments "signposts to life" for us?
8. How did Jesus express the essence of the Law?

(Contributed by Larry J. Michael, Rockville, MD)

# Signs of the Times

This idea uses traffic signs as symbols of faith in Christ and can start good individual sharing and discussion. Collect several highway and traffic signs, either packaged or made by the kids themselves, and place these on the walls of the room. Ask the kids to choose a sign that best describes their own life as a Christian and to tell why. Discuss each of the signs and their relationship to Christianity with the group. Encourage new ideas and creative thinking—no comments are considered wrong. Here are a few examples:

An ideal time for this discussion would be during summer or Christmas vacations, or when the group is about to embark on a trip or retreat. Road signs would then take on new meaning. Other signs include:

(Contributed by Barbara Farish, Columbus, GA)

# Slide Studies

Many youth groups have discovered that producing a slide show can be a unique and captivating way to get into the Gospels. Besides being fun to do, the finished product is always a hit when presented at a worship service or youth banquet. To get the most out of a slide show, have the kids create the whole show as a response to a theme you have been studying. Have them write the script, design the slides and take the pictures.

Of course, you will need to have a 35mm camera, a photographer who knows how to use it, a slide projector and enough time to get the slides developed before the presentation.

The following drawings are an example of how you might prepare a slide show script. This particular show was created to communicate the unity of the Church as seen in 1 Corinthians 12. (Contributed by Kim Jackson, Roseville, IL)

(Title)

(Title)

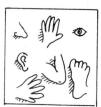
Our Bodies have many parts

But many parts make up only one body when they are all put together

So it is with the Body of Christ

Each of us is a part of the one body of Christ

Some of us are Jews

Some are Gentiles

Some are slaves

Some are free

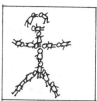
But the Holy Spirit has fitted us all together into one body

Yes, the body has many parts

Not just one part.

If the foot says, "Because I am not a hand, I am not a part of the body" that doesn't make it any less a part of the body.

And what would you think if you heard an ear say, "Because I am not an eye, I do not belong to the body"?

Suppose the whole body were an eye?

How would you hear?

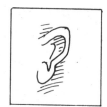
Or if your whole body were just one big ear . . .

How could you smell anything?

But that isn't the way God made us.

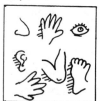
He has made many parts for our bodies

And has put each part just where He wants it

What a strange thing the body would be if it only had one part.

So He has made many parts

74

But there is only one body.

The eye can never say to the hand "I have no need of you".

The hand can't say to the feet "I have no need of you."

The head can't say to the hand, "I have no need of you."

God has put us together in such a way that if one suffers

All parts suffer with it.

And if one part rejoices,

All the parts rejoice.

Now what I'm saying is this: All of you together are the one Body of Christ.

And each of you is a separate and necessary part of it.

(THE END)

# Spirit Balloons

Here's a unique idea that can be used for planning meetings or for youth group discussions on goal-setting for the future. Since this idea involves the role of the Holy Spirit, begin by defining the word "spirit." It is used both in the Old and New Testaments and means "breath" or "wind." With this short definition in mind, have everyone write down a long-term goal that they have, a career they would like to pursue, or anything that involves dreaming **big** about things to come.

Take these dreams, fold them up, and place them inside a balloon. As everyone blows up the balloons, remind them of the definition of "spirit"—they are surrounding their dreams symbolically with the Holy Spirit. Discuss how all of our dreams and goals are made possible by the Holy Spirit and how dependent we are upon Him.

Tie all of the balloons and place them in the middle of the room. Using a game or random selection, pop some of the balloons, read the goals out loud and discuss what is necessary in order for a person to accomplish that goal. (Contributed by Mark Christian, Santa Rosa, CA)

# Spiritual Growth Chart

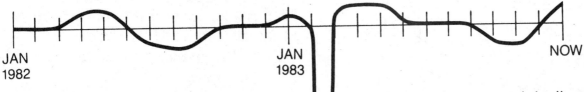

JAN 1982     JAN 1983     NOW

Here's a creative way to get your kids to think about spiritual growth and to evaluate their own walk with God. Pass out paper to your kids and have them draw a straight line to represent the last two years of their lives, labeling the months and years on the time line. Next, ask them to draw a flexible line charting their spiritual ups and downs. Anything above the time line represents a time of growth, anything below indicates decline and anything along the line represents no change in their spiritual progress.

After the charts are complete, have the group circle any major "high," "low" or "no change" periods and write down why that condition existed. Discuss these findings together. Some questions to consider are: What causes growth in our spiritual lives? Is there anything wrong with a chart that looks like a roller coaster? What have we learned about ourselves from these charts?

After the discussion, you might want to chart the spiritual progress of some colorful characters in the Bible (David or Peter, for example) and compare their struggles. (Contributed by Phil Print, Denver, CO)

## Thanksgiving Exchange

This is a good discussion starter for Thanksgiving or for any time when you want to teach a lesson on gratitude. It works best with a group that knows each other fairly well. Begin by having each person share one or two things that they are thankful for. These will usually be the kind of things that are most obvious to them.

Then have each person write his or her name on the top of a sheet of paper. Collect the sheets and redistribute them so that everyone has a sheet with someone else's name on it. Now have each person write on that sheet what he or she would be thankful for if they were the person whose name is on that sheet. They can list as many things as they want. Next, pass the sheets back to the person whose name is on each sheet and discuss the following questions:

1. What things are written on your sheet that you haven't thanked God for lately?
2. What things are written on your sheet that you had never even thought about thanking God for?
3. Is anything written on your sheet that you disagree with? That you didn't think you should be thankful for?

This exercise works great to help young people to realize that they often take for granted many things that they should be thankful for. (Contributed by Randy Wheeler, Portales, NM)

KRISTEN
can be thankful for:
1. Having a sister
2. Good health
3. Doesn't need glasses
4. Has lots of friends
5. Got a summer job

# The Thir-Teen Commandments

Here's a good exercise that could be tied in with a study of the Ten Commandments, although it could be used any time. Divide the group into smaller units and ask each group to think of as many "commandments" as they can that would apply to today's teenagers. For example, one might be "Thou shalt not cheat on exams" or "Thou shalt choose your friends carefully."

After all the groups have come up with their lists, share them and select those that everyone agrees upon. These can then be published by the group as the official Thir-TEEN commandments (or Four-TEEN, etc.). The group can then discuss them, rank them easiest to hardest, and hopefully apply them to their lives. (Contributed by Kevin Richardson, Sheridan, AZ)

# Time and Life

This skit is a great way to point out the importance of giving **all** of our time to God, and to spend it wisely. The narrator begins by introducing the theme of "Time and Life" while someone in the background holds up **Time** or **Life** magazines at the appropriate mention of it. As the narrator relates the findings of a recent study, various young people act out each segment.

All of the participants then hold up signs indicating the number of years they represent. The narrator explains that these are all important years, none of which should be lived without God's guidance. (Contributed by Jimmie L. Hancock, Montgomery, AL)

"The average person spends 23 years sleeping . . ."
  *(Person appears wearing pajamas, carrying a teddy bear and pillow and lays down to sleep)*
". . . 11 years working . . ."
  *(Person appears dressed in work overalls, carrying tools)*
". . . 8 years recreating . . ."
  *(Person appears in a gym suit, bouncing a basketball, etc.)*
". . . 6 years eating . . ."
  *(Person with stuffed body comes out eating potato chips, bananas, etc.)*
". . . 6 years reading and being educated . . ."
  *(Person in graduate garb appears frantically flipping through a large book)*
". . . 5½ years grooming . . ."
  *(People appear in rollers, wearing cold cream, combing hair)*
". . . 3 years talking . . ."
  *(Two people come out excessively talking to each other)*
". . . and a half year worshipping God."
  *(Person comes out with a Bible and kneels)*

# Tract Man

No doubt you have seen gospel tracts or booklets that have made you wonder whether your young people could do a better job creating them. Well, why not let them give it a try? Show them some tracts, such as the "Four Spiritual Laws" booklet, or those from Chick Publications, and ask your youth group to be creative and write their own. Have them aim the tracts at their own age group, and encourage them to use some Scripture in their works. (Contributed by Phil Print, Denver, CO)

# Travels In The Church

This is a good discussion starter on the church and worship that would also be great for an intergenerational group meeting or family retreat.

Pass out a diagram of your church, showing the location of each pew or chair, and some pencils. Have the group chart their "travels" of their church-going life, labeling the various positions where they have sat in church, from nursery to the hearing-aid section with specific dates.

Once the charts are filled in, discuss why people sit where they do in church, the habits and attitudes in your church, reasons for moving onward or staying in one place in church. Have everyone say where they expect to sit in the future of their church-going, where they would never sit and what sections of the church make them uncomfortable. (Contributed by Keith Curran, Huntington, PA)

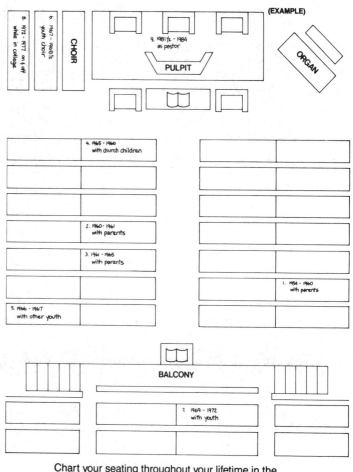

Chart your seating throughout your lifetime in the church. Starting with number 1, mark each pew where you regularly sat (for more than 1 month).

What does this say about you?

# Understanding Disability

Lack of awareness and lack of knowledge concerning disability are the two primary causes of harmful attitudes we sometimes show toward those who are disabled. The following outline can be used with youth to help them look at this problem, see their own attitudes, learn about disability, and hopefully bring about a change which will ultimately improve the quality of life for this very important segment of our population.

The following course of study is designed to take place in five different sessions, perhaps at a camp or spread over several weeks. Some of the sessions could be combined or dropped, however, or others of your own creation added.

### Session I: "How Do I Feel About Disabled Persons?"

*Objectives:*
1. To begin to look at how we feel about those who are disabled.
2. To begin to look at how we react to disabled individuals and how we tend to treat them.
3. To discover how ablebodied and disabled people are alike, instead of different.

*Step 1:* Hand out 3x5 cards and ask each person to write the first few thoughts that come to mind when they think of a person who is disabled or handicapped. Give them about 5 minutes, collect the cards and read them out to the group. Summarize the main things you learned from this exercise and write them on a chalk board or a large piece of newsprint. Keep this for future reference.

*Step 2:* Role play one or more of the following situations:
A. Two or three students are talking in the hall at school. A new student walks in the door with a parent and is looking for the office. They stop to ask directions. The boy speaks with an unusual voice and you notice hearing aids in both ears. How do you react to this situation? What are your thoughts about this new boy?
B. You are at the mall and it is very crowded. You get behind a girl who walks with crutches and has braces on both of her legs. She is walking very slowly and you are in a hurry. How do you feel? What do you do?
C. You are with a group of friends on the first day back at school. A boy with cerebral palsy (walking with an uneven gait and one arm seems to jerk continuously) approaches you for directions to the gym. He is difficult to understand because of a slight speech defect. How do you react to him? How do your friends react to him?
D. You are having lunch with some friends and notice a person in a wheelchair at the next table. He also has a device attached to his hand to help him eat by himself. He has finished eating and seems to be having some difficulty getting around the table to leave. What do you do?
E. You are walking down the street with a few friends and notice a girl with a cane walking in front of you. She makes a turn and comes to the wall of a building. She seems to be a little disoriented. What do you do? How do you feel?

After each role play discuss the feelings of all the individuals in the situation. How did it feel to be disabled? How did you want other people to react to you? What are some of the typical ways we react to those who are different from us?

*Step 3:* List the ways in which those who have disabilities are just like you and me. When we meet others who have a noticeable handicap, our first reaction many times is to see how different that person is from us. Actually, when we look closely, we can probably find many more ways we are alike than different. For example: (a) We all have the need to be loved and accepted. (b) We all need shelter. (c) We all need food. (d) We all want to be liked. (e) We all want to be entertained and have a good time. (f) We all need clothing. (g) We all want to look as nice as possible.

*Step 4:* Discuss ways you can begin to look beyond a person's disability and see a person with gifts, talents, expectations, disappointments, happiness, and sadness, just like anyone else.

### Session II: "What Is It Like To Be Disabled?"

*Objectives:*
1. To learn what life is like through the eyes of a person who is disabled.
2. To experience talking with a disabled person in a non-threatening situation.

Call your local State Division of Vocational Rehabilitation or a private rehabilitation agency in your area and invite a representative along with one or two clients to come and share with your group what it is like to be disabled and how they manage in your own community. Explain fully to the persons you invite exactly what you are doing and the objectives for this session. Hopefully your group will gain a better understanding of what it is like to have a specific disability.

**Session III: "What Is It Like To Be Disabled?" (cont.)**
*Objectives:*
1. To experience firsthand some of the difficulties disabled people encounter.
2. To become aware of the way our world has been built for the convenience of able-bodied people, and how it excludes the disabled population from many of the opportunities we take for granted.

Set up several simulaton experiences for your group to help build an awareness of the barriers disabled individuals face in our world today. For example, you might want to take the group to a mall, divide into small groups so as not to be disruptive and try the following experiences:
A. Take turns using a wheelchair and try to get in and out of stores, go to a movie, get into a restroom, get a drink of water, and get to the second floor of a store.
B. Put ear plugs in several persons' ears and have them try to communicate with others in the group, clerks in the stores, and so on.
C. Blindfold several of the people in the group. Have another person guide them in trying to take an elevator, find the restrooms, etc. You may want to also do this in a familiar setting too, as it can be just as difficult to find one's way around.
D. Supply a pair of crutches for several people to use to get from one end of the mall to the other.
E. Instruct the person in the wheelchair not to use his/her arms. Someone may need to push the wheelchair if it is manual, but that is the only thing the person is to be helped with.

There are many more examples you might use. Choose those which will be best for your group. A wheelchair or crutches might be available from a local rehabilitation agency if you explain your purpose. They can also be rented.

After the simulation experiences have taken place, come together and discuss what you have learned. What was most difficult? How did others react to you? Were there any surprises? How did you feel?

**Session IV: "What is Rehabilitation?"**
*Objectives:*
1. To learn about the facilities available to rehabilitate those who are disabled.
2. To learn to interact with disabled people in a positive way.

Visit a local rehabilitation agency and discover what is being done to help disabled individuals attain their highest level of functioning, adjust to their disability, and eventually find employment or some other meaningful activity in life. This would also be a good time to meet some other individuals with disabilities and talk with them. Call a local agency and arrange a tour of the facility as well as an opportunity to interact with the clients there.

**Session V: "How do I Handicap People with Disabilities?"**
*Objectives:*
1. To learn the difference between a disability and a handicap.
2. To learn how we handicap others.
3. To make a decision to act in the interest of disabled individuals, being sensitive to their feelings, wants, needs, and rights.

*Step 1:* Explain the difference between a disability and a handicap. A disability is the actual physical condition (loss of a leg, paralysis, blindness, etc.). That disability becomes a handicap when it keeps a person from doing something he/she needs or wants to do. All disabilities do not have to be handicaps. The unfortunate thing is that due to our attitudes toward disabled people, *we* are the ones that handicap them. That is, we are the ones who prevent them from living and working up to their potential.

*Step 2:* From the experiences you have had in the past few sessions, can you think of ways we might handicap a person with a disability? Some possible answers are:
A. By ignoring them, we keep them from enjoying regular interaction with others.
B. By discriminating against them and thinking that they can't do things as well as able-

bodied people, we keep them from enjoying feelings of accomplishment and working for a living.
C. By not making sure buildings are accessible, we keep them from taking care of certain tasks for themselves, from enjoying some forms of entertainment, from shopping for themselves, and so on.
D. By continually doing work for them, we keep them from meeting us on equal ground and enjoying a relationship of equality.
E. By continually holding lower expectations of them, we keep them from attaining the most for themselves.

*Step 3:* Repeat the first step from Session I. Compare the answers. Have they changed? If so, how?

*Step 4:* Divide the group in to small groups of three or four people. Give each group a piece of paper on which to list at least three ways they can begin to act toward disabled individuals in a positive, sensitive way. Have them share these with the entire group.

(Contributed by Mary Jo Davidson, Sarasota, FL)

---

# Vice Versa

This is a great motivator for Bible verse memorization that can be used for a week-long retreat. At the beginning of the retreat, divide the kids into small teams and give each team a Bible verse. (There should be a fairly good number of verses, so in a small retreat you may want to assign more than one verse to each team.) The goal is for each person to learn as many verses from other teams as he can for points. And each team receives a point for every person that learns its verse.

During the course of the retreat, the verses will pop up in conversation, be hung on doors, put on beds, printed on toilet paper, etc., as each team tries to teach its verse to someone else. At the end of the retreat, have everyone write down as many verses as they have learned, giving a prize to the person who has learned the most, and to the team that has had the most people learn its verse. This can get very creative—and six months later, the kids will still know the verses.
(Contributed by Kathy Neese, Lyons, NY)

---

# Video Values

The next time you do a series on culture or media, try this idea for examining popular movies with your youth.

Rent a VCR and a popular movie, carefully chosen for good taste and meaningful interaction among the characters (i.e. *Chariots of Fire, On Golden Pond, Kramer vs. Kramer, Tex, Tender Mercies*). DON'T have much discussion after the viewing.

In the next few weeks, continue your Bible study series as usual. Show the movie AGAIN, this time for evaluation. Pass out paper and pencils and have the kids write down all of the Scriptural principles they see either followed or violated. If they can, have them include specific Scriptural references. After the showing, discuss any changes in their attitudes toward the film. Does the film reflect the Biblical principles at work in the world? How could certain characters have behaved differently? What difference would a Christian have made among them?

(Contributed by Ed Laremore, Lynchburg, VA)

## What Is a Christian?

The following true-false quiz makes a good discussion starter on the subject of "What is a Christian." It forces kids to think through some of their own assumptions as well as questions that are frequently raised by others.

WHAT IS A CHRISTIAN?

T F 1. The only thing one must do to be a Christian is to attend church on Sunday.

T F 2. The only thing one must do to be a Christian is to be a member of a church and attend its functions.

T F 3. A person becomes a Christian when he/she is baptized.

T F 4. A person becomes a Christian when he/she is confirmed.

T F 5. In order to be a Christian the only thing one must do is believe that Jesus Christ died for your sins.

T F 6. All real Christians are "Born Again" Christians.

T F 7. Every member of this church is a Christian.

T F 8. Jesus was a Christian.

T F 9. Only those people who belong to the _____ Church are Christians.

T F 10. Most people in my church only *say* they are Christians but they really are not Christians.

T F 11. To be a Christian one must read the Bible regularly.

T F 12. Everyone who goes to church is a Christian.

T F 13. All Christians believe the same things.

T F 14. Being a Christian means that I can't do all the fun things that my friends do.

T F 15. One can be a Christian and still believe that drinking alcohol is OK.

T F 16. Once one is a Christian, he/she never sins again.

T F 17. You can tell that a person is a Christian by the way he/she acts.

T F 18. Christians do not swear/curse.

T F 19. Christians love everyone.

T F 20. My parents are Christians.

T F 21. As a Christian, I must do the right things in order for God to love me.

T F 22. God loves Christians more than he loves non-Christians.

T F 23. God does not allow Christians to get hurt.

T F 24. Most of my friends are Christians.

T F 25. I am a Christian.

(Contributed by Eric Lohe, Burlington, NC)

## What Is My Gift?

Here is a great way to focus on the discovery and use of spiritual gifts. Before the meeting, print adhesive labels with description of gifts — usher, good listener, song leader, S.S. teacher, friend who cares, bakes good cookies, repairs books, group leader, intercessor, plays organ, plays piano, organizer, etc. When the kids arrive, place one gift label on their back without telling them what it is. Everyone mingles around asking "What is my gift?" and others try to

# GOOD LISTENER

pantomime the answer, but may speak only "yes" or "no." When someone discovers his gift, he can move the label to his arm.

After everyone has discovered their gift, the group can discuss and evaluate each one. If someone is sure that the gift they are wearing is not for them, they may remove it and give it to someone else. Extras should be available close by, and kids should be allowed to write their own gift, or write gifts to others. Some people may have one or two gifts—some more. The leader needs to make sure that everyone has at least one gift.

Once this is settled, the group sits down to discuss what happened. What did it feel like to ask, "What is my gift?" "What was it like to give someone else a gift?" "What was it like to receive a gift from another?"

After the discussion, pass an offering plate and have the kids offer their gifts to God. Close with a prayer of dedication and thanks. (Contributed by Doris Weber, Petersburg, ON, Can.)

## Word Pictures

Here's an idea that can help your youth do word studies, examine Bible characters or delve into theological concepts. Pass out worksheets with a word picture diagram printed on them. Have your group write the key word (which can be any word or name you suggest) in the center. Then, combining the key word with the guide words on the outside, ask them to write in additional descriptive words. It's easiest to write the first thing that comes to mind. When they are through, your group will not only have a better understanding of the key word, they will be able to see more of the implications involved in study of Scripture.

---

## WORD PICTURE

This is a worksheet for you to produce a Word Picture uniquely your own. You will be surprised at the new light you bring to the key word in the center of the picture. You may even be surprised at how creative you really are.

Directions: Write key word in center circle. Using the guide words, write a word or a phrase in each outer circle that best fits the mood of that circle. You don't have to put down opposites all the time. The two circles may make you think of two different ideas. Or you may see one as a "+" and the other as a "−." However you see fit to fill the circles is okay. It is your picture of the key word. Have fun.

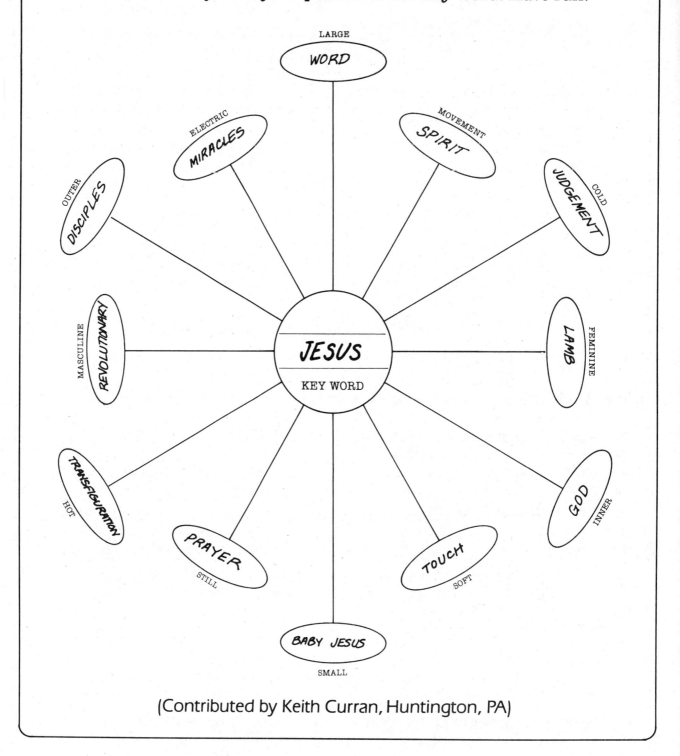

(Contributed by Keith Curran, Huntington, PA)

## Youth Group Revelation

For a valuable discussion-starter, try using this Bible study at the end of the year, or at a time when you think your youth group might have some hidden problems. It not only provides a good look at Scripture, but can be a sound basis for evaluation of your youth group as well. (Contributed by Randy Comer, Independence, MO)

# Youth Group Revelation

In Revelation 2:1-3:9, we find 7 letters to 7 churches, each with its own merits and problems. If John (in the power of the Holy Spirit) were writing to your youth group, what would he commend us for?

_____

_____

Look over this review of the 7 churches that the letters were addressed to:
  I. Review of the Seven Churches (Rev. 2:1-3:9)
     A. Ephesus (2:1-7). A church that was orthodox and doctrinally faithful; yet, it had forgotten its first love for the Savior. Faithful to doctrine ... but cold in its practice.
     B. Smyrna (2:8-11). Apparently a small, struggling church. Even though it was pure, it was a suffering assembly.
     C. Pergamum (2:12-17). A church of doctrinal compromise. It had begun to drift from the moorings of Biblical truth.
     D. Thyatira (2:18-29). An assembly that tolerated a Jezebel in its midst—a person who was leading people astray and winning a hearing, even though she was herself of false teaching.
     E. Sardis (3:1-6). A church that was big, impressive, and well-known ... but dead.
     F. Philadelphia (3:7-13). The most encouraging of all the churches. She had an open door for opportunity and ministry that God wanted her to use. The church was vital, very alive, and full of potential.
     G. Laodicea (3:14-19). A church that received no commendation ... one of lukewarm indifference. It was neither hot nor cold, neither dead nor zealous, but just bland and tasteless.

Which one is most like our group, and why?

_____

_____

Pray with your prayer partner now for areas where we are weak. Jot some of these down.

_____

_____

Write a word of appreciation for your youth leaders and share it with them today.

# SKITS

## Fun With Emcees

An often neglected part of a skit nite or talent show is the art of emceeing. Instead of doing the traditional thing of using only one emcee, why not try it with two. Here are a few possibilities:

1. **Stereo emcees:** The cohosts can each give a phrase of the introduction with both of them saying the last phrase simultaneously. For example:
    Cohost One: The next skit . . .
    Cohost Two:  . . . we would like to . . .
    Cohost One:  . . . present to you . . .
    Both cohosts:  . . . is entitled "The Stuntman."
2. **Bobbing emcees:** One cohost is to stand behind the other. The introduction is to be broken down word by word. The front cohost says the first word, squats down, and the second cohost stands and says the second word. This continues until the intro is finished.
3. **Echoing emcees:** Each cohost has a microphone. One cohost gives the introduction while the other echoes him or her.
4. **Singing emcees:** Both cohosts can sing the intro to their own made-up tune or the tune of a popular song or commercial jingle.
5. **Ventriloquist and dummy:** One cohost is the ventriloquist while the other is the dummy. The ventriloquist lifts the dummy onto his or her lap, tells a few jokes and then announces the skit.

(Contributed by Milton Hom, Richmond, CA)

# Future Banana

This short skit requires no words. A guy walks out on stage, sits on a chair in the middle of the stage, and takes out a banana. Meanwhile, the music from the movie **2001: A Space Odyssey** is playing in the background. The guy peels the banana and eats it to the music. If done properly, with appropriate facial expressions, the results are hilarious. (Contributed by Steve Siverns and Tim Criuckshanks, Arlington, MA)

# The Great Piano Recital

This skit can be a lot of fun if you have an upright piano, a spinet piano, a good pianist and a real good actor. Begin by placing an upright piano on stage or in front of the room. Then, place the spinet piano behind it so that the audience can't see it. Have the real pianist out of everyone's sight by the spinet piano and the actor at the upright piano (the actor should be a person who has no musical ability).

Announce to the audience that a guest pianist is going to entertain everyone. Then have the audience write their song requests on slips of paper which are collected. The guest pianist (the actor) should read the name of the request and then ham it up as if he were really playing it while a real pianist on the spinet is actually playing. This can be hilarious as the visible pianist will be guessing where the next notes will be on the piano keyboard.

For added fun, substitute the following crazy song titles for the titles suggested by the audience:
1. "You broke my heart, but I broke your jaw"
2. "She was a moonshiner's daughter, but I love her still"
3. "They operated on Father and opened Mother's male"
4. "When you wore a tulip and I wore a big red rose, and we both got arrested"
5. "Let's go behind the rock pile baby . . . we can get a little bolder there"
6. "Let me call you hinges, for you are something to adore"
7. "Old Arabian Ballad: Oh, What a Bag Dad Had"
8. "Lord, send me a blonde, cause I'm tired of squeezing blackheads"
9. "I was riding high in the saddle till my blister broke"
10. "Red snails in my swimsuit"

(Contributed by Dallas Elder, Portland, OR)

## Howdy Buckaroo

If the kids in your group have a tough time memorizing lines, this skit might be perfect for them. Four characters are needed: a mechanical quick-draw cowboy dressed in full cowboy garb, two warehouse employees dressed appropriately and a third employee. Only the mechanical quick-draw cowboy need remember any lines. They should be spoken in a mechanical manner: "Howdy Buckaroo. So you think you can beat me, eh? Put on the holster at my feet and on the count of three, draw! Are you ready? One . . . . Two . . . . Three!"

The only props you will need are two gun-and-holster sets, one of which should be loaded with blanks.

The play begins with the two warehouse employees rolling in the mechanical slot-machine cowboy for storage. The extra gun-and-holster set is placed at the feet of the mechanical cowboy.

The third employee walks in and, seeing the robot, decides to try his luck. He reads the instructions printed on the chest of the mechanical man and then places a quarter in the slot. The robot winds up and gives the memorized spiel. The employee is unable to pick up the extra gun-and-holster set because it's trapped under the boot of the mechanical cowboy. He panics and turns to run as the robot counts to three and shoots the employee.

Not to be outdone, the employee lifts the robot's leg and puts on the gun set before inserting another quarter. He even practices his quick-draw skills several times. Feeling quite secure with himself, he inserts another quarter. The message is repeated but this time the gun sticks in the holster and again he is shot.

For the final attempt, the employee pulls his gun, stands to the side and, holding his gun to the robot's head, inserts another quarter. The robot repeats the message except that this time the mechanical cowboy winds down in the middle of "two." The employee bangs on the robot a couple of times to get him moving again, but no response. Disgusted, he takes off the gun, sets it down at the robot's feet and turns to walk off. The robot continues suddenly with the rest of the pre-recorded message, says "three," and shoots the employee. (Contributed by Keith Herron, Grand Prairie, TX)

## Marching Kazoo Band

This is a great activity for the entire youth group at a large rally or talent night. Give every kid in your youth group a kazoo and a marching band uniform (party hats and all-white clothing will work just as well). Practice some simple marching drills and formations and finish with a high-kicking chorus line to bring down the house. As you perform, it might help to have recorded march music playing in the background (such as "Stars and Stripes Forever") to add some quality to the music and to help the band stay in beat. (Contributed by Janice Parylak, Deer Park, New York)

## The Mona Lisa

Here's a skit idea which is guaranteed to bring a faint, yet enchanting smile to everyone at the very least. Have someone memorize the words to the old Nat King Cole favorite "Mona Lisa." Then dress someone up as the Mona Lisa herself in a long, black wig, black robe and black shawl. Build a picture frame out of some old boards and have the "Mona" sit behind it. Drape a sheet from the bottom of the picture frame to the floor so that the audience cannot see the Mona Lisa's feet.

He is going to sing a very serious song for them. As the song begins, the curtain opens to reveal the Mona Lisa. The singer turns to see the Mona Lisa and begins to sing to the picture. During the song, however, the Mona Lisa comes out of character; she picks her nose, sneezes, cleans out her ear, shoots water pistols at the singer, blows a kiss to the singer, eats a banana, and does any other things which you might think of. All of this should be done every time the singer turns away from the Mona Lisa to face the audience. The skit ends with the singer getting a whipped cream pie in the face, at which point the singer jumps through the picture frame and chases the Mona Lisa. (Contributed by E. Paul Albrecht and Roy J. Delozier, Philadelphia, PA)

## More Fashion Follies

This idea can be combined with "Fashion Follies" **Ideas #24** for a really spectacular show. Simply choose several guys and gals to be models and design the following apparel for them to wear. Have a talented announcer describe the various fashions to the audience as the models walk across the stage.

1. **Brush-Denim Jacket:** A denim jacket with a brush sewn onto it.
2. **Popcorn Weave Sweater:** A sweater with popcorn attached.
3. **Checkered Skirt:** Plastic checkers sewn onto a skirt.
4. **Tank Top:** A box painted to look like a fish tank (cut a hole for the head).
5. **Pancake Makeup:** Real pancakes taped to one's cheeks.
6. **Lipstick:** Lips on a big stick.
7. **Orange Belt:** Oranges in cellophane tied around one's waist.
8. **Bib Overalls:** A baby bib sewn onto jeans.
9. **Jump Suit:** The model jumps up and down all of the time.
10. **Saddle Shoes:** Ropes from feet to hands.
11. **Standard Pumps (shoes):** Make pumps and tape them on the skirt.
12. **Hand Bag:** Make an outline of a hand on a purse.

13. **Grass Skirt:** Tape small packages of grass seed on a skirt.
14. **Cotton Blouse:** Put cotton balls on a blouse.
15. **Straw Hat:** Attach drinking straws on a hat.
16. **Colorful Choker:** Someone runs on stage and appears to choke the model.
17. **Picture Hat:** Have small frames and pictures on a hat.

(Contributed by Sheila Busboom, Urbana, IL)

---

# Monk Monotony

The following skit is an easy one to pull off as you will need only three characters (the Main Monk, Monk Monotony, and a sign carrier) and one prop (a large sign which reads "Ten Years Later"). The audience is asked to imagine a monastery where Monk Monotony has just taken a vow of silence.

| | |
|---|---|
| *Main Monk:* | So Monk Monotony, you have just taken a vow of silence? (*Monk Monotony shakes head "yes".*) Do you know what this vow of silence means? (*Monk Monotony shakes head "yes".*) That's right, you cannot say anything but *two words* for the next ten years. You may go now.<br>(*Monk Monotony exits. After about 20 seconds in which the Main Monk does nothing, the Sign Carrier enters slowly from right and exits slowly to the left, carrying the sign which reads "Ten Years Later." Monk Monotony enters.*) |
| *Main Monk:* | Yes, Monk Monotony your first ten years are up, and you may now say your two words. |
| *Monk Monotony:* | Hard Bed. |
| *Main Monk:* | You may go now.<br>(*Monk Monotony exits. After about 20 seconds in which the Main Monk does nothing, the Sign Carrier enters slowly from right and exits slowly to the left, carrying the sign which reads "Ten Years Later." Monk Monotony enters.*) |
| *Main Monk:* | Yes, Monk Monotony your second ten years are up, and you may now say your two words. |
| *Monk Monotony:* | Bad Food. |
| *Main Monk:* | You may go now.<br>(*Monk Monotony exits. After about 20 seconds in which the Main Monk does nothing, the Sign Carrier enters slowly from right and exits slowly to the left, carrying the sign which reads "Ten Years Later." Monk Montony enters.*) |

90

| | |
|---|---|
| *Main Monk:* | Yes, Monk Monotony your third ten years are up, and you may now say your two words. |
| *Monk Monotony:* | I quit. (*He begins to exit immediately.*) |
| *Main Monk:* | (*To Monk Monotony as he is leaving.*) Well, I am not surprised. You've been complaining ever since you got here. |

(Contributed by J. Russell Matzke, Colorado Springs, Colorado)

---

# One Fine Day in a Disastrous Flood

Only two characters are needed for this one, Noah and his son Ham. Unless you are able to get a hold of a 450 foot ark made out of gopher wood, the only other prop you will need is a can of Coke. The play begins with Noah and Ham walking onto the stage; both rocking back and forth as though they are on a boat. Ham looks sick.

| | |
|---|---|
| *Ham:* | (*groan*) Ohhhhh . . . |
| *Noah:* | What seems to be the trouble, Ham my boy? |
| *Ham:* | I'm nauseous; I don't feel so good. |
| *Noah:* | You don't look so good either. What seems to be the problem? |
| *Ham:* | It smells in here. These animals smell worse than a dead skunk in a heat wave. |
| *Noah:* | Oh, come now. It couldn't be all that bad, just because we have two of every animal in the world in this ark. |
| *Ham:* | Well, that's not all. This boat is going back and forth and back and forth. We've been in here three hundred and twenty-six days, twelve hours, three minutes and seventeen seconds. We've been floating in this water for so long I'm starting to feel like a teabag. |
| *Noah:* | Hey, don't worry son. I don't think God is going to keep us in here too much longer. You must have patience. |
| *Ham:* | Maybe for another forty-nine days, eleven hours, and possibly fifty-seven minutes and and forty-three seconds — counting leap year — don't you think? |
| *Noah:* | Yes, maybe . . . |
| *Ham:* | Using math-o-matics of course. |
| *Noah:* | Quite right, but you know you must learn to be patient, patient, patient, patient . . . |
| *Ham:* | Dad, Dad, Dad; you're starting to sound like a |

91

|        |                                                                                                                    |
|--------|--------------------------------------------------------------------------------------------------------------------|
|        | doctor.                                                                                                            |
| *Noah:* | I'm sorry. Is it still raining outside?                                                                            |
| *Ham:*  | Does it ever rain on the inside?                                                                                   |
| *Noah:* | No respect, no respect.                                                                                            |
| *Ham:*  | Take a peek and see.                                                                                               |
| *Noah:* | (*Looks out window*) It's raining so hard I can't see what the weather's like.                                    |
| *Ham:*  | Let me see, Dad. (*Looks out window*) Why, it's raining cats and dogs outside.                                    |
| *Noah:* | Son, I told you to keep those animals inside the ark.                                                             |
| *Ham:*  | That was only a figure of speech. It sure rains a lot.                                                            |
| *Noah:* | Yes son, I think we're over the future site of Seattle, Washington. That reminds me, I think I left the water running in the bathtub back home. |
| *Ham:*  | Uh oh Dad. When we get the water bill, Mom's going to kill you!                                                   |
| *Noah:* | I hope you meant that as a figure of speech.                                                                      |
| *Ham:*  | Hey Dad, do boats sink often?                                                                                     |
| *Noah:* | Only once.                                                                                                         |

|        |                                                                                                                    |
|--------|--------------------------------------------------------------------------------------------------------------------|
| *Ham:*  | What if we get a hole in the ark and it sinks?                                                                    |
| *Noah:* | Impossible. For one thing, God wouldn't allow us to sink; that would ruin the whole story. Besides, I can't swim. |
| *Ham:*  | What if we did sink? We don't have any life preservers big enough to fit the elephants.                          |
| *Noah:* | Oh, you're such a ham, Ham. Trust God. He's holding this boat together just like He holds our lives together. He will safely float you through any flood waters of life if you just put your trust in Him and let Him be your captain. |
| *Ham:*  | But things are just so dull around here. I wake up in the morning to the rooster's crow, to the pig's oink,       |

|        |                                                                                                                     |
|--------|---------------------------------------------------------------------------------------------------------------------|
|        | and to the zebras . . . whatever noise they make. Have you ever tried to get a six hundred-pound Siberian tiger to use a kitty litter box? Don't. Also Dad, you've got to do something with those dive-bombing birds. I have to wash my hair every hour because of them. Speaking of which, have you seen my hair dryer lying around the ark anyplace? |
| *Noah:* | Yes, I have. While I was drying my beard with it, the ostrich swallowed it . . . shocking sight. |
| *Ham:* | You're kidding. I don't know how much more of this I can handle. |
| *Noah:* | What, this ark? |
| *Ham:* | No, your jokes. |
| *Noah:* | Like I said before, you must have patience. |
| *Ham:* | Oh, I have patience. I've always had patience. Ever since I was born I've had patience. (*pause*) What's patience? |
| *Noah:* | Patience is the suffering of affliction with a calm, unruffled temper. When you're patient through times of trial and tribulaton, God will shape and mold you into a new and better you. |
| *Ham:* | But Dad, I'm so bored. This whole place is totally boring. I want off this ark. |
| *Noah:* | But son, don't you want to grow? |
| *Ham:* | What do you mean? Does being bored help me to grow? That's totally wild; I suppose if I was excited it would stunt my growth. |
| *Noah:* | No son, I don't mean that kind of growth. I'm talking about your spiritual growth. You see, through each trial and tribulation we should praise God because we can benefit spiritually and grow to be a stronger Christian for God. |
| *Ham:* | I see, we should rejoice in our sufferings because we know that suffering produces patience, patience produces character and character produces hope. |
| *Noah:* | Exactly son. We benefit from our boredom. So just be patient until, until the great rainbow in the sky shines bright. |
| *Ham:* | Thanks Dad. I'll go finish cleaning out the stalls. |
| *Noah:* | Hurry up, Mom's cooking dinner. |
| *Ham:* | What are we having? |
| *Noah:* | What do you want? |
| *Ham:* | Barbeque barley with cheese sause. |
| *Noah:* | Want a side order of fries with that? |
| *Ham:* | No thanks, maybe some alfalfa sprouts topped |

|            | with ketchup. |
|------------|---------------|
| Noah:      | You've got it. |
| Ham:       | Oh, by the way Dad, have you see any sight of dry land yet? |
| Noah:      | I sent a raven out earlier this morning to find dry land, but that raven had aquatic phobia. (*To the audience*) That's the fear of water. With the water below him and the rain around him, that bird totally freaked out. |
| Ham:       | Why don't we try it again, only with a smaller animal. |
| Noah:      | I know, I'll use a snake. |
| Ham:       | Naaa, Harold's got a cold. Besides, that snake is so near-sighted he fell deeply in love with a rope. |
| Noah:      | I bet his love life is all tied up. |
| Ham:       | Why don't we use a dove? |
| Noah:      | Naaa, that won't work. (*pause*) I know, we'll use a dove. |
| Ham:       | (*To himself*) Why didn't I think of that? |
| Noah:      | Here pretty bird. (*Noah acts as if he was reaching into a cage for a dove*) Now listen carefully, I want you to fly out and find dry ground, and if you do find dry ground, bring something back as proof. Good luck and God be with you. (*Throws the dove out the window*) Fly and be free. (*Mime watching the bird fly, then fall down into the water*) Swim, swim, flap your wings like this. (*Flap arms*) That's it, go, go, go. (*To son*) Remind me to sign that bird up for the next Olympics. |
| Ham:       | Right. |
| Noah:      | Look. |
| Ham:       | Where? |
| Noah:      | Up there, the dove returns, and it has something in its beak. (*A can of Coke is thrown on stage, Noah catches it*) Look, the dove has found land. |
| Ham:       | (*Graps the Coke can and holds it out to the audience*) It's the real thing. |
| Noah:      | (*Noah sings part of the Coke jingle*) Coca-Cola . . . oh, anyway, I knew God wouldn't let us down, you just got to have . . . |
| Ham:       | I know, I know, have a little patience. |
| Noah:      | You've got it now, my boy. Oh no . . . ! |
| Ham:       | What? |
| Noah:      | I just thought of something. |
| Ham:       | What? |
| Noah:      | Oh no. |
| Ham:       | WHAT!? |

| Noah: | I hope we can find a hotel with a vacant room. |
|---|---|
| Ham: | Don't worry, I bet a lot of people stayed home because of the rain. (*They exit*) |

THE END

(Contributed by Frank Walker, Bellevue, WA)

---

## Senior Superman

Have you ever wondered what happens to comic book super heroes when they get old? Is it true that most of them are now in Ft. Lauderdale playing shuffleboard? In the following skit, one well-known defender of law and order talks about his life as a senior citizen. You will need to arrange the stage to look like a talk show studio, and you will need two actors: Abner Theobald Knuklenose III (the talk show host) and Senior Superman. Superman should have a cane, be dressed in a raggedy, tattered Superman suit, and look very old, run-down and senile. Knuklenose could be dressed with a large African safari hat and wearing thick glasses and a big plastic nose.

| A.T.K.: | Good evening ladies and gentlemen. i'm your famous interviewer, Abner Theobald Knuklenose III presenting another in an ongoing series of (da-dat-da-da), 'Famous Interviews.'
This evening, ladies and gentlemen, we have a very special treat for you. We will be interviewing a person whom I am sure all of you will indeed recognize and look up to . . . that world renowned man of steel, that man who is faster than a speeding bullet, more powerful than a locomotive, able to leap tall buildings in a single bound. Look up in the sky, it's a bird, it's a plane . . . no, it's Superman! Yes! It's Superman, that strange visitor from another planet who came to earth with powers and abilities far beyond those of mortal men. Superman! Who can change the course of mighty rivers and bend steel in his bare hands. And who, disguised as Clark Kent, mild-mannered reporter for a great metropolitan newspaper, fights a never-ending battle for truth, justice, and the American way. Ladies and gentlemen, may I introduce to you . . . Old Man Super! (*pause*) Old Man Super! (*pause*) Hey, uh Sup . . . hey Superman, are you coming? (*Slowly Superman walks out. He is wearing his Clark Kent glasses and hat by mistake.*) Here he is, ladies and gentlemen, |
|---|---|

95

that super man himself, Old Man Super! (*A.T.K. realizes Superman is wearing his Clark Kent glasses and hat and quickly takes them off of him.*)

Superman: Hey, I can't see, ya young whippersnapper. Give me back my glasses! (*A.T.K. whispers to Superman, obviously explaining why he did what he did. Superman gives A.T.K. a big wink and the "high sign" to indicate "okay."*)

A.T.K.: It certainly is a delight to have you with us this evening, Mr. Superman.

Superman: Yes, it is.

A.T.K.: It is certainly kind of you to come and break away from your busy schedule to be with us.

Superman: Yes, it is.

A.T.K.: Indeed, it is a real thrill for me to personally meet and talk to such a famous person as yourself.

Superman: Yes, it is.

A.T.K.: Oh?? I'll bet many of our folks this evening have never had opportunity to see you in person. I'll bet many would have thought seeing you in person would be disappointing. What do you think?

Superman: Yes, it is.

A.T.K.: Let me direct a few questions your way, Mr. Super.

Superman: Just send 'em slow, ya' young whippersnapper.

A.T.K.: Certainly. I couldn't help noticing that you walked in and didn't fly. Why is that?

Superman: I don't fly anymore.

A.T.K.: Could I ask why?

Superman: Yes.

A.T.K.: Well?

Superman: Well what?

| | |
|---|---|
| A.T.K.: | Well why? |
| Superman: | Well why what? |
| A.T.K.: | (louder) Well, why don't you fly anymore? |
| Superman: | Well, why don't you ask me? |
| A.T.K.: | (very loud) Okay, I will . . . |
| Superman: | (very soft) You don't have to holler. I'm sitting right next to you and I'm not deaf. |
| A.T.K.: | Oh, I'm sorry. (calmer and softer) What is the reason for your not flying anymore, Mr. Superman? |
| Superman: | What'd you say? |
| A.T.K.: | (soft still) I said, 'What is the reason for your not flying anymore, Mr. Super? |
| Superman: | Speak up, I can't hear you. |
| A.T.K.: | (upset) Why don't you fly anymore? |
| Superman: | It's too greasy. |
| A.T.K.: | (confused) It's too greasy? |
| Superman: | Yea, and besides I keep burning the bacon. |
| A.T.K.: | (more confused) You keep burning the bacon? |
| Superman: | Yes, you know; when you get older, fried foods are too greasy and then I'd turn the heat up too much and burn the bacon. |
| A.T.K.: | I don't mean "fried," I mean "fly!" |
| Superman: | Oh, why didn't you say so? |
| A.T.K.: | I did. |
| Superman: | You did what? |
| A.T.K.: | I did say so. |
| Superman: | You did? I though you said "fly." (to audience) Didn't you think he said "fly?" |
| A.T.K.: | Okay, okay. (very clear and distinct) Why don't you fly anymore? |
| Superman: | Too dangerous. |
| A.T.K.: | What do you mean, "too dangerous?" |
| Superman: | It might be clearer if I told you about the very last time I flew. |
| A.T.K.: | Yes, please do. |
| Superman: | I was cruising at 20,000 feet, doing about 1200 miles an hour, heading north. I was up there minding my own business when all of a sudden, what's in front of me but a flock of 500 geese heading south for the winter. These were the biggest "honkers'" I'd ever seen. I tried to stop on a dime, but it slid into a quarter and those geese knocked me to the ground. |
| A.T.K.: | You really got "down" from a goose, huh? Ha! Ha! |
| Superman: | Sick! Sick! That's bad! But I never flew again. |
| A.T.K.: | But you're still a crime fighter, aren't you? |

| | |
|---|---|
| *Superman:* | Oh, yes! Always was, always will be. In fact, I caught me a desperate criminal just last week. |
| *A.T.K.:* | You did? |
| *Superman:* | Yes. |
| *A.T.K.:* | Oh, please tell us about it. |
| *Superman:* | I captured a sixty-eight year old lady professional pick-pocketer. |
| *A.T.K.:* | Wow! How did you catch her? |
| *Superman:* | She tried to pick-pocket me, and I don't have any pockets. He! He! |
| *A.T.K.:* | She sure wasn't very picky to pocket you. What other adventures in crime fighting have recently come your way? |
| *Superman:* | Well, I'm kept pretty busy defending society from the scum who ignore "No Smoking" signs on public transportation, from jaywalkers, from the villains who don't wash their hands before leaving a public restroom . . . that kind of stuff. But you know, recently, a lot of those criminals have been eluding me. |
| *A.T.K.:* | Why's that? |
| *Superman:* | Well, when crime strikes, I can't jump into a phonebooth and change in a second like I use to. It takes at least ten minutes to get out of my Clark Kent outfit and into my super hero uniform. I usually only get halfway through the process before a squad car arrives and I'm carried away for indecent exposure charges. |
| *A.T.K.:* | Don't people recognize who you are? |
| *Superman:* | No, and when you're from the planet Krypton, it's difficult to show them the proper identification. |
| *A.T.K.:* | One thing I am sure our audience would like to know . . . |
| *Superman:* | (*Interrupting and getting up to leave*) I'm sorry. I must go now. |
| *A.T.K.:* | But I was just going to ask . . . |
| *Superman:* | No. No more questions. It's time for my afternoon nap. A big game of gin rummy tonight at the Senior Super Heroes Home and I've got to be rested. |
| *A.T.K.:* | Well, ladies and gentlemen, I guess that wraps up our show for tonight. Join us again soon for another (*da-dat-da-da*) "Famous Interviews." |

(Contributed by Russ Matzke, Colorado Springs, CO)

# Some Do

This simple skit involves a guy, a girl, and a park bench.

(Contributed by Nancy and Robb Mann, Arlington, MA)

He:     (*nervously*) Some night.
She:    Yeah, some night.
He:     Some moon.
She:    Yeah, some moon.
He:     Some stars.
She:    Yeah, some stars. (*They sit down on the bench*)
He:     Some park.
She:    Yeah, some park.
He:     (*Moves closer to her, then, using his fingers, notices dew on the bench*) Some dew.
She:    Well I DON'T! (*She slaps him across the face, knocking him off the bench*)

# Sumu Wrestlers

For this skit you will need two guys, preferably of a muscular or flabby physique, dressed in diapers (use a white sheet for the diapers). You will also need an announcer with a good voice and something he or she can use as a microphone, such as a vacuum hose.

Have the two wrestlers come stomping into the room, circling each other and snorting at each other with deep voices. The announcer introduces the first man as Yamahaha, who then steps forward, bows with folded hands and slowly laughs with a deep voice and a Japanese accent, "ha ha ha ha ha." He then throws rice over each shoulder. This procedure is repeated when the announcer introduces Korimot-ho who responds with a "ho ho ho ho."

After their introductions, the two wrestlers begin fighting. They are never to touch each other or to speak, except for occasional "ha ha's" and "ho ho's." The fight is conducted by each fighter doing to himself what he really wants to do to his opponent. The opponent responds—at the same time—by reacting to whatever the hold or punch was as if it had really happened to him.

While this is going on the announcer calls the play-by-play describing finger bends, nostril lifts, toe stomps, navel jabs and armpit hair pulls. With some good actors this event can be hilarious. (Contributed by Bob and Doug McKenzie, Calgary, AB, Can.)

# CHAPTER FIVE

# SPECIAL EVENTS

## After-Church Salad Bar

Many youth groups provide coffee and donuts for the church after the morning worship service. Another great variation of this is to provide a salad bar. It's easy to do and the adults love it. Have the youth purchase and prepare all the ingredients — lettuce, tomatoes, mushrooms, sprouts, sunflower seeds, salad dressings, etc. — and set it up in the fellowship area after the service. People can pay a set price for the salad bar, or just make a contribution of any amount to the youth group. (Contributed by Dave Hicks, Palo Alto, CA)

## Anti-Prom Night

The annual high school prom is still a big deal on a lot of campuses, but unfortunately many kids are excluded because of their social status or because of expense. Here's a tongue-in-cheek alternative to the prom that will probably go over great with your kids. Even though it is called "Anti-Prom Night," it should not be seen as a negative response to the prom but a positive one. The key is to make it as ridiculous as possible, and to emphasize the idea of having a great time without spending a lot of money for it. The theme can be "Poverty with Style." No dates are allowed and no dress-up clothing is allowed, unless, of course, it's all done as tacky as possible.

The planning and the program can be patterned after the typical prom, only worse — or better, as the case

Trudy Moody, Lori Schneider and Wendy Rosene have an informal bubble blowing contest during "Anti-Prom Night" activities Thursday evening at the United Methodist Church. About 50 Storm Lake High School students attended.

Mike Bell and 'Jaggar'

### 'Anti-prom night' attracts 50 teenagers

By LORI GUNTHER
Staff Writer

Tables arranged under a canopy of streamers. Tall decorative centerpieces, place mats and dinnerware in position. Happy guests, dressed for the gala event, parade in. The queen is crowned and the banquet begins. Music fills the room throughout the meal.

The scene brings to mind the most exciting and colorful event of the high school year — prom night.

For this particular occasion, the canopy of streamers was made of toilet paper. Fluffy pink Kleenex and toothpicks stuck in paper cups made creative centerpieces, placemats were various color book pages, and the dinnerware included paper plates, Coke cups, and plastic forks—not quite the image of an elegant and elaborately decorated prom.

Obviously this was not prom, but rather "Anti-Prom Night." The event, sponsored by the United Methodist Youth Fellowship (UMYF), was designed to give the students a "cheap alternative to prom", according to UMYF Director Michael Bell.

"Poverty With Style," theme for the evening, included the rules: No dates or couples allowed; No expensive prom dresses or tuxedos allowed; Weird clothes are encouraged; No monetary expense will be tolerated.

"We wanted to prove that you can have fun without all the pomp, the pressure and expenditure," explained Bell.

Nearly 50 Storm Lake high schoolers gathered in the Fireside Room of the Methodist Church Thursday night to prove that they could indeed have a good time without the sophisticated dress and five-course meal that makes a Prom.

The attire, as they paraded into the decorated room, included sweats, jeans, peddle-pushers and black tights. There were students wearing cat glasses, purple glasses, paper corsages, headbands, baseball caps—the guest dog even had a bow in her hair.

The satire of prom was carried to the fullest as Bell crowned his dog, Jagger, Anti-Prom Queen 1983.

A prayer thanking the fact "that we can be fun and crazy" opened the banquet, consisting of chicken, chocolate milk, and chocolate cake.

There was even an alternative to the traditional after-prom party. Singing, blowing soap bubbles, and reading the ridiculous story of "Prom Night in Warm Cake, Iowa" entertained the students attending the after-anti-prom party.

Although named "anti-prom", the event wasn't meant as an insult to prom, said senior UMYF member, Tatiana Dierwechter.

"Prom is a good memory, but it leaves a lot of people out. It's getting real expensive, too. People need a chance to be themselves and act the way they want to without so much pressure."

Many students in attendance agreed that prom offers pressure from various angles — pressure to find a date, pressure to spend money

**Prom**

Continued on back page

may be. For example, decorations can come from the church supply closet with toilet paper streamers, paper placemats, table centerpieces with weeds or donated funeral flowers, etc. Activities can include:

1. A banquet of fast food chicken, fries, and other junk food.
2. The crowning of someone's dog as the Anti-Prom Queen.
3. An Anti-Prom "Mad Lib" (see below).
4. A special seven-and-a-half-minute Anti-Prom dance to the latest country and western hit or some silly song.
5. An "After-Prom" celebration that includes blowing soap bubbles.

Of course, you can add all kinds of crazy things to do to make this event a success. Play some games, put on some skits, show some great films— whatever it takes to make sure the kids have a good time. Be sure to advertise it well on campus and in the local paper, and be prepared for lots of true Anti-Prom sentiment that can be channeled into an appreciation of Christ's acceptance of everyone.

---

## Anti-Prom "Mad Lib"

*THE QUESTIONS: Begin by having the group come up with a name, word, or phrase for each of the following statements.*

1. Name a guy in the group.
2. Name a girl in the group.
3. Name something that you would hate to drink.
4. Name something that a girl wouldn't be caught dead wearing.
5. Name something a guy would hate to wear.
6. Name a guy in the group.
7. Name a girl in the group.
8. Name the last place, here in town, that you would want to go to.
9. Name someone in the group.
10. Name something to eat.
11. Name something bizarre that you wouldn't eat.
12. Give the title of one of the worst top forty songs you can think of.
13. Name what you had for lunch today.
14. Name a guy in the group.
15. What would you really like to say to your mother when she asks you to clean your room?

### PROM NIGHT IN GOMER, IOWA

Once upon a time in that beautiful city we all dream of going to called Gomer, Iowa there were two lovely people who were extremely, incredibly, madly, passionately, and ridiculously in love. These two were; of course, ___1___ and ___2___.

One day while they were sitting around after school picking fleas off ___2's___ dog and watching reruns of "Leave it to Beaver" on T.V. they began to discuss what they would be doing on the night of Gomer High's Prom. Well, ___2___ got so excited that she had to go get a glass of ___3___ and ___1___ got so excited that he had to go to the bathroom. The Gomer Iowa Prom was a big deal for these folks . . . Upon returning they began to discuss what they were going to wear to the Prom. ___2___ said she was going to wear ___4___ along with her mother's purple garter belt and large pink triangle earrings. ___1___ said he was going to wear ___5___ along with his dad's fishing cap, wading boots, and gold chain necklace.

While they were talking, two other Gomer High School students appeared at the door. (They wanted to watch "Leave it to Beaver" too.) These two were infamous for doing weird things together like sitting and reading *The Adventures of Heroic Cows* together or gazing into each others eyes while listening to old Barry Manilow records. These two were, of course, ___6___ and ___7___. They said that after the Gomer Prom that they would be going to ___8___ where they would kiss each other twice on the cheek then they would be off to ___9's___ 's house where they would play Chinese Checkers and drink hot grapefruit juice. After these exciting events they would finally go to their respective homes at around 11:30 p.m.

Well, at the Gomer High Prom later that week here is what happened: First, they had a banquet where they served ___10___ and ___11___. After that they all had their pictures taken in their lovely outfits. ___1___ and ___2's___ 's were the most outstanding. Their Prom theme was ___12___. To top things off they all danced to the music of that famous band: ___13___

And so goes another exciting adventure of the Gomer High School Prom. Join us next year when we will report on how ___14___ talks Jessica Lange into going to the Prom with him.

So goodbye, so long, and ___15___!

(Contributed by Michael Bell, Storm Lake, IA)

# Arcade Lock-In

Here's an idea that combines youth outreach, incredible fun and fundraising, all at the same time. Arrange with a local video arcade to have an overnight lock-in for your youth group. Contact the owner or manager and ask him to figure his cost for eight hours and the number of kids you expect to show up. Next, calculate what you need to raise, plus the cost of an all-you-can-eat snack bar and some video movies. Sell tickets at the adjusted price.

That night, everything will be completely free (that is, included in the price of the ticket). You've

already met your budget goal, so everyone can relax and have a blast. Not only that, there will probably be lots of new kids who will be introduced to your ministry.
(Contributed by Andy Harvey, Knoxville, TN)

# Awful Waffle Party

For this activity, you'll need a few waffle irons and a huge batch of waffle batter. As the waffles come off the irons, have a table ready with various toppings —syrups, ice cream (a must), nuts, jelly, peanut butter, whipped cream, fruit, and the like. You might also want to include some "awful" toppings, and dare kids to try them—pickles, onions, catsup, beets, spinach, whatever. This would be a great refreshment after an afternoon event or a swimming party, or you could do it all by itself! (Contributed by Dan Gray, West Lafayette, IN)

# Back-to-School Night II

Here are a few more activities you can use with the "Back-to-School Night" event found in **Ideas #29-32**. The event is a great way to begin a new school year.

1. Biology Class: Have teams "dissect" an avocado. Give each team a plastic knife, spoon, avocado, needle, and thread. Instruct them to remove the pit and sew up the avocado. The first team to complete the task is the winner.
2. Between Classes: No school day is complete without a trip or two to the locker. For this event, make a number of lockers out of hanging clothes bags. Inside each of the bags put a stack of books, magazines, a coke can, a tennis racket and a pair of gym shorts. Each member of a team must open the locker (unzip the bag), take out all the contents, and hold them while putting on the gym shorts. They then must close the locker, run to a specific point, and return back to the locker and repeat everything they have done in reverse (open the locker, take off their shorts, replace the contents, close the locker), then run and tag a teammate who then goes and does the same.

(Contributed by Dan Craig, San Diego, CA)

# Back-to-School Scavenger Hunt

Here's a list of items which might be fun to find as part of a Back-to-School Days scavenger hunt. Divide your kids into groups and assign an adult sponsor to drive each group around. You might wish to stipulate that they can only go to their own homes for the supplies. Whatever you do, make sure all of the items are returned following the hunt as some of them may be expensive.

---

*School Supply List*

1. PENCILS — 100 points (*limit 25*). 500 extra points for the longest, shortest, and fattest pencils. 50 extra points for pencils with advertising on them.

---

2. RULERS — (300 points (*limit 5*). 500 extra points for the longest).
3. LUNCHBOX — 500 points (*limit 1*). 1,000 extra points for the "most original" decoration.
4. THERMOS — 500 points (*limit 1*). 300 extra points if it leaks.
5. SANDWICH — 200 points (*limit 1*). 500 extra points for the one with the most condiments.
6. ERASERS — 200 points (*limit 5*). 500 extra points for the biggest.
7. NOTEBOOK BINDERS — 300 points (*limit 5*). 500 extra points for the thickest.
8. PAIR OF GYM SHORTS — 300 points (*limit 2*) 500 extra points for the largest and the smallest size.
9. TENNIS SHOE — 300 points (*limit 1*). 500 extra points for the smelliest.
10. FOLDERS — 200 points (*limit 5*). 100 points extra for ones with pockets; 500 extra for most "artistic".
11. STACK OF NOTEBOOK PAPER — You LOSE 500 points if the stack is less than 6 inches thick.
12. PAPER CLIPS — 25 points (*limit 25*). 300 extra points for the largest.
13. PEN WITH ERASABLE INK — (*limit 1*). 500 points.
14. FOUNTAIN PEN — (*limit 1*). 700 points.
15. DICTIONARY — (*limit 1*). 1,000 points. 1,000 extra points for the biggest.

(Contributed by Dale Hill, Fairbanks, AK)

# Bat and Putt Night

Here is an idea for a group of teenagers if you have a miniature golf course and batting cages in your area. Rent the location for about two hours so you can have it to yourselves. To spice up the fun, put some competition into your evening by guaranteeing special prizes for all the winners. Here's how you can arrange your competition:

Divide your youth into different competitive levels (junior high girls; junior high boys; senior high girls; senior high boys) so that each person competes with those on his or her own level. The competitions can be arranged in several categories such as (1) golf score for whole round; (2) holes-in-one; (3) best score left-handed; (4) highest number of strokes on one hole; (5) highest number of strokes for a whole round (these last two categories are for those who aren't as skilled as the others). If you have batting cages, you can add two more categories to your competition: (1) most hits in 25 tries; and (2) most consecutive hits.

For each category you should award four "minor" prizes. Then four "grand" prizes should be awarded to the kids who have done the best in all categories. To determine this you have to establish a system of points awarded for their scores, number of hits, and holes-in-one, and so on.

Another fun approach is to ask if the owner of the golf and batting course will give you some free passes (assuming that you pay him a fair price for your evening's fun). If he does, you can have fun awarding them to kids who meet the challenges you set before them, such as making a certain putt or making holes in one. Also, another aspect of having a successful evening rests in your ability to "sell it" to the kids. Advertise it with posters saying "**1st Annual (City or youth group name) Golf Open and Batting Championships**." Build it up, excite the kids and prepare to have a fun-filled time with your youth. (Contributed by Doug Graham, Kalispell, MT)

## Boob Tube Bash

Here's a special event for Halloween or any time of the year. Have everyone come dressed up as their favorite TV character, past or present, and award prizes for the most original, the oldest TV show, best lookalike, and so on. You can have everyone vote on these, and then announce the ratings.

Activities can include take-offs on TV game shows (like **Family Feud, Hollywood Squares, Name That Tune, Beat the Clock**), skits that make fun of well-known sit-coms and soap operas, and perhaps a film featuring out-takes of TV shows like **M*A*S*H*** or **Happy Days** (available from film distributors or your local public library).

Serve TV dinners or hot dogs ("tube-steaks") and finally, play a video tape of a favorite TV show. If you have some video equipment, you can videotape the entire event and then play it back for the kids to conclude the evening. (Contributed by John Erwin, Eureka, CA)

## Bust-In

Having trouble with attendance in Sunday School? Send a letter to all of your youth assigning each one a Sunday that they HAVE to be there, or have them sign up on a calendar in your room. If they are not there on that day, the entire class will come by to visit them during the Sunday School hour! Be sure to publicize who is supposed to attend for the following week. Not only will those kids come, but others will come in case they get to help bust in on the absent ones! (Contributed by Bill Ross, Blacksburg, VA)

## Cake-Bake Night

You can't lose whenever you use an idea that involves food. Get a good recipe for flat pan cakes and large cookies and spend an evening baking and decorating. Have all sorts of decorating items on hand, such as jelly beans, frosting, redhots, sprinkles, and so on. Let the kids use their creativity and come up with their own designs, or else have them decorate everything around a certain theme. You might

want to make some extras and deliver them to shut-ins or to the pastor and

his family. (Contributed by Richard Moore, Vista, CA)

## Car Rally Starter

Here's a clever (and frustrating) way to get kids started off on a car rally or treasure hunt. Before you give the

teams their first instruction or clue, you give them a sheet like the one on the next page. They must complete it before they are allowed to leave.

**TO RECEIVE YOUR FIRST CLUE, COMPLETE THE INSTRUCTIONS BELOW.**

1. Please read all the directions on this sheet before doing anything else.
2. Total up the ages of everyone in your group: _____
3. List the middle names of everyone in your group: _____
4. Have someone in your group do ten push ups.
5. Have your group yell as loud as they can: "We're Number One!" three times.
6. Write one Bible verse of your choice here: _____
7. If you followed direction number one, and read all the directions first, then you do not have to do instructions two through six. Just turn in this sheet with an "x" in the upper right hand corner, get your first clue, and you may take off. Good luck!

(Contributed by David Beguin, Rocky Hill, CT)

## College Survival Kit Scavenger Hunt

Here's a good way for your high school group to have a great time, while reaching out to college students at the same time.

Divide the group into teams— one for each of last year's seniors now in college—and send them out into the community to obtain the items on the list below. When they return with their completed collections, they write notes to mail to last year's seniors who are now in college, along with the "survival kits" they have assembled.

Here is a suggested list of items:

- Cookies (various kinds to tickle their innards). Each team must get three dozen cookies, no more than six at any one house.
- A pizza discount coupon (**very** valuable to a college student!)
- Two tea bags (for mellow evenings)
- Two toothpicks (to hold their eyelids open after an all-nighter!)
- One package instant soup (for those rushed lunches, or if they are bored with cafeteria food)
- Hot chocolate (to drink as they're thinking of home)
- Kleenex tissues (in case they're crying as they're thinking of home)
- A flashlight battery (for "burning the midnight oil" when they study for a test)
- A stamp (so they can write and tell you how blessed they are)
- A church bulletin (so they know that we're all still there)
- A quarter (so that if they're lonely, they can call someone who really cares)
- And anything else you think would be appropriate.

(Contributed by Leroy Tucker, Greeley, CO)

---

## Concentration Clues

Next time you do a treasure hunt which incorporates the use of clues, try your hand at making up clues using letters and symbols similar to those used on the television show **Concentration**. Almost any clue or location can be written this way. Kids really enjoy trying to solve them. Here are some examples.

under office stairs

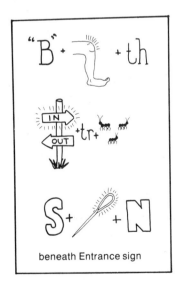

beneath Entrance sign

(Contributed by Stephen K. Weaver, Angola, IN)

## Fast Food Frenzy

Here's a fun activity that gives a new twist to the old scavenger hunt idea.

Divide your group into smaller units that can travel together in a vehicle. (The size of these groups will obviously be determined by the size of your vehicles). Each group begins with $5.00 (or any amount you choose) and a list of instructions. Their objective is to spend **some** of their money at ten fast food locations of your choosing, returning with the least possible amount of change left over. You might select locations like these:

1. Pizza Hut
2. Orange Julius
3. Seven-Eleven
4. Mr. Donut
5. Kentucky Fried Chicken
6. Taco Bell
7. Baskin Robbins
8. Arby's
9. McDonald's
10. Burger King

Groups are not allowed to add, subtract or exchange money from their original $5.00 or the change they receive from their purchases. They may stop at each location only one time and purchase only one item at each stop, and they must obtain a receipt to verify their purchase. They do not have to follow the order listed above and may stop at any location of these stores throughout your city.

Make sure the kids understand that **speed** is not a factor in this event (to avoid hurried driving). In case of a tie, the group with the lowest total mileage will be declared the winner. (Contributed by Dick Gibson, St. Petersburg, FL)

## Foot Faces

On your next long drive to or from camp, take along some felt pens (some large, some pen-size) and have those with artistic talent create some wild drawings on the feet of volunteers. If they can draw faces, have them do so on the bottom of the feet . . . . that is, if the person is not too ticklish! Be sure to take pictures of the finished masterpieces for the next youth slide show. (Contributed by Richard Moore, Vista, CA)

## Garbage-In, Garbage-Out Party

Here's an activity many of your kids can relate to. Hold it in a garage or some other "junky" place, with lots of old furniture and trash around for "decorations." Have the kids dress in their worst clothes. Make "punch" out of watered-down lemonade with orange peels, lemon peels, apples, peppers, celery, and other "garbage" floating around in it. Serve it in a (clean) garbage can. Have parents provide plenty of "leftovers" for refreshments.

One good game to play is "Garbage Bob," which bears a striking resemblance to "bobbing for apples," but which obviously has a different object. You can award points for various kinds of garbage retrieved with the teeth from the tub of floating goodies.

A "Trash Scavenger Hunt" also works great for this event. Just send the kids out in group with a list of stuff that is going to be (or should have been) discarded. A variation of this would be to have a "Bigger and Worser" Hunt, in which kids keep trading down at each house for something "worse" than they had before. Use your own imagination, and you can make this the absolute awfullest event of the year! (Contributed by Tim Smith, Fresno, CA)

## Group Birthday Party

If your kids enjoy celebrations, one you would not want to overlook is the birthday of your youth group. After you have made a good guess on when the very first youth meeting at your church was ever held (you might have to make up a day if you don't know) make it a point to celebrate that birthday with a party every year. Order a cake from the local bakery with appropriate decorations. Be sure that the place is decorated with streamers and balloons and that everyone has party hats and favors.

For games you might want to play a new version of the old favorite, "Pin the Tail on the Donkey." Each person can write on a paper tail some of the shortcomings of the previous year. These tails are then pinned to the donkey's posterior while blindfolded. Voting may decide the single most "donkey" event of the year with prizes given for the best gripes.

Other games can also be played, of course. Prizes can be given to the first one to stand and spell "Kum-ba-ya," or the first to identify the make of the guitarist's guitar, or the first to remember the name of any hymn sung in church during the past month, or the first to guess the number of "praises" in the song "Praise Ye the Lord."

For a western flavor add "Crack the Pinata." On slips of paper designed to look like bats, solicit ideas for the upcoming year. These ideas should be designed to open up the youth group. The kids should be admonished to "give their best crack" at thinking up new ideas. As each idea is read and discussed, candy from a pinata can be passed around.

The presents are always opened last at birthday parties. At this time the youth leaders can share pleasant memories of each youth from the previous year as a present to the group. The youth may wish to share their favorite memories as well. Or, if you wish, the youth leaders can use this time to present the group with a gift which they have gone in on together, such as athletic equipment, a game, or something else that can be used by the group for years to come. (Contributed by Albert Frederico, Temple City, CA)

## Hang Out Party

Sometimes kids just need a place to "hang out," so why not have a "Hang Out Party?" Pick a place where kids will feel comfortable, provide some music, a TV set, some video games, card or board games, refreshments (very important), and some very inconspicuous chaperones. Encourage kids to come and just "hang out"—bring a friend, a favorite game to play, or even homework.

This event requires little or no

preparation and very little expense, while it meets a genuine need for kids who want a place where they can be with their friends without getting into trouble. (Contributed by Dave Shaheen, Silver Springs, MD)

## Heartburn on the Run

Here's a fun activity that combines a progressive dinner with a car rally or treasure hunt. Be sure to have a number of drivers with permission to drive.

Choose four homes to visit, one for each course of the meal (soup, salad, main course, and dessert). The foods should be as hot and spicy as possible. Create some clues that the kids must figure out in order to get a complete meal. Clues should be clever, and should reveal the next house without being too obvious or too impossible. At each home, they receive a new clue. As the youth arrive at the starting point, explain the rules for the evening: 1) you must eat all of the food at each house; 2) you may not drink water; 3) the car that returns first wins. When all of the teams are ready, pass out the first clue and let the carloads take off.

When they make it back to the starting point you might want to have some crackers or bread and butter and lots of water on hand. The prize: paid Mexican dinner for the winning carload. (Contributed by Stephen May, Elk Grove, CA)

## Is It Spring Yet?

If you live where spring weather is slow coming, then you might want to speed things up with an "Is It Spring Yet? Party." Depending on your climate, this question may be relevant either in March or April.

Here are some games and activities for the event.

1. **Kite Flying Contest**—Kids can make their own kites and try to get them up in the air. Give awards for the most unusual, largest, smallest, best flight, and so on.
2. **Lawn Mowing Race**—This is done with the chassis of a power lawn mower. (You can find them in repair shops with the engines removed.) One kid rides on the lawnmower and makes engine noises while the other person pushes.
3. **Earthworm Race** (or **Caterpillars**)—All players lie down on their stomachs, side by side. The end person rolls over everyone and places him or herself on the other end. The next person follows, and soon the earthworm rolls to its destination.
4. **Tricycle Races**—Every kid wants to be out on his or her tricycle in the spring, so have some trike races of various kinds.
5. **Flower Picking**—Have the kids go on a scavenger hunt to see

who can come back with the most spring flowers, dandelions, or whatever.

The devotions for this event could center on the newness of life in Christ, or the Resurrection. With a little creativity, you can add other elements to this idea to make it a big success. (Contributed by Dan Van Loon, Clearlake, IA)

## Junk Food Potluck

Since churches are famous for having potluck dinners, why not try an appropriate version for your youth group. Have a junk food potluck and encourage your kids to bring generous amounts of their favorite junk food to share with others. Anything healthy or nutritious should not be accepted. To add to the fun, plan to show a movie along with the dinner. You might find that this would be a good time to encourage everyone to bring along a friend who has never been to a youth meeting. (Contributed by Philip Popineau, Lodi, CA)

## Lifesaver Tournament

With a little creativity, you can build a very successful event around the theme of "lifesavers" (those little candies with the hole in the middle). Have everyone bring a roll of their favorite flavor as their ticket to the tournament and then play games like these:

1. **Ring Toss:** Construct two ring toss pegs by nailing a long, thin nail through a small wooden base. Kids then toss lifesavers onto the nail for points. It can also be played like horseshoes.
2. **Distance Roll:** This game can also be called "Holey Roller." The idea is to see who can roll a lifesaver along the ground the farthest. It may not leave the ground, and it must roll on its edge.
3. **Life Saver Shuffleboard:** Draw a shuffleboard court on a tabletop or on the ground, and make some small "pushers" out of sticks. Play regular shuffleboard, only smaller.
4. **Guess the Flavor Relay:** Put some lifesavers in a bag and have the teams line up relay style. Team members crawl to the bag blindfolded and take out one lifesaver (or are handed one by a leader). They must guess the color by tasting. They get only one guess. If they are wrong, they must go back and try again. Each person on the team must do this.

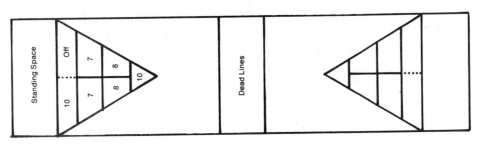

5. **Broom Hockey:** Play regular indoor broom hockey using a lifesaver as a puck. Brooms are used as hockey sticks. It's really wild.
6. **Life Saver Barnyard:** This is like the old "Barnyard" game, only you use different flavors of lifesavers, rather than animals. Give lifesavers to the kids so that there is an equal number of flavors distributed evenly. Then have the kids suck on the lifesaver or just place it on their tongue, and without speaking, they must get into groups of the same color. They do this by sticking out their tongues. The first group to get together completely wins.

In addition to these games, you can create others which incorporate the use of lifesavers. Or, you can add other things that are round with a hole in the middle, like doughnuts and inner tubes. The possibilities are endless. (Contributed by Lynn Petrie and Juli Sutton, Milwaukee, WI)

## Lock-Out

The idea of having a lock-in is great. But why not give it a bit of a twist and hold it outside the church. The church grounds or parking lot would work great, although you could also hold your lock-out in an old barn or at a park. Do everything you would normally do at a lock-in with the additions of star gazing, outdoor cooking and an early morning sunrise service. (Contributed by Mark Evans, Lake Charles, LA)

## Lucky Lunches

This idea works well for a quick after-church or before-the-event meal. Have everyone bring a can of lunch food with the label removed. If they bring in a can that has the label painted on, or a can that is particularly easy to recognize, then put it in a lunch bag. Stress that the item should be suitable for a meal. No dog food, coffee grounds, pickle relish, or other less-than-tantalizing fare. If desired, you may elect to allow boxed meals, like pizza, macaroni and cheese, and the like.

Take all of the items and number them, and have the kids draw numbers. Then allow each person to claim his or her lunch. The fun is in discovering what you'll be having for lunch. Of course, eating it can be a whole different matter!

Provide some "accompaniments" to the meal, like chips, jello, drinks, or a salad. Allow the kids to trade and share as they wish. If you're near a kitchen, you may want to provide some cooking utensils for those who need them.

This could also be done as a "Lucky Progressive Dinner," with your youth sponsors as stations, handing out each course without telling what the food items are. (Contributed by Mark Simone, Ravenna, OH)

# Mini-Pool Party

Here's a way to have "cool" discussion on a hot summer day.

Borrow or buy several inflatable childrens' pools, one for every four kids in your group. Blow them up and scatter them around someone's backyard. Assign the kids to a pool, giving them some specific questions to ask each other. Every five or ten minutes, make them rotate to another pool, so that everyone has a chance to talk to everyone else. You might also want to play a few games and, of course, have lots to eat. (Contributed by Sharon Shaw, Birmingham, AL)

# Missionary and Youth Night

Instead of the traditional preaching and slide shows, here's a way to involve your youth group with visiting missionaries in a personal and realistic way. Sponsor an afternoon or night activity when several missionary families can be with the group for a time of light interaction, games and refreshments. With a little creativity, most of the activities can sneak in some good, solid information about missions. Some games to include are:

1. Missionary Squares: Same as Hollywood Squares, except that all of the questions pertain to particular mission fields or common misconceptions about missionaries.
2. Missionary Bingo:

**Instructions:** See how many squares you can get signed by someone who fits that square's description.

| A teaching missionary: | A missionary who was originally from Wisconsin: | A missionary who has been helping a lot with administrative work: | A missionary who likes sports: | A missionary to the Philippines: |
|---|---|---|---|---|
| A missionary whose mission field is on tropical islands: | A missionary who speaks Japanese: | Someone who has been a missionary for more than 15 years: | A missionary who has two children: | A missionary who has taught kids in Venezuela: |
| A missionary who has eaten raw fish: | A missionary who hasn't yet been to his/her mission field: | You: | A missionary to South America: | A missionary who has also been pastor of the Loomis E.F.C.: |
| A missionary who graduated from Trinity College: | A church planting missionary: | A missionary who is not from Nebraska: | An M.K.: | A missionary who speaks Spanish: |
| A missionary to Japan: | A missionary who only knows how to speak English: | A missionary to Africa: | A missionary who has been to the field for only one term: | A missionary who plays the flute: |

3. Missionary Mad-Lib:

Once upon a _____ there was a _____ young man named
                NOUN                    ADJECTIVE

_____ . One _____ _____ _____ decided that the
BOY IN GROUP         ADJECTIVE      DAY     SAME BOY

Lord wanted him to be a missionary to _____ . The only problem
                                    NAME OF PLACE

was _____ was _____ in love with _____ , and he
   SAME BOY      ADVERB             GIRL IN GROUP

knew she would never _____ to live in a _____ place
                VERB           ADJECTIVE

like _____ . What was _____ to do?
  SAME PLACE        BOY'S NAME

After _____ thought, he decided to _____ it straight.
     ADJECTIVE              VERB

"_____," he said, "you know I _____ you _____ , but the
 SAME GIRL                VERB      ADVERB

Lord has told me to go to _____ as a _____. Will you go with
                 SAME PLACE      NOUN

me as my _____?" "_____," she exclaimed, "I'd _____ to
      NOUN    EXCLAMATION              VERB

_____ in _____ . They eat _____ _____, and _____
  VERB     SAME PLACE        ADJECTIVE PLURAL NOUN

_____ and _____ _____ there, and those are my favorites.
PLURAL NOUN     ADJECTIVE PLURAL NOUN

Of course, I'll _____ with you."
           VERB

And so they lived _____ ever after.
               ADVERB

You may want to wrap-up the time with a question period, asking things like, "What made you think God wanted you to become a missionary?" "Do you LIKE living in a foreign country?" "Why did you go so far away when there are spiritual needs here?" A time like this can really create some interest and a sense of responsibility for missionaries from your church. (Contributed by Rich Starcher, Sumner, NE)

---

## Mystery Car Rally

Here's an idea for a car rally that requires solving clues in order to read the prescribed route. Key words and numbers are left out of the instructions, and the group must solve the "clues" to know where to go. Here's an example:

1. Turn right into _____ street.
2. Take the first left after you pass
   _____.
3. Go _____ blocks and turn right.

The "clues" needed to fill in the blanks can look like this:

1. in the middle (Answer: Central)
2. Guys with a lot of energy (Answer: Pep Boys)
3. 144 divided by 6 minus 14 plus 2 times .5 (Answer: 6)

Obviously, if the kids make a mistake and get the key word wrong, they'll get off course and it will cost them time. As with any car rally, make sure the kids are in cars with responsible drivers and that all traffic laws and safety precautions are taken. (Contributed by Gary Nicholson, Corpus Christi, TX)

---

## A Night In The Tropics

Here's a good way to take the boredom out of the winter months, especially if you live in a cold climate. Have a Tropical Party, and make believe you are on a South Pacific island for a night. Decorations should include posters of Hawaii and Tahiti (available from a travel agency), fishnets on the wall, potted green plants and palms (borrow from a nursery, if possible), sea shells, wicker chairs, tropical fish, and the like. Background music should be Hawaiian or steel band music, like Don Ho, Arthur Lyman, or the Beach Boys.

An extra attraction (if you can get the needed equipment) might be a "tanning beach," with lights that simulate the sun's ultraviolet rays. Provide suntan lotion.

On the invitations, ask kids to dress appropriately—shorts, "aloha" shirts,

muu-muus, sandals, beachcomber hats, puka shell necklaces, and so on. Have some extras on hand for kids who can't get any on their own. When the kids arrive, give them a flower lei (paper or real), and play some appropriate games. Good ones include the limbo walk (walking with only knees bent under a stick that is lowered with each try); bobbing for bananas; hula dancing contests; and clik-claks (dancing between sticks as they are "clicked" together and on the floor in rhythm by two people holding the stick ends just above the ground).

For refreshments, be creative with the theme. Have a giant fruit tray, tropical punch bowl and appropriate goodies like lemon bars, coconut granola and fried bananas. You might even want to put on a complete luau, serving barbecued pork, rice, and all the trimmings.

You can conclude the evening with some music, skits, or a film that features surfing and water sports. Kids will love it, especially if you do it in January or February. (Contributed by Steve Burkey, Eaton, CO)

## Nike Night

Most kids have shoes, shirts, jackets, or **something** with a "**Nike**" emblem attached. So ask everyone in the group to wear their own or borrowed **Nike** apparel to your "**Nike** Night."

With a little imagination, you can put together an evening of races and other athletic competition that everyone will enjoy. Then, toward the conclusion of the event, sit the group down and explain to them what the Greek word "**Nike**" actually means: "victory."

You might deliver a short message on victory, using a passage from scripture like I John 5:4–5. You can also sing some songs or hymns about victory (like "Victory in Jesus") and substitute the word **Nike** for the word "victory"

throughout the song.

The event can be lots of fun, and the lasting impact will be that whenever the

kids see a **Nike** emblem in the future, it will take on new significance. (Contributed by Richard Crisco, Milton, FL)

## Noise Night

Here's an event that gives your young people a chance to make as much noise as they want. For a change, the kids will have a legitimate excuse to really let loose. Some suggested activities are listed below,

and perhaps you can create some of your own:

1. Screaming Contest: Set up a microphone to a tape recorder with needles and lights that monitor the volume. Have each

kid take a turn standing about twenty feet from the microphone and making as loud a noise as possible using only his mouth (no clapping or other such noises). See who can register the loudest scream. This could be done by teams also.

2. Identify the Noise: In advance of the event, make a tape recording of a variety of noises and have the kids try to identify them.

3. Yeller Relay: Team members try to yell instructions to each other from a distance of about twenty feet while the opposing team is yelling and making as much distracting and contradictory noise as possible. For example, the first person runs to a point away from the team and receives an instruction (like "Run with your right hand up over your head!"). He must yell that instruction to the next person in line until that person gets it and follows the instruction;

meanwhile, opposing team members are yelling and trying to prevent comprehension. Both teams do this at the same time.

4. Night Contest: Divide into teams, and each team tries to come up with the most obnoxious, disgusting noise it possibly can. Judge determines the winner.

5. Skits: Try "Beautiful Bessie" or "Wild West Show" from previous volumes of **Ideas**. Both require that the group make a lot of noise.

6. Cap Smash: Get a hammer and a roll of caps for each person. He or she then gets ten seconds to see how many caps they can set off while the group counts. (Hint: This works even better when the contestant is blindfolded.)

7. For Dessert: How about some "Ice-Scream?"

(Contributed by Jim Walton, Rochester, NY)

---

# Non-Violent Softball League

Many times church softball leagues fail to achieve the fellowship and positive interaction between church members which was originally intended. In fact, the intense competitiveness of the game often leads to arguments, hurt feelings, and even fights between the players. As a summer project, your youth group might attempt to organize a more enjoyable and constructive softball league centered around different game rules. One group, for example, amended the rules so that each team pitches to itself and women receive three pitches and guys two; that no stealing or bunting was allowed; and that the players could not wear cleats. Another version would be to have a "Polish Baseball" league as described in **Ideas #13-16**. (Contributed by Dave Sauder, Paradise, CA)

# Parade Pantomime

This idea will probably work best in a "small town" atmosphere. It's very effective as a promotional event, or just as something crazy and fun to do with your youth group. Contact a local radio station and ask them to play about 15 minutes of John Philip Sousa marches at a given time on Saturday afternoon. If they agree to do that for you, you're in business.

Obtain a parade permit (if necessary) and then get all your kids together to march down the street as a "marching band." If they can get uniforms, or make band costumes, so much the better. But no musical instruments are needed. Each parader carries a radio instead of an instrument. At the appointed time, the kids begin marching down the street with their radios turned up loud all on the same station. It looks ridiculous but sounds great. If it's advertised in advance, it will attract lots of attention.

A variation of this (if you can't get a radio station to cooperate) is to put the music on a sound truck or big loud-speaker. The kids then march down the street pantomiming the instruments. (Contributed by Dave Emmrich, Brainerd, MN)

# Parents' Night Out

This is a good way to give the adults in your church a night out, provide a service project for your youth, plus make a little money for your next retreat or trip fund.

Offer the parents and/or adults a night out that gives them dinner, a movie and babysitting all for one low price. Movies can be rented in 16mm, or you could set up a VCR and TV to show a video.

Have the group prepare and set up for the dinner, then divide them in half. One half serves the adults, while the other half feeds and cares for the kids in another room. Then they switch. Half the group does clean-up, while the other half babysits. Afterward, all the youth work together to put everything away. You might want to show the movie to them, if there's time! (Contributed by Rodney Puryear, Birmingham, AL)

# Party Passports

A great idea for a progressive dinner would be to use the theme of an around-the-world cruise. Each of the homes visited could be decorated as a different country and could offer a unique ethnic dish. You could even rig the church bus as a ship and have a bon voyage at the church before

leaving.

To enhance this idea, why not print up mock passports for each of the travelers. These could be used in the place of a ticket and would then be stamped at each of the homes visited. You could use one of the visa pages as an itinerary listing of all of the stops, giving a brief story about each of the "countries" which will be visited. (Contributed by R. M. Naron, Pasadena, TX)

# Political Action Night

Only a few items are needed for this stimulating evening of political action and discussion: stationery, envelopes, and postage stamps provided by the youth fund; and a complete listing of the names and addresses of the politicians representing your area in the local, state, and federal governments. (Note: This list may be obtained from your local public or college library, or your county courthouse.)

Every youth leader would like to promote political action and social awareness in his or her youth group. But implementing political action is a problem because of differing political convictions, both within the youth group and among their parents and congregational friends.

A good way to avoid this polemic is to have your youth group turn one of their regular meetings into "political action night," when the kids spend an hour writing to congressmen and senators; city and county officials; or even the President of the United States. The young people express only their **own** opinions about issues of their choice and then sign the letters, putting their own return addresses on them. Many of the young people in your youth group who share

similar opinions may want to collaborate on one letter and send it to as many officials as they can.

Political Action Night should be promoted a few weeks in advance in your church bulletin or newsletter, making it clear to the congregation that the views expressed will not be those of any particular political persuasion, but rather those of the kids individually. The group may even want to invite the rest of the congregation to join them on the night of their letter writing to have fellowship and feedback from the adults' political points of view.

The purpose of this activity is threefold: first, to increase young people's political and social awareness, especially in regard to ethical issues that may affect them now and in the future; second, to promote discussion and expression of their individual convictions about these issues; and third, to emphasize that they can become involved in social and political change (even if it is just a letter) for the sake of Christ and righteousness.

In most cases, the letters your group writes will be answered either by a computer-printed response or personally from one of the official's assistants. Even though the responses may be rather impersonal, a young person gets a chance to discuss, get feedback, and observe a little bit of how the political process goes on. (Contributed by Michael Bell, Storm Lake, IA)

## Scripture Search Scavenger Hunt

This scavenger hunt is not only fun, but it gets kids into the Bible as well. To discover the items that must be brought back, the kids need to look up the verses and answer the questions. Use this list or create your own!

1. **Luke 15:8** - A woman had ten of something. You bring in the same. (10 silver coins)
2. **Matthew 16:19** - Jesus said he would give Peter something. Bring one back. (a key)
3. **Revelation 11:1** - Bring in something we use today like the thing John was given. (measuring instrument)
4. **Mark 14:20** - Jesus dipped bread into something. Bring one in. (dish)
5. **Isaiah 24:12** - Bring back one of the two things you could eat. (olive or grape)
6. **Matthew 5:13** - Bring in what Jesus says we are. (salt)
7. **1 Peter 2:2** - Bring in some of the drink found here. (milk)
8. **Hebrews 1:9** - God has anointed thee with the _____ of gladness. Bring any kind. (oil)
9. **Luke 15:17** - Bring in what the servants have plenty of. (bread)
10. **James 1:11** - Something falls off. Bring one in. (flower)

(Contributed by Deb Norman, Union, IA)

## Service Scavenger Hunt

Throw tradition into "reverse" for this scavenger hunt. Instead of collecting a list of items, as in a regular scavenger hunt, this one allows the kids to give! Each team of scavengers is given an identical list of service projects to do (i.e. mow one lawn, sweep three driveways, wash two cars, empty four wastebaskets, etc.). The first team to complete the list wins. You'll be surprised at the different feelings your kids will have when they're finished. The neighborhood may feel pretty good about your group too. (Contributed by Steve Illum, Niagara, NY)

## Shopping Mall Tag

This event is obviously held in a shopping mall. It's simple and lots of fun. After taking the group to the mall, give each person a blank index card. Two of the cards will have holes punched in them. Whoever receives them are "It," but they won't tell anyone who they are.

When the game begins, everyone gets about five minutes to scatter and hide, but they must stay inside the mall at all times. The "Its" may begin tagging people after the five minutes are up. When a person is tagged, he or she must go with the "It" to one of the youth sponsors, stationed in a designated place in the mall. The sponsor will punch the tagged person's card, making that person an "It" also. He or she may then go out with the original "Its" and try to tag someone else who has not yet been tagged. The game lasts for one hour or as long as you choose.

The winner (or winners) are those who can go the entire hour without being tagged, or the "It" who tags the most number of people. Every time an "It" brings someone in to have is or her card punched, the "It" also gets another hole punched in his or her own card. Another important rule is **no running** at any time. (This is grounds for disqualification.)

Winners can be rewarded appropriately, and to make things even more difficult you can let one of your youth sponsors also be an "It" who can tag kids. As with any event of this sort, it is wise to gain prior permission from the shopping mall management before turning your kids loose there. If this is impossible, the same event can be conducted in any busy place where there are lots of people. (Contributed by Bill Curry, Telford, PA)

## Snow Carving

This is a new way to use the "Snow Sculpturing" idea found in **Ideas #1–4.** First, you need some snow. Second, you divide up into snow-carving teams of three or four kids per team. Then you assign a theme, like "food," and have the kids create large snow carvings of their choice for judging.

To make the carvings more realistic, provide spray bottles of water colored with ordinary food coloring, and allow the kids to "paint" their masterpieces. It works great and looks terrific.

Encourage your young people to be creative, and they will probably come up with some interesting ideas. One group, using the food theme, carved a 20-foot hot dog (complete with mustard and catsup), a bag of french fries, a banana split, a bowl of spaghetti with meatballs, and a giant taco.

After the judging, take a few pictures, and serve snow cones for dessert. (Contributed by Dave Washburn, Brockport, NY)

## Social Graces

Many young people feel like complete idiots when they go on their first big date or attend a formal dinner for the first time. They just don't know how to act. So, why not have a special banquet, planned and arranged by the youth group, that teaches some of the social graces to your kids in a fun and non-threatening way? Part of the program can be done in a tongue-in-cheek

fashion, but overall it should be a serious attempt to help kids feel confident when they find themselves in a formal social setting.

Before the banquet, divide the group into committees, each researching etiquette on table manners, serving, introductions, seating, decorating, table setting, etc. Then put the committees to work in their area, getting the room ready before the banquet. Appoint two young men to act as hosts.

As the kids arrive, they will be greeted by the hosts. Hosts or dates are to seat the girls properly — and do it several times for practice. Girls practice taking off their coats gracefully and sitting without awkwardness. Before the meal starts, the hosts briefly discuss how to make restaurant reservations, how to enter a restaurant, how to use the napkin, and how to read the menu and order from it.

When the soup is served, have a group quickly explain proper etiquette for eating soup — what to do with crackers, which spoon to use, where to place the spoon, etc. Everyone practices during the course.

Next is salad. A couple of young people explain how to properly cut the lettuce, what fork to use, how to eat a cherry tomato, how to handle olive pits, bread sticks, and so on.

For a main course, try chicken, baked potatoes, rolls and butter. Groups can explain how to manage the rolls, butter, sauces for the meat, bones, and how to complain gracefully to a waitress if something is wrong. After the main course, there can be a short program, speaker, or entertainment.

Finally, dessert is served and again, practical matters are brought up. Topics include tough pie crust, drips and crumbs, what to do with the napkins, if something falls on the floor, tipping, paying for the check and how to leave the table.

This activity can be extremely helpful for the kids, parents will love it, and it can become an annual event.

(Contributed by Roger Davis, Wausau, WI)

## Soup-er Sunday

If it's difficult to draw a crowd on "Super Sunday," try this. Have your group get together to watch the game (or a videotape of it) on a wide-screen TV. (You can rent them in most cities). If you live in the East and normally have Sunday night church about the same time the game starts, get someone to tape the game during church and have it ready to show **after** church.

Also ask each kid to bring a can of his or her favorite soup or favorite vegetable, and mix them all together in a big pot for a soup feast. Provide some fresh-baked bread and a beverage, and you'll have a "Soup-er Sunday." (Contributed by Kelvin Richardson, Sheridan, AR)

## Spaghetti Slobfest

Here's an unusual banquet idea that is great for laughs. Set up tables and assign places at the tables for each person. Set the tables with the most unusual eating "dishes" and "utensils" you can find. For example, one person may have to eat out of a vase with a wooden spoon. Another person eats out of a coffee creamer with an ice-cream scoop. Someone else gets a fruit jar and chopsticks. Each place setting should be as crazy as possible. Then, cover everything up with a sheet. Try not to let anyone in the room until you are ready to seat the entire group. Then, let everyone in. When each person is seated in their spot, remove the sheets and watch the look on their faces.

Now is when you need a camera. The hosts can serve the spaghetti, and the kids are instructed to eat only with the utensils provided. You can also serve bowls of salad and some bread. It will be a night they'll remember for a long time. (Contributed by Pat Christmas, Tarpon Springs, FL)

## Tator Night

Here is an idea that is an expansion of "The Tator Family" discussion (IDEAS #17-20). Why not have a whole evening devoted to "tator" events? Here are some suggestions:

**Tator Contest:** Have a tator-tasting contest, using several different brands of potato chips (most cities have at least a dozen). Put the chips in numbered bowls, and have each kid fill out an evaluation form (next page) judging the taste. Ask them not to "reveal" any brand that they guess. Afterward, tally the evaluations, and then disclose the brand names from best to worst.

**The People's Tator:** This skit is a take-off on "The People's Court." You will need 12 different people to play parts from the "Tator Family" (IDEAS #17-20) and one to play Judge Tator. Choose some kind of court case to be debated by the defendant, plaintiff and jurors. Have the judge ask questions of all the "characters," so that their personalities are revealed. The rest of the group tries to write down what personality they think everyone is exhibiting. Afterward, reveal the "tator" names, and discuss how people give off certain impressions, or reveal certain attitudes by their personalities.

## The Jury Box

| SPECK TATOR | DICK TATOR | AGI TATOR | HESI TATOR | EMMY TATOR | COGI TATOR |
|---|---|---|---|---|---|
| COMMON TATOR | IRRI TATOR | VEGI TATOR | DEVIS TATOR | FACILI TATOR | MEDI TATOR |

# "TATOR CHIP" CONTEST!
## "Choose your Spud, Bud"

"Tator" Night wouldn't be complete without "tator chips." This is your chance to say what **you** think! Rate the chips on a scale of 1–20 considering taste, appearance, texture, etc. Please taste each brand only once, so rate your brand right!

| This chip is related to a buffalo chip | | | | | | | | | | | | | | | | | | This chip should be in the bag of fame | |
|---|---|---|---|---|---|---|---|---|---|---|---|---|---|---|---|---|---|---|---|

**1.** 1 2 3 4 5 6 7 8 9 10 11 12 13 14 15 16 17 18 19 20
**2.** 1 2 3 4 5 6 7 8 9 10 11 12 13 14 15 16 17 18 19 20
**3.** 1 2 3 4 5 6 7 8 9 10 11 12 13 14 15 16 17 18 19 20
**4.** 1 2 3 4 5 6 7 8 9 10 11 12 13 14 15 16 17 18 19 20
**5.** 1 2 3 4 5 6 7 8 9 10 11 12 13 14 15 16 17 18 19 20
**6.** 1 2 3 4 5 6 7 8 9 10 11 12 13 14 15 16 17 18 19 20
**7.** 1 2 3 4 5 6 7 8 9 10 11 12 13 14 15 16 17 18 19 20
**8.** 1 2 3 4 5 6 7 8 9 10 11 12 13 14 15 16 17 18 19 20
**9.** 1 2 3 4 5 6 7 8 9 10 11 12 13 14 15 16 17 18 19 20
**10.** 1 2 3 4 5 6 7 8 9 10 11 12 13 14 15 16 17 18 19 20
**11.** 1 2 3 4 5 6 7 8 9 10 11 12 13 14 15 16 17 18 19 20
**12.** 1 2 3 4 5 6 7 8 9 10 11 12 13 14 15 16 17 18 19 20
**13.** 1 2 3 4 5 6 7 8 9 10 11 12 13 14 15 16 17 18 19 20

**Tator Teams:** If you want to divide the group into teams, there are lots of funny names to use that fit into the theme. Try naming your teams some of these: Red Potatoes, Russet Potatoes, Sweet Potatoes, Idaho Potatoes, New Potatoes, French Fries, Scallops, Hash Brown or Potato Skins.

Other games that you might want to include in your "Tator Night" are potato sack races, potato printing (IDEAS #9-12), potato sculpturing, potato bowling, the "hot" potato game, and so on. (Contributed by Mitch Olson, Rockford, IL)

## The Tie That Binds

Here's an idea for a theme dinner which you can organize around the verse, "Blest be the tie that binds." Seat people in a row at tables as they come in. Tie the right arm of each person to the left arm of the person next to them, all the way down the row. Thus, when anyone wants to eat he will have to ask his neighbor to lift her arm so that he can pick up his food. A simple menu such as hoagies and potato chips is best for this. To carry through with the theme, you might want to prepare a program on community cooperation and mutual dependence. Of course, if you do a skit or special music, don't be too shocked when your audience doesn't applaud! (Contributed by Kathie Taylor, Carpentersville, IL)

## Timed Car Rally

Here's a car rally that does not emphasize speed, but rather following directions—and enjoying the sights if done during daylight hours. A rally course is mapped out ahead of time and a detailed set of directions written out and duplicated for each vehicle. The directions should include 50 to 100 instructions (depending on how long you want to make it) similar to these:

1. Go east to the first stop sign.
2. Turn right.
3. At the traffic light, turn left, then go straight.
4. At the first traffic light, turn right.
5. Proceed under the trestle at 25 m.p.h.
6. Confirm water tower and the red-sided building on the left.
7. Turn left at the next stop sign.
8. Make a U-turn at the first opening in the middle divider.
9. Turn right at the stop sign.
10. Etc.

Make it clear to the kids that this rally is not a race. Each car will leave at five minute intervals and will be timed. The course has been previously and accurately timed by the leaders, and the winner is the carload coming closest to that predetermined time.

Tell the drivers that they are to observe the posted speed limits, or to drive at the speed specified in the directions. This speed will help them to arrive at the winning time. You can include some landmarks for the group to confirm (see item 6 above) just to make sure that they are still on the right course.

Have the rally end up at the church or at someone's house where you can reveal the winning car, award prizes, and serve refreshments. (Contributed by Bob Miller, Corinth, MS)

## Tin Man Triathlon

This activity is a scaled down version of the famous "Iron Man Triathlon." It is not only a test of endurance, but an opportunity for the group to help one another accomplish a tough goal. Any high schooler can enter the event, participating in one event, or all three. You can promote participation with "Tin Man" T-shirts, buttons, or posters.

The course should be challenging, such as a half-mile swim, a 20-30 mile bike ride and a 2-4 mile run. But the real emphasis should not be on winning as much as helping one another finish the course. It shouldn't be too grueling if they spend a couple of weeks on conditioning, but make sure you have on hand a nurse, salt pills and plenty of good old Gatorade.

You might want to top off the "Tin Man" with a spaghetti feast celebration, inviting a Christian professional athlete to be a special speaker. (Contributed by Keith King and Steve Fortosis, La Mirada, CA)

## Tourist Trap

If you live in an area with local tourist attractions, have a party that makes fun of them all in a lighthearted way.

For example, one group in Canada did

a takeoff on several of their local tourist spots. The "St. John to Digby Ferry" became the "Digby Fairy" (see photo). The "World Famous Tidal **Boar**" became the "World Famous Tidal **Bore**," and so on.

You can play games based on the ride or themes of your tourist attractions. If you live near a zoo, for example, you could play "The San Diego Zoo Game" (or whatever the name of the zoo), which is actually "Barnyard," found in **Ideas #1–4**. For prizes, you can give away souvenirs from a few of your local tourist traps.

Kids can also come dressed in tourist outfits: "Aloha" shirts, Bermuda shorts, cameras, sunglasses, and the like. Set up a few "backdrops" depicting tourist spots, and take some instant photos of kids standing in front of them "to send back home." (Contributed by Beth Power, River Glade, N.B., Canada)

# Trip Packets

One great way to save kids from boredom and to help redeem the time on long bus trips is to provide each young person with a creative "Trip Packet." If you plan ahead, these are easy to put together and fun to create. Items to include are:

**Trip guidebook:** This can be printed and produced by the youth leadership. It should be as factually informative and graphically interesting as possible. Include a list of trip counselors, a trip schedule, new choruses, a letter from the youth pastor, announcements for future youth group events, a "principle page" (rules for the trip), and pages for taking notes, devotional notes, and getting autographs and addresses.

**Brochure of retreat center or motel.**

**Christian music cassette:** This could be a contemporary Christian music tape of a group or artist that will soon be coming to town or to church to present a concert. When the tapes are used this way as a promotion tool, you can often buy them from the artist's record company at a lower cost.

**Puzzles and games:** Activities to keep them busy and interacting with each other. Offer prizes to whoever can solve them first.

**Fliers of upcoming events:** Jesus-festival fliers, rallies in the area, high school outreaches, Christian skate nights, etc.

**Interesting tracts:** There are some that are really creative and which communicate with young people. Check with your local Christian bookstore.

**Candy:** A few snacks to satisfy the ever-present youth sweet tooth.

All this stuff can be placed inside a big envelope or paper bag. It is definitely worth the extra effort to provide the group with an orderly schedule of activities, some guidelines to follow on the trip and a little extra spark of excitement. Use your imagination to come up with additional enclosures that are unique to your group. (Contributed by Robert Crosby, Rochester, NY)

# Turkey Bowl

The next time you're planning events around the football bowl games, beat the rush by hosting your own "Turkey Bowl" over the Thanksgiving holidays.

The "Turkey Bowl" is a football game played by your youth group (boys and girls), or with another youth group in your town. It should be touch, flag, or "Flamingo Football" (IDEAS #1-4) rules. But more than just a game, make this event special by having a "Bowl Breakfast" to kick off the day. Invite the kids and parents to a light breakfast where a local Christian football coach can share his testimony. If a coach is not available, check your local or state chapter of the Fellowship of Christian Athletes to secure a speaker.

To make this an annual event, rig up a special "Turkey Trophy" that can be used each year. You may be able to publicize this in a local newspaper to receive lots of participation. (Contributed by Phil Anderson, Macon, GA)

# Window Shopping

Here's a variation of the "Shopping Center Game" found in **Ideas #13-16**. It can be held in a shopping mall or along the main street of your community. The advantage to this version is that your kids won't have to go in and out of stores looking for items but can find them simply by window shopping.

To prepare for the hunt, go to the shopping area prior to the day of the activity and pick out some interesting items from the store windows that you want the kids to identify. Then create some clues or questions that can be listed in a random order. For example:

1. What color hair does the shortest mannequin have in the store window offering tennis balls for only $2.00 a can?
2. How many pairs of shoes have rubber soles in the Kirby's Shoe Store window?
3. Which item can be bought for only $2,367 at Jessop's Jewelers?

To begin the hunt, divide your group into teams of two or three people. Hand each team a list of clues and give them about an hour to hunt the answers down. Be sure to remind them that they are not to enter the stores or to run from place to place. The winner is the team which has the most correct answers in the allotted period of time. (Contributed by Gary Pettyjohn, Ft. Lauderdale, FL)

## Y'no

Y'no how everybody says "Y'no" all the time? Well, here's a good way to take advantage of that. Next time you have a party or special event, y'no, you just call it "Y'NO" which stands for "Youth Night Out." It's a pretty simple idea, y'no, but the group will love it. (Contributed by Robert Crosby, Rochester, NY)

# YOUTH GROUP LEADERSHIP

## Anonymous Elections

This idea can help solve one of the problems that youth groups always seem to face—how to elect officers without holding a popularity contest. This method should help the most capable and deserving get elected.

Before you hold elections, take time to receive nominations for each office. Encourage anyone who wants to run for office to nominate themselves, and encourage others to nominate anyone who they feel would do a good job. Then, all the nominees need to write a short statement answering these questions: 1) Why do you want to run for this office? 2) What special talents, abilities or qualifications do you have that would help you in this office? 3) What would you do or change if you were elected?

During the week, compile these statements and categorize them according to the office sought. Type them up and make enough copies for each youth, but DO NOT ATTACH A NAME TO ANY STATEMENT. On election night, pass out the statements, and use these sheets as your ballots.

The kids must vote for the statements and qualifications that they like, rather than the most popular names. After the election is over, the group finds out who wrote the winning statements. This approach should result in an election that allows the most capable people to win. (Contributed by Mark Christian, Santa Rosa, CA)

## Christian Tape Library

Contemporary Christian music is a positive addition to the lives of your young people, but it is also expensive. Records and tapes are usually costly and teenagers normally don't have the money to spend.

Why not set up a first-rate tape library at your church which has most of the current music in it? The kids in your group can purchase a "library card" for a nominal amount and use it to check out tapes for one week at a time. You can also ask the kids to leave a deposit on the tape to insure its safety. Catalog the tapes and run the whole thing just like a regular lending library. You can even have fines for late returns. Some kids may want to buy more than one library card so they can check out more than one tape at a time.

The money that is collected can buy more tapes. Some of the Christian record companies have tape and record clubs that reduce the cost of the tapes a little bit. You can also include a few selected secular tapes if you wish. Most kids have tape players and will probably take advantage of this. (Contributed by Todd Wagner, Hermiston, OR)

## Clip-Art File

This idea will save you lots of time and will be fun to use. Have your youth leadership and advisors keep on the look-out for funny, interesting or strange pictures in the newspaper or in magazines that can be cut out and kept in a file. Look also for unusual letters or catch phrases. When it comes time for a flyer or mailer for your youth activities, you will then have a great resource for creating unique, eye-catching graphics. You may want the whole group to be on the look-out for good stuff. Keep a box in your office or in the group meeting room for any contributions. (Contributed by James Taylor, Bellevue, NE)

## College Sweep

Once a year, take your high school juniors and seniors on a week-long, intensive tour of Christian liberal arts colleges and universities in your part of the country. You can go during the school year, as most schools will give excused absences to kids who want to participate.

This type of trip is relatively inexpensive since you'll find that colleges are eager to give your kids not only a tour, but also room and board for the visit. Usually the months of March and April are ideal for colleges to host groups.

Set up meetings with administrators at each stop, and encourage your young people to ask them questions. In addition, take advantage of the time you have with these youth to strengthen your relationships. Be sure to plan a day of recreation in the midst of this informational week.

Such a tour will help your youth make their college choices more wisely. Typical confusion and indecision over which college to attend result in part because their knowledge of colleges is only as deep as the catalogs are thick. Stepping onto a campus, mingling with the students, asking questions of the students and administrators, eating in the cafeteria, sleeping in the dorms, and sitting in on classes all combine to make the approaching transition much more easy to understand and prepare for. (Contributed by Robert Crosby, Rochester, NY)

## Computer Slides

One quick and easy way to make sing-along or announcement slides is with a personal computer and a 35mm single reflex camera. Most churches have at least one member who owns a personal computer, and many computer owners have word processing software. Simply type in the words you want to display. Format the output so that it looks exactly like you want your slide to look. If your computer offers color, utilize it to spice up your slides.

When your screen appears the way you want it, take a picture of the screen with your camera using standard 64 or 100 ASA film. Video images are flashed so quickly you will have to set the shutter speed to 8. This will require the use of a tripod and timer (or shutter bulb) to avoid blurred images. With a little imagination you can make creative, colorful slides quickly. (Contributed by Ben Sharpton, Kissimmee, FL)

## 50 Phrases To Bury a New Idea

Next time you have a planning session, give all your leaders the following list ahead of time. Tell them that you just wanted them to come prepared. Chances are they will be less likely to use any of these phrases on your new ideas when you bring them up.

1. We tried that before.
2. Our church is different.
3. It costs too much.
4. That's beyond our responsibility.
5. That's not my job.
6. We're all too busy to do that.
7. It's too radical a change.
8. We don't have the time.
9. Not enough help.
10. Let's do research first.
11. Not practical.
12. The congregation will never buy it.
13. Bring it up in six months.
14. We've never done it before.
15. Christians don't do that.
16. We don't have the authority.
17. That's too ivory tower.
18. Let's get back to reality.
19. That's not our problem.
20. Why change it, it's still working O.K.
21. I don't like the idea.
22. You're right, but . . .
23. You're two years ahead of your time.
24. We're not ready for that.
25. We don't have the money, equipment, room, personnel.
26. It isn't in the budget.
27. Can't teach an old dog new tricks.
28. Good thought, but impractical.
29. Let's hold it in abeyance.
30. Let's give it more thought.
31. The elders would never go for it.
32. That's what liberals (fundamentalists . .) do.
33. Not that again.
34. Where'd you dig that one up?
35. We did all right without it.
36. It's never been tried before.
37. It would take away from our missions emphasis.
38. Let's form a committee.
39. Parents won't like it.
40. I don't see the connection.
41. It won't work in our church.
42. What you are really saying is . . .
43. Our denomination doesn't do it that way.
44. Don't you think we should look into it further before we act?
45. Remember, this is a church.
46. It can't be done.
47. It's too much trouble to change.
48. I know a church who tried it.
49.
50. We've always done it this way.

(Contributed by Michael Tucker, Tempe, AZ)

# Fun Fact Sheet

It's always a good idea to keep good up-to-date information on all the kids who attend your youth group meetings. The following form works great for getting a few pertinent facts out of your youth group that you can then use for planning and getting kids involved. It can also be used for all first-timers as a visitor's registration form.

## WELCOME

NAME _____
ADDRESS_____
CITY _____ ZIP _____
SCHOOL _____YEAR _____
PHONE NUMBER _____

_____ I WOULD LIKE TO KNOW ABOUT THIS GROUP'S ACTIVITIES.
_____ I WOULD LIKE TO KNOW ABOUT THE BIBLE STUDIES.

_____ I CAME WITH A FRIEND.
_____ I CAME WITH MY FAMILY.
_____ I CAME ON MY OWN.
_____ I CAME BECAUSE MY PARENTS MADE ME.
_____ I CAME BY ACCIDENT.

_____ I WORK AT_____
_____ I DON'T WORK, BUT WISH I DID.
_____ I DON'T WORK, AND HOPE I NEVER WILL.

_____ AT SCHOOL I'M INVOLVED IN _____
_____

_____ I DON'T ATTEND ANOTHER CHURCH
_____ I ATTEND _____ CHURCH
          _____ OFTEN
          _____ NEVER
          _____ NOW & THEN

**I LIKE TO:**

| | |
|---|---|
| _____ H$_2$O SKI | _____ BASEBALL |
| _____ SNOW SKI | _____ FRISBEE |
| _____ READ | _____ SEW |
| _____ DRAMA | _____ PAINT |
| _____ BASKETBALL | _____ DRIVE CRAZILY |
| _____ VOLLEYBALL | _____ BACKPACK |
| _____ SOCCER | _____ ROCK CLIMB |
| _____ FOOTBALL | _____ HANG AROUND & BE COOL |
| _____ CHESS | _____ PICK MY NOSE |
| _____ SKATEBOARD | _____ PICK MY FRIEND'S NOSE |
| _____ RUN | _____ GET STRAIGHT A's |
| _____ LOOK AT GUYS | _____ SPIT ON PEOPLE WHO GET STRAIGHT A's |
| _____ EAT | _____ TENNIS |
| _____ LOOK AT GIRLS | _____ SWIM |
| _____ LISTEN TO MUSIC | _____ SURF |
| _____ WRITE ON BATHROOM WALLS | _____ ROLLERSKATE |
| _____ READ BATHROOM WALLS | _____ GOLF |
| _____ WORK ON CARS | _____ FILL OUT LONG QUESTIONNAIRES |

(Contributed by Michael Maples, St. Paul, MN)

## Generic Greeting Cards

It's always a good idea to remember your young people by sending them birthday cards, get well cards, thank you cards, and the like. But keeping an inventory of all those cards can put a strain on storage space, right?

Why not create your own "Generic Card?" Printed on yellow paper (like all those "yellow brand" products in the grocery store), it serves as an all-purpose card, no matter what the occasion. A good way to let kids know you care about them, plus it's fun to receive. Here's how to lay it out.

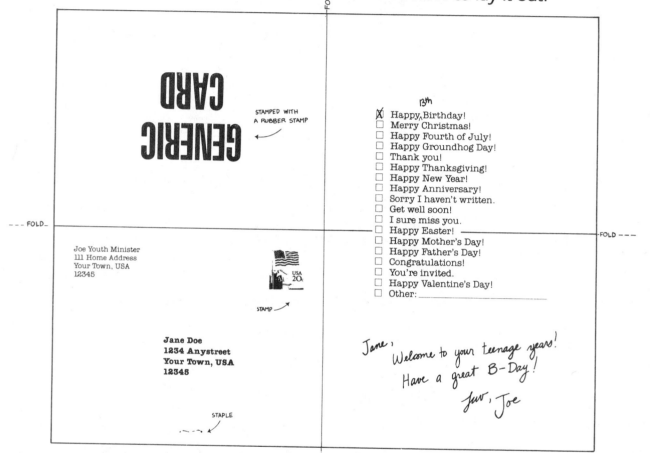

Of course, when you send the card, you'll want to add a personal note on the back. (Contributed by Alan C. Wilder, Jacksonville, FL)

---

## Get Started and Get Acquainted

This idea is designed to help newly recruited youth sponsors and advisors have more personal interaction with kids in the youth group. Most volunteer adult sponsors work full-time and don't have time to "hang out" with the kids at their events and favorite places.

Early in the school year, structure some time for each youth sponsor to have dinner (at their home, if possible) with small groups of kids, just to get to know them better. You can provide the sponsors with a list of questions they should ask each young person which will give them insight into his or her personality and background.

134

If these dinners are conducted over a period of a month, have a get-together at the end of the month. Include a light-hearted "roast," and a time of sharing some of the things said and done at the dinners during the month.

Some sponsors might find it more convenient to take kids to breakfast, go on a picnic lunch, or whatever. If your church has a youth budget, you might want to provide your sponsors with money for their food expenses. (Contributed by Malcolm McQueen, El Cajon, CA)

## Great Graphics

One great way to promote your activities in a big way or to redecorate your meeting space is to use billboard art. Notice the billboards in your area, and try to think of some creative applications to get your message across. Next, contact your local outdoor advertiser and see if they will let you look through their stock. Often they will just give you a billboard, or part of one, if you have your church write a letter stating that it will not be used for any money-

making venture or commercial advertising. You might also want to offer a donation receipt to the company.

Use your billboard as a wall decoration for your meeting place as part of a skit, or as a promotion for a particular activity. There are lots of possibilities. (Contributed by Gary Ogdon, Minneapolis, MN)

## Group Baseball Cards

Collecting baseball cards is still one of America's favorite pastimes. Now there are companies that will make custom baseball cards for high schools and colleges featuring their student athletes (see clipping). This opens up all kinds of possibilities for the creative youth

worker.

Why not make up baseball cards of all the kids in your youth program? Cards can include their picture and name on one side, and on the other their "vital statistics" (age, grade in school, likes and dislikes, right- or left-handed, "batting

135

# Hermitage celebrities card faces

**By Vic Fulp**
Times-Dispatch staff writer

In recent years, baseball card collector shows have become quite popular. Swarming from table to table are those looking for their favorite stars, while the more serious seek to improve their collections.

A New York Yankee fan may be looking for a deal on a Mickey Mantle card, while a diehard Giant follower flips through books and stacks of cards for Willie Mays.

How about a Jeff Wingrove card, or one of Keith Jasper? Maybe Jay Lane or Rodney Cowans? Or even Chester Fritz.

Who?

Wingrove and Jasper play baseball for Hermitage High School. Lane and Cowans played basketball for the Panthers and Fritz, the former

Continued on page 4, col. 3

Staff photo by Lindy Keast Rodman

**TRADING CARDS** — Hermitage student-athletes who are selling and trading cards of themselves display their wares. They are (front, left to right) Theresa Talley, Ron Carey, (rear, left to right) Danny Bowman, Susan Dixon and Keith Jasper.

average.") They can be funny and fun for your kids to collect and trade. They also help kids get to know each other better.

You can have them printed locally and help finance them by selling advertising space (in small print) on the back of the cards. Each kid in the group gets a stack of his or her own cards, and then kids trade with each other until they have everyone's card in their collection. Or you can give each young person a complete set of cards to begin with.

Another idea is to take photos of all the athletes at your local high school, get the information you need on them, and print up decks of cards to be sold or given away to the student body. Include a Bible verse or a positive slogan from your church or youth group. The possibilities are unlimited.
(Contributed by Craig Buxton, Richmond, VA)

## Group Mascot

One good way to build identity and unity in your youth group is to adopt a mascot. First make up a funny name, such as WUMY (for Wesley United Methodist Youth). Then, announce that there will be a contest to design the mascot. Try to get lots of ideas generating. Have the youth vote on the best design. At future meetings, make T-shirts for the group using liquid embroidery or a silk

screen. You can also have patches made for ski caps, jackets, baseball caps, or any other team identity the group might need. Once the design is established it can have all kinds of uses — stuffed animals, needlepoint, stationery, posters and the like. A mascot can be a good morale raiser for your kids, and can help the group feel an increased sense of unity. (Contributed by Don and Pat Habersberger, Bethlehem, PA)

## Heartboards

One way to build communication and positive relationships among your group is to have a bulletin board or "heartboard" up where notes can be exchanged, needs advertised, giveaways posted. It can also be a good way to make announcements and can save lots of postage once kids are in the habit of finding and picking up their notes.

Cut one or two large hearts (4' x 8') out of masonite and paint them bright red. Drill evenly-spaced holes around the edge of the hearts and mount metal clips with nuts and bolts to the board. Each clip can have someone's name on it. These "heartboards" should be hung up in areas that receive the most youth traffic.

Be sure to encourage the exchange of personal notes, so there is lots of interaction with the boards. You might even want to provide some special "youth notes" printed up for use on the boards. Have the kids use the board for exchanging birthday cards, Christmas cards, and be sure to see that everyone in the group gets a personal note with their name on it regularly. The more the kids receive, the more they will think to give. (Contributed by James Gilbert, Jr., Kaufman, TX)

## Honor Thy Sponsor

One reason it's hard to recruit and keep adult sponsors and volunteers is that they don't feel appreciated. Good sponsors are hard to find, so it makes good sense to take good care of them. You can do this in several ways:

1. Give them free tickets to concerts and events which they chaperone.
2. Give them money for meals and other expenses when they're required to be at events that cost money.
3. Include them in your planning sessions. Ask for their advice and act on it when you can.
4. Recognize them publicly in the youth newsletter, the church bulletin, and from the pulpit.
5. Provide them with funds, personnel, equipment, and resources to carry out the task assigned to them. Don't force them to go it alone.

(Contributed by Randy Nichols, Sumter, SC)

## Invisible Ink Groups

Here's an easy way to get kids into groups or teams. When they arrive, mark on their hands or their necks with invisible fluorescent ink (like the type used at amusement parks to stamp your hand for re-entry). Don't tell them what it says. You can use a rubber stamp to apply the marks, or you can put them on with a pen or brush. The ink is available in stationery, art, or novelty shops.

When it's time for the kids to get into groups, turn off the lights and have them get under a "black light" to see which group they're in. You can use codes, like an "O" for group one and "X" for group two, and so on. Kids enjoy the mystery that's involved, and it's an effective way to get them into groups without lots of arguing and changing from one group to the next. (Contributed by Mitch Olson, Rockford, IL)

## Junior-High Ticket Program

Here's a creative way to control the behavior (or misbehavior) of highly exuberant junior high youth using ordinary, double-rolled tickets. It basically rewards them for good behavior and penalizes them for bad behavior in a fun and non-threatening way.

When youth arrive at a meeting, they receive five tickets that they keep with them throughout the entire evening. Place the matching stubs in a container. You can usually buy these numbered tickets in local stationery stores, paper supply companies, or party supply stores.

The youth keep the tickets with them throughout the night, but when they misbehave, the counselor or adult leader then takes a ticket away from them. The behavior that is not allowed should be determined ahead of time, and all youth should be informed as to what they can and cannot do. For example, the leader is talking and two kids are talking, and it disturbs the group. They each lose a ticket. This goes on throughout the evening, during the game time and recreation, free time, Bible Study, devotions, and anything else that is

planned.

At the end of the meeting 10-15 prizes are brought out. A drawing for the prizes is held using the ticket stubs in the container. Prizes can be candy or soft drinks, or anything else of interest to junior high youth. The counselors who took tickets away from kids use those tickets to participate in the prize drawing. It makes the youth think when a counselor wins a prize from a ticket he took away from a kid for bad behavior.

The youth are encouraged to keep their extra tickets after the night is over, and then after six months, an auction can be held in which the youth bring all the tickets they have collected, and then make bids on some extra special prizes. This way, youth who always behave and have lots of tickets, have a reward for their good behavior.

Difficult discipline problems are not going to be solved with this kind of program, but it might be helpful to make kids more aware of the fact that their behavior does matter in a group setting. (Contributed by Steve Christopher, Long Beach, CA)

## Library Courtesy Cards

If you have a personal or church library which sometimes suffers from the "disappearing book syndrome," then this idea might help. Print up some small cards like the one below, and ask book borrowers to fill one out when they borrow a book.

The card is not so much for your benefit, however, as it is for the borrowers'. Have them keep it to use as a bookmark and also to remember where the book came from. Usually books aren't returned because people forget that they borrowed them from someone. You can, of course, keep a list of who has which books, but the cards help the books to come back on their own. A humorous touch makes them easier to fill out. (Contributed by Scott Welch, Wilmore, KY)

Hey Scott,

I borrowed your book, and I wanted to let you know. I need it to: (Please check one)

☐ Raise the movie projector for our home movies tonight.

☐ Put under my little sister to help her reach the table.

☐ Flatten out leaves for my leaf collection.

☐ Help in witnessing to a Moonie.

☐ _____
_____

I'll be sure and return it as soon as I'm done. Thanks!

Your friend,

## Photo Blowups

Here's a good idea for this year's grad night celebration. Have each of your graduates give you their senior picture (or any good portrait photo) and have giant poster-sized blowups made to decorate the room. The posters can line the walls with a professional-looking name tag underneath each one. The result is quite impressive, and the posters make nice gifts for each grad when the celebration is over.

Check the telephone directory for photo studios in your area that will do this, or write: Wallet Photo Co., P.O. Box 2000, Dept. 473, West Caldwell, NJ 07006. This company will make posters from small photos by mail order for a surprisingly low cost. (Contributed by David Mahoney, Jr., Portland, IN)

## Picture Postcards

This idea can be a great way to communicate with kids in your group, or to make newcomers feel more included. Using a 35mm camera, take several pictures of each young person individually and also some of the group together. When a new person joins the group, be sure to take a picture of him or her as well. When you get the film developed, order "jumbo size" prints.

When you need to communicate, send these photos as postcards. Simply put a message on the back with an address and stamp, and drop it in the mail. It will be instantly personal and fun to receive. (Contributed by Roger Gales, Lawrence, KS)

## Poster Diary

At the beginning of the school year or at your first youth meeting of the new year, distribute to each young person a piece of heavy-duty poster board. After letting them personalize their board, explain to them that this is their "diary" for the year. They should attach to it items of meaning or interest as they happen throughout the year. They can pin or tape name tags to it, ticket stubs, event programs, worship bulletins, athletic event identifications, rodeo "remains" or anything else they want.

At the last meeting of the year, the kids can bring them in and share their creations. The group can then spend some time discussing in retrospect the growth, changes, impressions that the past year brought.

This idea works best with senior high kids, and chances are, it will be necessary to remind them of their poster diary at times throughout the year. For a few dollars more, you might want to purchase a large quantity of small, white bulletin (cork) boards that can be used for the same purpose. (Contributed by Mark Simone, Ravenna, OH)

## Purple Heart Award

Here's a thoughtful and humorous way to encourage and thank an adult youth sponsor after a particularly difficult or demanding activity. Present him or her with a "Purple Heart" award which bears an inscription similar to this: "In recognition for service above and beyond the call of duty in Youth Ministry."

The award can be made out of purple construction paper and framed. You can even have a presentation ceremony of some kind.

In recognition for service above and beyond the call of duty

Your sponsors will enjoy the attention and appreciate your thoughtfulness. (Contributed by Mark Skorheim, Bullard, TX)

## Sponsor Search

Here's a good system for recruiting adult sponsors for your youth group. It deals with the two most basic objections that adults have—feeling that they don't have anything to contribute, and not knowing what is expected of them.

First, develop a booklet or series of handouts on your youth group, giving an overview of the youth ministry, and spelling out exactly and specifically what the advisor is to do. Make it simple and attractive. Next, meet with the church staff or your board to put together a "hit list" of good prospects. Be sure to have a good number of them—more than you need so that some may gracefully decline.

Contact each person on this list by phone or in person, asking them to consider working with the youth of the church. Emphasize that you will not need their decision for several weeks. During this time, ask them to attend a few youth meetings, an outing, and an advisors' meeting. Then meet with them personally to answer questions and to gain an impression of their commitment to Christ and their special gifts and abilities. Be sure to pray together. Finally, make the decision **together** about their involvement. Even if the person decides not to make a long-term commitment, there is always an opportunity to enlist their help with special events, camp counseling, and the like. In a few months, they may be able to help full time. (Contributed by David C. Wright, Vienna, VA)

## Sticker Post Cards

Here's a quick way to create your own personalized postcards to send members. Go to any stationery or art supply store and purchase a variety of stickers with positive messages like "Good Work!", "Terrific!", or "U-R-Tops!" They're usually available individually or in rolls or sheets. Use them to add color to ordinary, drab post cards. Then add a personal note, and you've got a great way to encourage and congratulate your kids. (Contributed by Joy Jones, Canton, NC)

It's AMAZING

3-21-83

Linda,
Thanks for a super job as Sunday School teacher for Senior Adults during Youth Week! They appreciate you, and so do I—
Love,

Matthew 6:33

It's Fantastic!

Jim,
Congratulations on being honored as "Student of the Month" by the Rotary Club! I am proud of you—
In His love,

Psalm 37:4-5

## Summer Exchange Program

This idea is patterned after foreign exchange programs that are common in the public high schools. The same thing can be done between churches in neighboring towns, states, or even other countries. What you do is set up an exchange program in which individual young people are traded for a short period of time (one month is ideal) between two churches. The exchange need not be simultaneous (yours may go in June; theirs may come in July). The young person who is "traded" then becomes an "apprentice" to the youth minister at the new church. While he or she is there, that young person will learn to develop their leadership potential and to share his or her abilities with another part of the body of Christ.

Make it clear with your church and the exchange church just what the duties of the youth will be. These may include working in the office, running errands, planning youth nights, working on files, helping with visitation, leading Bible studies, giving devotionals, helping with Vacation Bible School, or just being a part of the regular youth program. Try to immerse the youth in the program of the church without drowning him or her! If this is a full-time exchange, with the kids staying in the homes of church members, be sure that they have their own cars and that their schedule does not upset their "host family." The churches should provide some spending money and plan to pick up all church-related expenses, such as retreat costs and costs of all youth activities.

To select a youth for this program, have those who are interested apply and write an essay, or give a brief biographical sketch, with a Christian testimony and a photo. Send these to the exchange church and let them choose which youth they would like to sponsor.

When your exchange youth arrives, you might want to introduce him or her in your church service and present him or her with a key to the church, an honorary membership certificate, or some other token of welcome. This will give the youth maximum exposure to the congregation and may open avenues for service. Having a responsible and committed young person may do wonders for the kids in your group and the leader that you send off will return with new perspectives and greater maturity in Christ. (Contributed by Daryl and Carole Eldridge, Arlington, TX)

## Teen of the Week

Here's a great way to make your kids feel important, and also to help everyone to get to know each other better. Each week you choose a teen of the week who is the honored guest at that week's youth meeting.

Here's what is involved: contact the chosen teen's parents secretly and have them provide you with family photos, baby pictures, awards, report cards, toys, articles of clothing, or anything that would be of interest to the group. One bulletin board in the church can be set aside for the teen of the week, and all those items can be hung up on the board. When the young people arrive for the meeting, they will all head straight for the teen-of-the-week board to find out who it is this week. In addition, the chosen young person can be honored in some special way during the meeting. It's a good way to have fun and to let kids know that they are special. (Contributed by Roger Davis, Wausau, WI)

## Terrific Team Titles

Here's a good way to get your young people involved in some kind of ministry in the youth group. Think up all the possible ministries or jobs that someone could do, decide how many people could do them, and then give those jobs some clever names. Print up a list of the job titles with a brief summary of what is involved, and then let the kids sign up. This approach will usually get better results than just waiting around for kids to volunteer.

At the end of the school year, or when appropriate, you could have an awards night and recognize the accomplishments of each person who was involved in one of these jobs. (Contributed by Michael Anderson, Minneapolis, MN)

| POSITION | PEOPLE | DESCRIPTION |
|----------|--------|-------------|
| Refreshment Refresher | 1 | Fill pop machine and keep track of the money. |
| File Flies | 2, 3, 4 | Work around my office, espeically filing and reading various articles once every 2, 3, or 4 weeks after school. |
| Physical Plant Plaintiff | 1 | Make sure heat is turned off, Sunday School books collected, windows shut, yell at people who are messy, etc. |
| Greeter Getter | 2 | Say hello to newcomers, introduce them, have them fill out visitor cards. |
| Pictorial Personage | 1 | Take photographic images of Sr. High or Jr. High events. |
| Senior Sitizen Savers | 2, 3, 4, 5 | Once a month go with adults to Senior Citizen's home and help in the worship service. (Just helping them find verses or hymns or leading if you feel comfortable, etc.) |
| Call Committee | 2 | Call and invite visitors, send "We Missed You" cards to people who didn't show. |
| Periodical Pusher | 1 | Distributes Christian magazines. |

## Volunteer Job Description

Whether a youth program is large or small, volunteers are usually the lifeblood of the program. But when volunteers are recruited, they often don't realize just what they are getting into. This can be remedied by providing a written job description to the volunteer similar to the one below. This will help the volunteer to know immediately:

1. What is expected of the volunteer.

2. What the purpose of the job is.
3. Who the volunteer is accountable to.
4. What kind of person is needed for the job.
5. What kind of resources are available for the volunteer to carry out the job.

In addition, it lets the volunteer know that:

1. Good planning has gone into the event.
2. He or she has been chosen specifically for the task because of their job qualifications.
3. The job is important to the event and to the youth program.
4. There are people and resources to help accomplish the job.

The following is a simple form which can be modified to fit your own needs. It doesn't take long to fill out, and it is guaranteed to save time spent chasing down missed communications and hurt feelings.

---

JOB DESCRIPTION FOR _____
(title of position)

_____ , _____
(name of event or program)         (beginning and ending dates)

FILLED BY: _____
(name of volunteer)

ACCOUNTABLE TO: _____
(name & position of supervisor)

BASIC PURPOSE: _____
(state basic purpose of job in one sentence)

DUTIES OF THIS POSITION: (list duties)
1.
2.
3.
4.
etc.

QUALIFICATIONS NEEDED TO FILL THIS POSITION: (list qualifications)
1.
2.
3.
etc.

RESOURCES AVAILABLE TO YOU: (list resources)
1.
2.
3.
etc.

---

Here are a few additional helps for writing job descriptions:

1. Make the position title reflect what the job is. Keep it simple.
2. State as simply as possible the purpose for which the job was created.
3. Begin statements of duties with verbs. Make them measurable.
4. Qualifications should include personal, spiritual, and ability qualities needed to perform the job well.
5. Be creative in listing resources. Volunteers need to know that they are not being asked to be the "Lone Ranger."
6. Any job, no matter how small, can be described in writing — and is more likely to be understood if it is.

(Contributed by Jim Steele, Lake Oswego, OR)

# Weekly Planning Sheet

If you have trouble getting organized each week for your youth group meetings and activities, try a weekly planning sheet like the one below. It will help not only you to think through what needs to be done, but others as well. Fill it out and give copies to your youth advisors, the pastor, youth council, and others. The example here is only a suggested format, though it has been used with good results. Create your own to fit the needs of your program.

YOUTH EVENING PLAN SHEET

NAME: _____

TIME ALLOCATION

GOAL FOR THE EVENING: _____ DATE: _____

MEAL PREPARED BY: _____

ANNOUNCEMENTS: _____

ACTIVITY: _____ PHONE #: _____

  1. MATERIALS NEEDED: _____

  2. COST: _____

  3. TRANSPORTATION BY: _____

SONGS: _____

SCRIPTURE TO STUDY: _____ PHONE #: _____

TITLE: _____

FURTHER EXPRESSIONS OF WORSHIP: _____ PURPOSE: _____

LESSON OUTLINE: _____

ALTERNATE BACKUP ACTIVITY: _____

  1. MATERIALS NEEDED: _____

  2. COST: _____

THINGS I NEED TO DO FOR NEXT WEEK: _____

PEOPLE I NEED TO BE WITH OR PHONE: _____

CONCERNS I NEED TO PRAY FOR: _____

YOUTH'S RESPONSES TO THE EVENING: _____

CREATIVE THOUGHTS AND IDEAS FOR THE FUTURE: _____

EVENING RATING

1  2  3  4  5  6  7  8  9  10

PITIFUL

EXCELLENT

(Contributed by Bill Hughes, Georgetown, NY)

# YMTV

Home video is gaining in popularity as the equipment becomes cheaper and easier to use. Why not create your own video library featuring special youth concerts, fellowships, dramas, and other activities for future viewing? All it takes is a video camera borrowed from someone in your youth ministry. When you host singing groups, speakers, or other special guests, videotape them (with their permission, of course) and then allow the kids to check out the video cassettes whenever they want to see them again. Many young people are into **MTV** (Music Television), so you can call yours **YMTV**—Youth Ministry Television! (Contributed by Darrel Brock, Wichita Falls, TX)

## Youth Group Application For Admission

The form below is an "Application for Admission" to your youth group, a tongue-in-cheek way of collecting vital statistics on your youth group members.

It's also a great way to test your kids' sense of humor. Make it look very "official," have all your kids fill it out, and give one to new kids as they come.

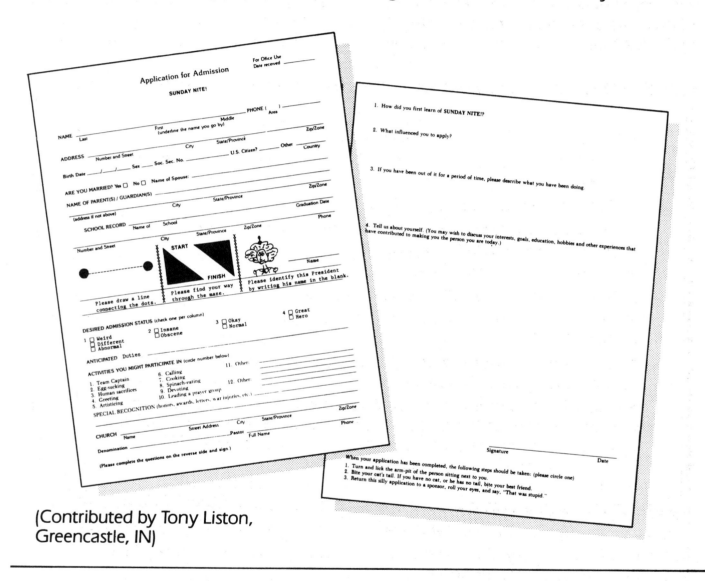

(Contributed by Tony Liston, Greencastle, IN)

## Youth Group Dollars

Here's a good way to increase attendance at your youth group activities and meetings. Award some custom-designed "play money" for each event that can be redeemed at a later date for discounts on camp, special outings, prizes that kids can bid on, or whatever. Every time they attend a youth group function, they get one dollar bill. (Have them sign it so no one else can use it.) With a little creativity, you can come up with your own kind of money—"Baptist Bucks," "Covenant Currency," "Youth Group Gold," and so on. Just print up your own on a copying machine or have it printed at a local print shop. (Contributed by Molly Halter, Youngstown, OH)

## Youth Leader's Coupon Book

Most youth workers can't afford to give every young person in their group a Christmas or birthday present. Here's a gift idea that is cheap and yet valuable.

Create a coupon book which offers a variety of services to the young people, redeemable any time during the year. Think up as many coupons as you like:

- Good for one free dinner at my house.
- Good for one free "rap session." Void between 11:00 p.m. and 7:00 a.m.
- Good for prayer for any prayer request.
- Good for one free ride (in an emergency) to the destination of your choice (within reason).
- Good for one "encouraging word." Redeemable any time.
- Good for one free "Pat on the Back" when needed.
- Good for one pretty good answer to your most burning question.
- Good for one evening of babysitting: We have the baby, you do the sitting (free, of course).
- Good for one treasure map: A free treasure will be given to anyone who visits the youth pastor's office Monday through Friday between 9:00 a.m. and 4:30 p.m. Call for an appointment.

These coupons not only offer the kids something for free: they also make them aware of the kinds of things you're willing to do for them. (Contributed by Larry J. Stoffel, Danbury, CT)

# CHAPTER SEVEN

# CHRISTMAS

## Caroling Scavenger Hunt

Here's a new way to go Christmas caroling this year. Divide up into caroling groups, and give each group a list similar to this:

Sherrif's station—300 points
Convalescent hospital—250 points
Shopping center—200 points
Airport (as people are arriving off a flight)—500 points
McDonald's restaurant (inside)—
100 points

This list can include as many locations as you want. Some can be easy to reach and some can be hard. The object is for the group to go Christmas caroling at as many locations on the list as they can within a given time limit. At each location, they must sing three Christmas carols all the way through, and then have someone in authority at each location sign their list to verify that they were actually there.

All the caroling groups may then return to a meeting place at the end of the time limit to determine the "winning" group, and to enjoy some refreshments and sharing of experiences (Contributed by Gerry Blundell, Lancaster, CA)

## Christmas Post Office

Here's a good idea for a Christmas service project to raise money for missions. Construct a box (like the one shown) out of plywood, with little compartments large enough for letters and Christmas cards. There should be at least 25 compartments.

After it's built, painted, and labeled, place it in a prominent place in your church, announcing that "The Christmas Post Office is now Open." People are invited to "mail" their cards and letters to each other simply by placing them in the appropriate compartment and by paying five cents (or whatever) per card. Each week until Christmas, church members are to check the compartment with the first letter of their last name, and pick up their Christmas mail.

The money that's raised can then be used for missions or some other Christmas project. One church has done this for three years in a row, and each year it's more successful than the last. (Contributed by Larry Lawrence, Jonesboro, GA)

CHRISTMAS POST OFFICE

## Christmas Words

In advance, make up a list of words associated with Christmas, and assign each word a value in points. For example:

| | |
|---|---|
| Nativity | 10 points |
| Santa Claus | 3 points |
| Yule | 12 points |
| Gift | 5 points |
| Angel | 9 points |
| Shepherds | 10 points |

Your list should be as complete as you can make it, but it doesn't need to be exhaustive. Points can be assigned randomly, or you can assign them according to how common they are, the number of letters in each word, or some other criterion.

Next, ask each person in your group to make a list of the first 20 Christmas words that come to mind. When they're finished, distribute your pre-printed list of Christmas words with the points for each word. Each person should determine the point value of their own words by locating them on the master list. Any words not on the master list can receive extra bonus points.

Next, find out who won the most points, and award a prize of some kind to that person. You can also find out who had the fewest points, and award that person a booby prize.

Finally, ask the kids to take the words on their lists and to assign points to them in order of their importance to them, with 1 being most important and 20 being least important. Or, give them another list of Christmas words containing a variety of both religious and secular words, and ask them to do the same thing. This way, all the kids are working on the same list, and they can share their results with each other and compare the points assigned to each word. It's a good way to open up discussion on what Christmas means to each person. (Contributed by Jim Olia, Eagle Bend, MN)

## Crazy Carols

Tired of singing the same old Christmas songs year after year? Try turning those old songs into new ones by playing "Mad Libs" with them.

Have the kids give you some crazy words (specify noun, verb, adjective, and so on), then use these to fill in the blank as in the examples below. Put the finished product up on an overhead projector, and sing the song with gusto! The kids will love it.

---

### I'm Dreaming

I'm dreaming of a(n) _____ _____, just like the ones I
                     adjective     noun

used to _____. Where the _____s _____, and
       verb            noun      verb

_____s _____, to hear _____s in the _____.
noun     verb           noun         noun

I'm dreaming of a(n) _____ _____, with every
                     adjective     noun

_____ I _____. May your _____s be _____
noun     verb          noun         adjective

and _____; and may all your _____s be _____.
   adjective              noun       adjective

---

### Who's Coming To Where?

Oh! You'd better not _____; you'd better not _____;
               verb               verb

you'd better not _____; I'm telling you why: _____ is
           verb                 person in group

coming to _____! He knows when you've been
      name of a place

_____ing; He knows when you're _____. He knows
verb                  adjective

if you've been _____ or _____; so be _____ for
         adjective      adjective      adjective

goodness' sake.

Oh! You'd better not _____; you'd better not _____;
               verb              verb

you'd better not _____; I'm telling you why: _____ is
           verb                same name as above

coming to _____!
    same place as above

(Contributed by Richard Starcher, Sumner, NE)

# Get Acquainted Christmas Tree

Here's a mixer idea for a Christmas party. Print up a "Christmas tree" similar to the one below, with a variety of descriptive statements on each "ornament." Like other games of this type, the object is to mill around the room and find people who fit each description; then have them sign their names on the ornaments. Different colored marking pens can be made available to make the tree decorating process more colorful. (Contributed by Tim Smith, Fresno, CA)

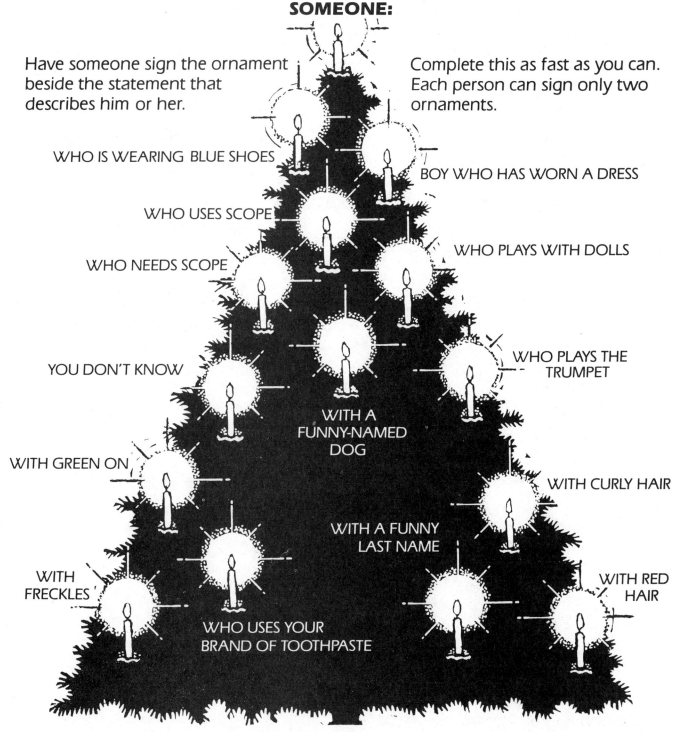

**SOMEONE:**

Have someone sign the ornament beside the statement that describes him or her.

Complete this as fast as you can. Each person can sign only two ornaments.

WHO IS WEARING BLUE SHOES

BOY WHO HAS WORN A DRESS

WHO USES SCOPE

WHO PLAYS WITH DOLLS

WHO NEEDS SCOPE

YOU DON'T KNOW

WHO PLAYS THE TRUMPET

WITH A FUNNY-NAMED DOG

WITH GREEN ON

WITH CURLY HAIR

WITH A FUNNY LAST NAME

WITH FRECKLES

WITH RED HAIR

WHO USES YOUR BRAND OF TOOTHPASTE

## Gifts For Jesus

This year, why not invite your kids to do a Christmas gift exchange in which they actually purchase gifts and give them to Christ? Set a price limit on the gifts, or have the kids make them by hand. They should be wrapped like any Christmas gift would be, and placed in a manger at the party or meeting. Allow each young person to open his or her gift, explain why it was chosen, and tell how Christ can use it. For example, someone might give a pair of new tennis shoes, and tell about an orphanage which needs new shoes for its children. By giving to "one of the least of these," the gift is actually given to Christ. This can be a meaningful way for kids to understand the true meaning of Christmas. (Contributed by Randy Pierce, Mt. Prospect, IL)

## The Guest

Here is a short Christmas play which is an adaptation of the poem "How the Great Guest Came" by Edwin Markham. While the original poem's setting was in Europe a few centuries ago, the setting for this version of the story is the present. (Contributed by Dan Johnson, Allison Park, PA)

### THE GUEST

**Characters:**

| | | |
|---|---|---|
| Conrad | The Woman | Two passers-by |
| Ellspith | The Old Man | Narrator |
| Barclay | The Kid | |

**Props:**

| | | |
|---|---|---|
| street lamp | bread | chairs or sofa |
| fireplace | milk | lamp |
| table | honey | other furnishings |
| bookshelf | door | costumes |
| shoes | | |

### THE GUEST

Narrator:    Before the cathedral in grandeur rose
At Ingelburg where the Danube goes;
Before its forest of silver spires
Went airily up to the clouds and fires:
Before the oak had ready a beam,
While yet the arch was stone and dream—
There where the altar was later laid,
Conrad, the cobbler, plied his trade.

| Ellspith: | (knock, knock) |
|---|---|
| Conrad: | Bark! Bark! |
| Ellspith: | (knock, knock) |
| Conrad: | (as he walks to the door) Bark! Bark! Down, Fang! Bark! Bark! Quiet. Bark! Growl ... (Opens door.) Hello, Ellspith! Merry Christmas! Come in, come in. |
| Ellspith: | Conrad, old friend. A merry Christmas to you, too. Conrad, what was barking? You don't have a watchdog. |
| Conrad: | I know. I can't afford one. So when someone comes to the door, I have to bark myself. |
| Ellspith: | Oh, Conrad—we are all feeling the financial pinch. |
| Conrad: | Where's Barclay? |
| Ellspith: | He's coming any minute. |
| Barclay: | (knock, knock) |
| Ellspith: | That's him now. |
| Barclay: | (knock, knock) |
| Ellspith: | Who's there? |
| Barclay: | Snue! |
| Ellspith: | Snue! (Opens door.) What's Snue? |
| Barclay: | I don't know. What's Snue with you? Say, Conrad old boy—did you fix my sole? |
| Conrad: | Only the Lord can fix your soul, Barclay. But I did fix your shoe. (Hands him shoe, tapping on the sole.) |
| Barclay: | How delightful. Now I have my Christmas shoes to wear with my Christmas stockings. They were knit by my dear, dear aunt. Do you know what they call my aunt, Conrad? |
| Conrad: | Probably Marnie Farnstock. That was her name. |
| Barclay: | (exasperated) I mean after she died. |
| Conrad: | They called her the late Marnie Farnstock. |
| Barclay: | They called her Marner the Darner. She used to say, "The hand that darns the sock ..." |
| Ellspith: | "... is usually the one that socks the husband!" Come, Barclay. We have to get you home into your socks. (They start to leave.) |
| Conrad: | Ellspith. Barclay. |
| Ellspith: | Yes, Conrad. |
| Conrad: | Before you leave, I must share my heart with you. |
| Ellspith: | Conrad, please do. |
| Barclay: | Yes, we are your friends. |
| Conrad: | (dramatically, gazing heavenward) |
| | At dawn today |
| | As night slipped away ... |
| | The Lord appeared in a dream to me |
| | And said, "I am coming your Guest to be!" |
| | So I've been busy with feet astir, |
| | Strewing the floor with branches of fir. |
| | The wall is washed and the shelf is shined, |
| | And over the rafter the holly twined. |
| | He comes today, and the table is spread |
| | With milk and honey and wheaten bread." |
| Ellspith: | (staring blank-faced straight at Conrad) Why is he talking in poetry? |
| Barclay: | Too much Lutefish, I suspect. |
| Ellspith: | Listen, Conrad. It's Christmas and your thoughts are filled with Christ's coming. No doubt your dreams merely reflected what you have been thinking all day. |

| | |
|---|---|
| **Barclay:** | Ellspith's right, Conrad. I mean, Christ's not really going to come to your door. |
| **Conrad:** | *(pause)* Perhaps you are right. That *is* a little unusual. But it seemed so real. |
| **Ellspith:** | We have to go, old friend—have a delightful Christmas. |
| **Barclay:** | And if Jesus does come, send for us. We wise and royal beings will come bearing our gifts of mirth and frankenstein. *(Ellspith pulls Barclay out through door by scarf.)* |
| | *(appropriate farewells)* |

## POOR WOMAN

*(Conrad sees woman shivering in the cold, selling coal to passers-by. He invites her into his home to warm herself.)*

| | |
|---|---|
| **Woman:** | Thank you kindly, sir. The weather is miserable out there. |
| **Conrad:** | It certainly is foggy. |
| **Woman:** | The visibility is so bad even the birds are walking. *(She sneezes right in his face.)* |
| **Conrad:** | *(slightly put off, but polite)* Excuse me ma'am, but could you sneeze the other way? |
| **Woman:** | I don't know no other way. |
| **Conrad:** | Here. Sit down by the fire and warm yourself. Tell me how you came to such a wretched condition! |
| **Woman:** | I was raised in poverty. We had nothing when I was growing up. And then. And then I met John. He was rich. Sophisticated. He was the only banker unaffected by the crash of '29. |
| **Conrad:** | Really?! |
| **Woman:** | He went broke in '28. Ever since then we lived in a little dreary apartment in town. Our furniture was meager and shabby. We had one little worn rug on our cold floor. It looked so bad my mother would say, "That rug looks terrible. Sweep it under the dirt!" |
| **Conrad:** | What does your husband do now? |
| **Woman:** | Oh, he passed away last year. I told him that if he were to die, starvation would stare me in the face. He said, "Doesn't sound pleasant for either of you!" So now it is just me and my children. |
| **Conrad:** | Woman, how can I help you? |
| **Woman:** | You dear man. You can't help. *(Gets up to go to the door.)* I can see that you are not much better off than I. I am simply trying to sell some coal in order to purchase some fresh milk and bread for my family. |
| **Conrad:** | *(Turns and looks at the table.)* Here—take this. |
| **Woman:** | *(awed by this great sacrifice)* God bless you, my friend. |
| **Conrad:** | Merry Christmas. |

## THE OLD MAN

| | |
|---|---|
| **Man:** | *(knock, knock)* |
| **Conrad:** | Bark! Bark! Ah! It'll never work! I just don't sound enough like a dog. Coming! *(Opens door. Man throws bone in.)* What's that for? |
| **Man:** | I thought I heard a dog. |
| **Conrad:** | Ah, yes. He passed away. I just laid him to rest. What can I do for you, old man? |
| **Man:** | I am receiving Christmas donations for the Buford T. Ellis Memorial Fund. |

| | |
|---|---|
| Conrad: | And who, may I ask, is Buford T. Ellis? |
| Man: | At your service, sir. *(Bows dramatically with top hat.)* |
| Conrad: | *(chuckling)* Come in, Old-Timer; you look like you could use at least a rest. |
| Man: | Thank you, sir. Usually I am not received in such kindness. |
| Conrad: | It's the least I can do. Here. Sit down. |
| Man: | *(Sits down. Puts feet up on little table. Pulls out stogie.)* |
| Conrad: | So you are collecting money? |
| Man: | I am. I need some extra bucks for my expensive hobby. |
| Conrad: | And what hobby is that? |
| Man: | Eating. |
| Conrad: | You know it would be nice to have a lot of money. But really, money only brings misery. |
| Man: | But with money you can afford to be miserable. This Thanksgiving I asked myself, "What do I have to be thankful for? I can't even pay my bills." |
| Conrad: | Be thankful you're not one of your creditors. |
| Man: | That's true. You know, I used to get by fairly well with my small business. But I have suffered one financial disaster after another. |
| Conrad: | It's been a tough life for you, hasn't it? |
| Man: | It hasn't been easy, but God has helped me. |
| Conrad: | Listen, old man. I don't have much. But here—take these shoes. You could stand a new pair. |
| Man: | *(looking very happy)* You are very generous. *(Rips off his old shoes. They fall apart. Puts on new ones.)* They fit perfectly! Thank you, sir. *(He leaves. They exchange farewells.)* |

## THE KID

| | |
|---|---|
| Kid: | *(knock, knock)* |
| Conrad: | *(Opens door.)* |
| Kid: | *(sings)* While shepherds washed their socks by night, all seated on the ground ... |
| Conrad: | *(interrupts)* Hold it! Hold it! I think you have some of the words mixed up there. It's "watched," not "washed." |
| Kid: | While shepherds watched their socks by night ... |
| Conrad: | Wait! And it's "flocks," not "socks." |
| Kid: | What are flocks? |
| Conrad: | They're a bunch of sheep. Do you know what sheep are? *(Kid shakes head no.)* They're little wooly things ... kind of like socks!—Merry Christmas! What can I do for you on this blessed day? |
| Kid: | I'm collecting arms for the poor. |
| Conrad: | That's "alms." |
| Kid: | What are alms? |
| Conrad: | They're gifts—usually money. |
| Kid: | OOOH NOOO! |
| Conrad: | What's the problem? |
| Kid: | I've been going through the streets crying, "Arms for the poor; arms for the poor!" |
| Conrad: | Land o' Goshen! And what did you get? |
| Kid: | Strange looks. I'll *never* get any money. |
| Conrad: | Who are the poor you're collecting for? |
| Kid: | Conor Johnson *(pastor's kid)* Home for Wayward Children. |
| Conrad: | There's no home there. |
| Kid: | Well, there's the Agony General Hospital, too. |

| Conrad: | Never heard of it. |
| Kid: | Would you believe the Shuffleboard Retirement Center? |
| Conrad: | *(shakes head)* Why don't you just tell me where the money is really going? |
| Kid: | *(face down, ashamed of his poverty)* It's for me. |
| Conrad: | That's what I thought. It looks like you need it. |
| Kid: | But it's not really for me. It's for my sister. I want to give her a present this Christmas. We don't have very much, and, well … I love my little sister—I thought I might give her something special. |
| Conrad: | *(Looks at the table—gives the kid the honey.)* |
| Kid: | *(Looks inside.)* Wow! Is this real honey? |
| Conrad: | Yes. Give it to your sister. And here. Give her these shoes, and here is a pair for you. |
| Kid: | Wow! You are something, mister. Thank you. *(Excitedly leaves.)* |
| Conrad: | *(as he leaves)* Hey, lad! What is your sister going to give you for Christmas? |
| Kid: | I don't know. Last year she gave me the measles! Bye, mister! |
| Conrad: | Merry Christmas!, |

*(While the narrator reads, Conrad wanders around room looking sad; but as he realizes that Christ came to him in those three people, he begins to look radiant.)*

| Narrator: | The day went down in the crimson west |
| | And with it the hope of the blessed Guest, |
| | And Conrad sighed as the world turned gray: |
| | "Why is it, Lord, that your feet delay? |
| | Did You forget that this was the day?" |
| | Then soft in the silence a Voice he heard: |
| | "Lift up your heart, for I kept my word. |
| | Three times I came to your friendly door; |
| | Three times my shadow was on your floor. |
| | I was the beggar with bruised feet; |
| | I was the woman you gave food to eat; |
| | I was the child on the homeless street!" |

# Hum A Carol

This is a great way to split your group into teams for other games. As each person arrives, whisper the title of one of four Christmas carols to him or her. After everyone has been assigned a carol, everyone starts humming and walking around trying to find someone humming the same carol. Eventually, you have four groups all together humming the same carol. No words are allowed; only humming. You can choose as many or as few carols as you wish, depending on

the size of your group. A great way to break the ice. This can also be used at other times in the year using other songs. (Contributed by Judy Madtes, Frederick, MD)

# The Innkeeper's Wife

If you have someone in your group with some acting ability, this short "monologue" would be very effective at Christmas time. The lines should be memorized, and a few props would be helpful. Use your own imagination, and change or add any lines that you feel would improve the impact or delivery of the material. It could be followed up with a discussion about how we often are like the innkeeper's wife, and miss opportunities in our lives to be of service to Christ.

(Lady comes in with cleaning rag and apron, and mutters to herself while beginning to clean.)

I'm so tired of all this cleaning! Seems like that's all I ever do! (Phone begins to ring.) I'll **never** get finished if this phone doesn't stop ringing. (Answers phone.) Hello, Bethlehem Inn, may I help you? ... Oh, hi, Mable ... **Terrible**, just terrible! Hardly got any sleep last night! ... Why? ... You mean you haven't heard? ... Well, you know Caesar has passed this **amendment** about taxing! I just don't understand this government—it's such a mess! ... That's right ... Because of all this, so many folks have been traveling—we've just been **packed**! You should see the parking lot—it's **full** of camels and donkeys! And you know what a **mess** they make! Yes, David has been sick and the girls gave up their room to some travelers. Why, we even had folks sleeping in the hall last night ... and you know what a fire hazard **that** is! ...

Well, Joe had to cut some more wood so **I** had to get all the kids in bed and check in the guests. Got 'em all to bed, fixed Joe some supper, and **finally** got to bed myself! ... yeah ... uh-huh ... Along about two o'clock there was this **loud banging** on the door! I nearly flew out of the bed with heart flutters! Oh, goodness me! That was so **frightening** ... uh-huh ... So Joe goes down to the door and I peeped out the window ... Couldn't believe what I saw! There was a young couple on a donkey and she was **pregnant**! ... **Yes** ... uh-huh ... **real** far along! ... And out in that cold, too! I heard it got down to ten below here in Bethlehem last night ... **No**! We didn't have a choice! Every room was packed! They said that every inn for the past two miles was full, too ...

Yeah ... Well, Joe gave them the key to the barn so they could at least get out of that wind ... and she looked like she could have had that baby any minute! ... uh-huh ... uh-huh ... By that time the kids were awake and fighting over the pillows—**Man**, did I need an **Alkaseltzer**! ... uh-huh!

Just **barely** got back to sleep, and heard some more noise outside. Looked out the window and saw **more camels**! People looked kinda like shepherds—I figured they could just find their way back to the barn, too ... yeah ... (Starts to look at watch) ... uh-huh ... uh-huh ...

Who? ... Oh, Yeah, she had the baby all right ... I found out this morning ... A King after Caesar? ... Sure, Mable, you've really lost it this time! I'm sure a King is going to be born in a barn ... Well, I don't care **who** it is! I'm not going down there to help after all the trouble they've caused **me**! ... I'll just be glad when they're **gone**! ... **What**? ... Mable, I'm **sorry**! ... We just didn't **have room**! (Looks at watch) I **just don't** have time! I've got lots to do here. I'll probably be the one who has to clean up all this camel mess! **Yuk**! Yeah ... uh-huh ... I gotta go! **Bye**! (Hangs up and mutters.) Some people just don't understand! I've got work to do! (**Exit**.)

(Contributed by Mary Kent, Tyler, TX)

# Reindeer Hunt

This idea could be used a part of a Christmas party with great success. Have the entire group go to a shopping mall, or to some other place where there are lots of people (especially Christmas shoppers). Divide the group into small teams and give each team a list of Santa's nine reindeer: Dasher, Dancer, Prancer, Vixen, Comet, Cupid, Donner, Blitzen, and Rudolph.

Ahead of time, position nine people somewhere in the mall or store who look like ordinary customers doing their shopping. Each one of these people is one of the reindeer. The object is for the kids to find all nine of the reindeer and get their autographs on their sheet. But in order to do this, they must go up to anyone whom they think "looks like" a reindeer and ask, "Are you Dancer? Are you Prancer?" and so on. Rudolph can be disguised and worth extra points, or more difficult to find.

Use people whom the kids won't recognize right away, and it would be wise to get permission from the store's management ahead of time. Assure them that your group will be instructed not to run or to be rude to anyone in the store, mall, or wherever the event will be held.

Depending on location, you might want to make the game easier or tougher, adding clues, or somehow identifying your "reindeer" with a particular color of socks, a hat, or something like that. (Contributed by Tim Smith, Fresno, CA)

# Santa, Reindeer, Christmas Tree

This game is an adaptation of the old "Rock, Paper, Scissors" game. It's great with larger groups of 20 or more kids. Here's how it works.

Have the kids pair off and stand back to back. On a signal (a whistle, horn, or "sleigh bells?") the kids immediately turn around to face each other while taking one of three positions:

1. Santa—They hold a hand straight out in front of them, as if they were "whipping" their reindeer.
2. Reindeer—They hold their hands up over their heads like antlers.
3. Christmas tree—They hold their hands out to their side, like a tree that gets wider at the bottom.

Except in the case of a tie (when kids both take the same position), there will be one winner who stays in the game, and the losers are out. The winners and those who tied then pair off and play again, until there are only two people left for the championship round.

Here is how the winners are determined: **Santa** always beats

**Reindeer** (since he can "whip" the reindeer). **Reindeer** always beats **Tree** (since the Reindeer can eat the Tree). **Tree** always beats **Santa** (because the tree can fall on Santa and smash him.)

Make sure that kids take their positions **before**, not after, they turn around each time. (Contributed by Bruce Schlenke, Wexford, PA)

---

## The Spirit of Christmas

This discussion-starter on giving is best suited for camps and retreats around the holiday season, although it could be done at any time of the year. Put up Christmas decorations and decorate a tree complete with garland, ornaments, lights and tinsel. Get the entire group together to sing Christmas carols, and play two or three games associated with Christmas. After the games, divide everyone up into small groups. (Previously determined teams or families work best.) Pass out plenty of Christmas wrapping paper and tape. Announce that Christmas just wouldn't be Christmas if you didn't give and receive presents. At this point have each group return to their rooms and wrap something they brought with them to give away for Christmas. (Each group wraps one joint gift.) They can give anything they wish.

Place all the presents under the tree. Have the groups come up one at a time and choose a present for Christmas. Once each of the groups have their presents, wish them a "Merry Christmas" and have them open their gifts.

Some groups will receive nice gifts of value, while others will receive gag gifts that are totally worthless. The group that gave five dollars in cash may only get back an empty soda can. Of course, the reverse is also possible. People who gave worthless or joke gifts may get back very nice and thoughtful presents.

Discuss the following questions with the group, and any others that come to mind:
1. What was your first reaction when you were asked to give something away?
2. How did you decide what to give?
3. Was it hard to give something of value away?
4. Were you excited when you opened your present? Why or why not?
5. If you received a gag gift, but had given a nice gift, what was your reaction?
6. If you received a nice gift, but had given a gag gift, what was your reaction?
7. What does Christmas mean to you?
8. What do you think is the true spirit of Christmas?
9. God has given us the greatest gift, His only Son. How do you think God feels about the gifts we give to Him in return?

(Contributed by Tommy Baker, Florence, KY)

# Teenage Christmas Story

Here's a different approach to this year's Christmas play. Use the outline below to write your own script, based upon how your young people would imagine the events described in the outline might have actually happened, or would happen if they occurred today. In this way, a great deal of learning and discovery takes place as well as the enjoyment of putting on a Christmas drama.

As with any play, you will need to select a cast, design sets, obtain costumes if needed, conduct rehearsals, and so on. The outline of the play allows for a great deal of freedom in creating your own personalities and dialogue.

*Scene One: Mary's home*
Mary is a normal teenage girl. This scene can have her doing normal teenage things: talking on the phone, listening to the radio, combing her hair, and so on. Mary's parents can be in this scene, wanting her to do her chores—wash the dishes, clean her room, all the usual household stuff.

*Scene Two: Mary's room*
This is when the angel of the Lord announces to her that she has been chosen to be the mother of the Messiah. The angel could be dressed in a business suit, or any modern clothing. Mary should respond with typical unbelief, questions, and fear.

*Scene Three: At Elizabeth's house*
Mary has been with Elizabeth through the summer and now it is becoming more apparent that she is pregnant. People have been taunting her about her pregnancy. She has an engagement ring, but she and Joseph, her fiancee, have been apart while Mary has been with Elizabeth. Mary tries to explain everything to Elizabeth, and Elizabeth offers her advice and encouragement.

*Scene Four: Mary's home*
As Mary arrives home, she is noticed in her "condition" by her parents, and Mary tries to explain things to them. The parents should react as any normal set of parents would.

*Scene Five: Mary's home*
Mary is alone, sitting on the couch, when Joseph comes in. He learns for the first time about Mary's pregnancy. He reacts with disbelief and anger.

*Scene Six: Joseph's home*
Joseph is storming around, trying to come up with some kind of answer to his dilemma. An angel comes to talk with him. Joseph asks questions and expresses surprise and awe. This scene could end with Joseph agreeing to go to Mary and ask her forgiveness for doubting her.

*Scene Seven: The Birth of Jesus*
This scene could look more like the traditional nativity scene, with the manger, the shepherds, and so on; or it could be a "modern" manger scene, perhaps in a garage, an abandoned tenement house, or some other place that would be similar to the original, but possible today.

Keep in mind that this is only a suggested outline. The main point is that the young people themselves get involved in the creation of the script. It will be a Christmas play they'll never forget. (Contributed by Mary Ann Wymer, Dayton, OH)

## Mind Trip to Bethlehem

Young people have vivid imaginations, and this short meditation allows them the opportunity to use those imaginations to put themselves into the Christmas story. Simply read the script below while the group is seated or lying down in a comfortable position. Read it slowly and allow the kids time to let the scenes develop in their minds. Feel free to change the script as you see fit. You might want to adapt the references to mountains, snow, and the like, to fit wherever you live (plains, ocean, city, or whatever).

Sit back against the wall in a comfortable position. Close your eyes. In your thoughts you are getting up now to leave the room. Put on your coat and go out the front door. As you open the door a blast of cold air hits you. You go out the door and begin walking toward the mountains. It is early afternoon, and as you walk through the snow the warmth from the sun on your back feels good. As you walk along you notice the many beauties of winter around you. As you continue walking you notice the snow has melted away, leaving only patches here and there, and the mountains have become rolling hills.

It is late afternoon now, and you see a group of people at the top of a hill. You walk up the hill to join them. They have a campfire going. The heat feels good in the chilly evening air. You smell the food being cooked and it makes you hungry. The people invite you to eat with them and spend the night. The food is good, and as the stars come out you begin to feel tired from your long day of walking. You lay down and pull a blanket up over you. The sky is clear and a million stars are twinkling in the sky. You feel yourself falling asleep.

Suddenly the night is bright as day. Your heart is pounding. You are terrified. You have no idea what is going on. Then you hear a voice: "Don't be afraid." You are so scared that those words hardly calm you. The voice goes on: "A baby has been born in the nearby town, and this is a very special baby. It is God's Son. You can find this baby in a manger."

Then the night is filled with what sounds like a hundred voices singing the most beautifully you've ever heard. They sing, "Glory to God and peace on earth," over and over and over. "Glory to God and peace on earth." You feel your fear draining away. The light goes away and the sound fades away. You look at the people around you. You all know you have to go find this baby.

You run down the hill to the edge of town where the caves are, where all the animals are kept at night. A light comes from several of them. You begin running from one to the next, and suddenly you find people in this cave, and yes—a tiny baby. Almost on tiptoe you go in to see this baby. A cow softly moos at your intrusion, and the startled parents look up at you. You can only look at this tiny baby you have just been told is God's Son, this baby so tiny and asleep, this baby you have heard voices singing about. You just gaze on this baby. After a long while you tell this baby's parents what has happened this night. Then you slowly turn and leave. You walk back to the hill and up it. The others join you there, all quiet in their thoughts after having seen this baby.

When the morning light comes, you say goodbye to your friends and begin walking back home. The green grass gives way to brown and small patches of snow begin to appear. By noon you are walking through deep snow and are close to home. You enter the front door, take off your coat and enter the room you had left and sit down. When you are ready to join the group again, open your eyes.

(Contributed by Sandy Peterson, Butte, MT)

# Whose Birthday Is It?

The following skit opens up good discussion possibilities around Christmas. It features a family of four—the mom and dad, their son Ken and daughter Pam. Of course, you can add as many characters as you wish. The setting is a typical living room on Christmas morning.

**Pam:** (complaining) No birthday present again ... Why did I have to be born on Christmas Day? Did you know that nobody has ever remembered my birthday?

**Ken:** Considering the time of year, who's going to remember a mere birthday? It's Christmas!

**Pam:** (complaining even more) You get birthday presents every year, and so do Dad and Mom. But all I ever get is combination birthday/Christmas presents. It's not fair!

*(Dad and Mom enter.)*

**Dad:** Merry Christmas, Pam. Merry Christmas, Ken.

**Ken:** Merry Christmas, Dad, Mom.

**Pam:** It's also my birthday, you know.

**Mom:** We know, dear. Merry Christmas.

**Dad:** Well, let's all open presents, shall we?

**Mom:** I wonder what I got from Santa this year!

**Ken:** Here, Dad! (handing him a gift) Open this one!

*The characters can ad lib their parts at this point, with Mom, Dad, and Ken continuing to be enthusiastic about opening Christmas gifts, and Pam becoming more and more upset that her birthday is being ignored. Finally, Pam bursts into tears and leaves the room. The others act surprised and annoyed that Pam is making such a big deal over such a "little" thing.*

**Ken:** I wonder what's gotten into her! What a Scrooge.

After the skit, discuss what happened with the family. See how long it takes for the group to make the connection between this family's ignoring Pam's birthday and how we often ignore the birthday of Christ. (Contributed by Jim Ruberg, Burlington, IA)

162

# CAMPING

## Camp Charades

Here's a version of charades which is perfect for around-the-campfire fun. Hand out slips of paper to everyone in the group. Each person must then act out exactly what it says on their slip of paper without talking. They may use only actions and sounds. The group simply tries to guess who or what the actor is. Here are a few possibilities:

1. A light bulb burning out
2. The cracking campfire
3. One horrendous rain storm
4. A squeaky bathroom-stall door
5. A bug crawling on someone's plate
6. A snake in the grass
7. A rip in someone's pants (you are the rip!)
8. A sleeping bag being unrolled and rolled up
9. Someone being struck by lightning
10. Ten mosquitos biting you all at once
11. Gagging on the camp food
12. A popcorn kernel thrown into the campfire — it pops and burns up!

(Contributed by Michael A. Nodland, Chicago, IL)

## Crazy Coupons

On your next retreat, why not pass out "official coupon books" to all of the travelers. The books are great for laughs and for getting people to interact. The only rules are: 1) you cannot refuse to redeem a coupon

when asked, 2) a different person must redeem each of your coupons, and 3) the other person must sign the coupon when redeemed, but you get to keep it as a souvenir. (Contributed by Carolyn Roddy, Santa Barbara, CA)

## Fragile Friends

This exercise is a good one to help make kids aware of the fragility of other people and the importance of being gentle with each other. It can be used anytime, but it is especially appropriate for a camp or retreat.

Give each person a raw egg. Then have them try an "egg blow-out." To do this, use a pin or nail to punch a small hole in each end of the egg, and then blow on one end of the egg. The contents of the egg will be forced out the other end, leaving you an empty, unbroken eggshell. You can, if you wish, seal the egg up with a small amount of candle wax. The insides of the egg can be served next morning for breakfast.

Now, discuss with the kids the delicate nature of eggshells, and relate this to the delicate nature of our relationships with each other. Then give the group several thin colored marking pens that will write on the eggshells. Have the kids write the names of several kids in the group on the eggshell. While doing this, they need to be careful not to break the egg.

Now each person must carry his or her egg with them all day, devising some means of protection and accepting responsibility for its condition. At the end of the day, collect the eggs, whole or smashed, and discuss the feelings of responsibility, the task of caring, and the problems of protecting something so fragile. Tie this in with how we treat each other personally, and how we can avoid hurting each other. (Contributed by Sr. Audrey Quinn, Pittsburgh, PA)

## Guardian Angels

Here's a good relationship-building idea that would be great for your next camp or retreat. At the beginning of the camp, assign to each person a same-sex partner that they don't know very well. At the first meeting, the partners can be introduced and asked to sit together while the guidelines are explained. They can also be given some time at this first meeting to get to know each other.

From that point on, those two young people become each others' "Guardian Angel." They must sit together at a specified number of talks and meetings, as well as at several mutually agreed-upon meals. In addition, they are asked to pray for each other in specific terms each day of the retreat. Also, they should try to perform at least one act of Christian service for the other person during the retreat. At the end of the retreat, have some of the kids share what happened. Chances are some lasting friendships will have begun.

A variation of this would be to assign "Guardian Angels" secretly. The rules still apply, but the caring and acts of kindness are done anonymously. At the end of the camp, identities can be revealed. (Contributed by Paul Tonna, New York, NY)

## It's Hug Time

This little device will help campers open up to each other and have fun at the same time. During the times that the whole group is assembled, have an alarm clock inside a large coffee can decorated with the words, "It's Hug Time!" The alarm should be set to go off at some unexpected time. When it sounds, everyone jumps up and yells, "It's Hug Time!" and they hug as many people as possible before the alarm stops. By the second or third time, kids will hardly want to stop. (Contributed by Jan Schaible, Wichita, KS)

## It's Inedible

Here's a song parody that is a riot when sung at summer camp. It's to the tune of Perry Como's hit "It's Impossible," and it commemorates the glories of camp food.

*"It's Inedible"*

*It's inedible! Call it food if you desire, but it's inedible!*
*It's incredible how it sets my heart on fire — it's just incredible!*
*As I force it closer to me, I can feel it oozing through me;*
*With each mouthful I'm reminded that it's really quite inedible.*

*It's inedible! Just by looking you can tell that it's inedible.*
*It's incredible — oh, how dreadful it can smell; it's just incredible!*
*And tomorrow, when the aftertaste is gone, I'll still regret it,*
*For no matter how I try I can't forget it!*

*So believe me when I say it's just inedible.*

*It's inedible! Bring the stomach pumps with haste, 'cuz it's inedible!*
*It's incredible how offensive it can taste — it's just incredible!*
*And tomorrow, please forgive me if my state of health is dismal,*
*For it seems that I've run out of Pepto-Bismol;*
*And that proves beyond a doubt that it's inedible!*

(Contributed by Steve Jones, Colorado Springs, CO)

# Love Letters

After an overnight trip or a week long retreat, write each parent a letter telling them how their teen behaved on the trip. This is especially good for youth who never cause any problems.

This way, they are complimented for good behavior and parents hear about the good their child has done. (Contributed by James C. Harville, Jr., Louisville, KY)

# Personal Goal Setting

Before you leave on a retreat, pass out a personal goal-setting chart (see below) to each of the kids. Encourage them to list on the right-hand column their goals for the upcoming retreat. They may want to include goals like making new friends, controlling one's temper or growing closer to God. If they would like, they should share their goals with one other person. Then each evening during the retreat, give your group time to fill in their charts using the symbols found beneath it. At the end of the week, have everyone share their goals once again with their partners.

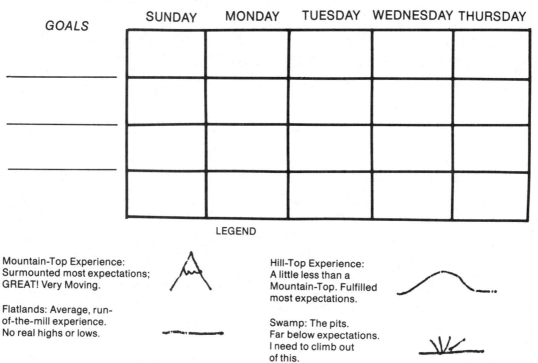

**RETREAT PERSONAL GOAL-SETTING**

In the column on the right, have each person list all of his goals (make new friends, meet some girls, grow closer to God, etc.) for an upcoming retreat. Share these in pairs. Each evening, give your group time to fill in their chart, using the symbols presented in the LEGEND. At the end of the week, have everyone share their goals once again with their partners.

| GOALS | SUNDAY | MONDAY | TUESDAY | WEDNESDAY | THURSDAY |
|---|---|---|---|---|---|
| ____ | | | | | |
| ____ | | | | | |
| ____ | | | | | |
| ____ | | | | | |

LEGEND

Mountain-Top Experience: Surmounted most expectations; GREAT! Very Moving.

Flatlands: Average, run-of-the-mill experience. No real highs or lows.

Hill-Top Experience: A little less than a Mountain-Top. Fulfilled most expectations.

Swamp: The pits. Far below expectations. I need to climb out of this.

(Contributed by Ben Sharpton, Gainesville, FL)

# Scripture Schedule

Here's a camp exercise you can use to get your kids into the Scriptures as soon as they get off of the bus. Give each camper a copy of the list below and have them begin searching through the Bible to figure out the week's schedule. It's an appropriate way for them to prepare for camp, and they will do it out of eagerness to discover what's in store for them during the week. The schedule, of course, can be easily adapted to fit your unique program, and additional verses can also be added. (Contributed by Herbert E. Saunders, Milton WI)

SAMPLE SCRIPTURE SCHEDULE

| Time | Verse | Activity |
|------|-------|----------|
| 7:00 | Jonah 1:6 | (Rise & shine) |
| 7:45 | Psalms 5:3 | (Morning Praise) |
| 8:00 | I Timothy 6:8 | (Breakfast) |
| 8:30 | John 9:4 | (Chores) |
| 9:00 | Isaiah 65:22d | (Craft Project) |
| 10:00 | Ecclesiastes 5:19 | (Class) |
| 11:00 | II Samuel 2:14 | (Recreation) |
| 12:00 | Ephesians 5:19 | (Chapel) |
| 12:45 | Matthew 4:4 | (Lunch) |
| 1:30 | II Thessalonians 3:10 | (Chores) |
| 2:30 | Job 40:20 | (Recreation) |
| 4:30 | Luke 11:41b | (Camp Clean-Up) |
| 5:30 | Revelation 19:9 | (Dinner) |
| 6:30 | II Chronicles 34:12a | (Chores) |
| 7:00 | Psalms 42:8 | (Vespers) |
| 7:45 | Psalms 100:1, 2 | (Music) |
| 8:30 | Zechariah 8:5 | (Recreation) |
| 10:00 | Psalms 63:5-7 | (Evening Devotions) |
| 10:30 | Psalms 139:8 | (Preparation for Bed) |
| 11:00 | Psalms 4:4 | (Lights Out) |

# Ski-Trip Affirmation

Here's a good community builder for a ski retreat. Pass out mimeo sheets with the categories listed below and ask the kids to write in one or two names from the group that fit each description. This is followed by an "affirmation bombardment" where everyone tells who they chose for each category and why.

Put the name of everyone in your group in one of the blanks below at least once. You can put two names in one blank if that's what you want to say.

_____ 1. Trail Signs — you show me the way.

_____ 2. Ski Partner — I just enjoy being with you.

_____ 3. A New Snow — you're a chance for a new start.

4. Chair Lift — you give me a "lift"!
5. Mogul — you're a challenge that helps me.
6. Like beginner's slope — comfortable, secure.
7. Skis — help me keep going.
8. Ski Boots — keep me stable; protect me.
9. Trees — make the trip beautiful.
10. Long Underwear — not obvious, but needed!
11. Poles — help me up when I fall/fail.
12. Parka — protect me from the bitterness around me.
13. Goggles — help me see when it's hard to see.
14. Mountain Stream — refreshing, cool.
15. Ski Patrol — always there when I need you.
16. Other

(Contributed by George T. Warren, Goodwell, OK)

# Sleeping-Bag Announcement

Here's a creative way to announce a slumber party, church Lock-In, overnight retreat, or camp. Send your invitations in a "sleeping bag."

Have an adult or youth who can sew make individual bags for each announcement. Two scraps of fabric, one of them a print and both of them about 9" x 7," should be sewn together to make a mini-bag. The announcements can be drawn with a sleepy face on top and then slipped into the bag. Pass these out or lay them out on a table for the kids to pick up and give to friends. (Contributed by Annette W. Glosson, Burlington, North Carolina)

Sewing directions:

Solid colored fabric    7''

9½''

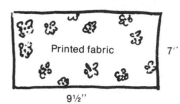

Printed fabric    7''

9½''

With right sides together, sew the solid colored fabric to the printed fabric. Sew around three sides.

168

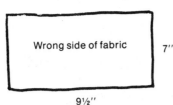

Turn this pocket inside-out, so that the right sides are facing out. Then fold the pocket together (solid fabric inside) and sew across the bottom and about two-thirds up the side.

Wrong side of fabric    7"

9½"

Fold    Printed fabric    7"

4¾"

Turn the pocket again, and you have a miniature "sleeping bag."

# Travois Races

A travois is a primitive vehicle which was used by the Plains Indians to move people and cargo. It consists of two trailing poles harnessed to a horse. A platform is then strapped to the back ends of the poles and is dragged along the ground. If you don't have a large stable of horses (using them might be dangerous anyway), why not have travois races using people for the horsepower?

You will need a big pile of slender saplings or small trees 8 to 12 feet long and trimmed of branches. Use only windfalls rather than stripping the branches from live trees. You will also need hammers, nails and heavy twine. Then map out a lengthy race course, preferably up and down hills and around obstacles.

Divide the group into teams of 12. Each team should choose eight "horses" and four riders for a four-part relay. The teams should be given forty-five minutes to an hour to build their travois.

When everyone is ready, line the travois up on the starting line and send the different relay teams to their respective stops. Each travois should be pulled by two "horses" and carry one rider seated on the platform. At the first stop, change crews and continue on to the next stop. The true test of durability will be how the travois withstand the race. (Contributed by Adrienne E. Anderson, Calgary, AB, Can.)

# CHAPTER NINE

# PUBLICITY & PROMOTION

## Adult Movies

Here's an eye-catching way to advertise your next youth film night at church:

(Contributed by Bob Hunt, San Clemente, CA)

DON'T EVEN THINK ABOUT BRINGING AN

**ADULT**

TO THIS GREAT **MOVIE** TO BE SHOWN

**AT CHURCH!**

## Announcement Charades

If you always have lots of announcements to make, and aren't sure that everyone will pay attention, try this. Divide your group into small teams of four or five kids each. You could do this by having them count off or by using some other creative method.

When the group is divided, give each team one or two

announcements written on 3 x 5 cards. Tell them they have three minutes to come up with a charade that will allow the others to guess the announcement. Give a prize to the team with the most creative and effective approach. If all of the announcements are about the same in length and difficulty, divide into two teams and play by regular charade rules, timing the charades and awarding a prize to the fastest team. It's a surefire way of getting your kids "involved" in the announcements. (Contributed by Mike Young, Mercer Island, WA)

## Bomb Squads

B.O.M.B. stands for "Bring Our Members Back!" and it makes a good theme for a drive to contact inactive members of your youth group. Using small groups of kids, form "BOMB Squads" to visit, write letters or make phone calls to kids who, for one reason or another, have stopped coming to the youth group. You might want to throw a BOMB BLOWOUT (party) inviting back old members or create BOMB T-shirts for your group to wear at school.

Another possibility would be to involve the other groups in your church in this campaign. You could fly a large helium balloon above your church with the word "BOMB" written on it. Of course, it would

be a good idea to "drop" it on your evangelism committee first. (Contributed by Scott Phillips, Fort Worth, TX)

## The Caterpillar Eating Contest

This idea is a real attention-grabber. Make some posters and send out a mailing advertising a "Caterpillar Eating Contest" at your next youth event. Be sure to include the note, "We provide the caterpillars!" The kids will be anticipating a relatively gross activity.

When it comes time for the contest, bring out the "caterpillars." These can be made individually, or in a long trough. Here's the recipe:

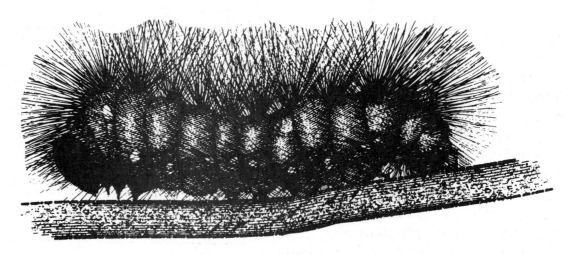

# CATERPILLAR EATING CONTEST
## We Provide The Caterpillars

Split a banana lengthwise and place it flat-side-down on a plate. Spray whipped cream in long lines down the back and sides. Decorate it with green sprinkles and chocolate syrup stripes. Use pretzels to make feelers, two cherry halves for eyes and rows of raisins for feet.

The contest can be based on speed eating, eating without hands, blindfold feeding, or team consumption. Kids will love it. (Contributed by Jim Larsen, Klamath Falls, OR)

## Commandment Cards

Here's an idea for a "get-well" card or announcement which you can print up yourself and you can customize for each young person. It can be printed on regular 8½ x 11 paper and folded, letter style. On the front, draw a picture of Moses or stone tablets and print the words, "It is written, 'THOU SHALT'…" Leave space underneath to complete the message, such as "come to youth group" or "pay your camp bill."

When the card is opened, the inside flap continues by saying, "Where is it written, you ask?" Then, that flap opens and the inside reads, "Page one of this card!"

Below that is more space for specific details or a personal message.

(Contributed by Don Warner, Los Angeles, CA)

It is written,
THOU SHALT
NOT
MISS OUR
YOUTH
MEETING

# Football Cards

This idea is good for outreach, relations with local schools, and group identification. Every fall, print up the local high school football schedules, using the school colors, on wallet-sized cards. On the back, put information about your youth group, a phone number kids can call, and perhaps a simple plan of salvation. Make these cards available to the schools to distribute, and for your kids to pass out to friends.

**MERRITT ISLAND MUSTANGS**
**1983 Football Schedule**

| HOME | | AWAY | |
|------|------|------|------|
| Sept. 23 | Miami Columbus | Sept. 9 | Titusville |
| Oct. 7 | Open | Sept. 16 | Cocoa |
| Oct. 14 | Satellite | Sept. 30 | Eau Gallie |
| Nov. 4 | Jax. Raines* | Oct. 21 | Lakeland |
| Nov. 11 | Martin County | Oct. 28 | Melbourne |
| Nov. 18 | Vero Beach | | *Mustang Homecoming |

1. God has a plan for your life. — John 10:10
2. Man is separated from God. — Romans 6:23
3. Jesus is the only way to God. — John 14:6
4. We must receive Jesus by personal invitation. — John 1:12
*You can receive Christ right now by faith through prayer.*

# CROSSOVER
## *A Youth Worship Experience*
FIRST BAPTIST CHURCH
140 Magnolia Ave., Merritt Island, FL 32952

(Contributed by Bobbi Cordy, Merritt Island, FL)

# The Four Laws of Dating

If your group is familiar with "The Four Spiritual Laws" booklet, here's a funny way to publicize a special Saturday night event, or to promote a series on dating. This could be printed as a flyer or hand-out, or you might want to go ahead and put it in booklet form.

Have You Heard of the
## Four Dating Laws?

**1**

Just as there are physical laws that govern the physical universe, so are there social laws that govern our relationship to the opposite sex.

**LAW ONE**

GOD LOVES YOU AND HAS A WONDERFUL SATURDAY DATE PLANNED FOR YOUR LIFE.

*Scripture references contained in this booklet should not be read in context from the Bible whenever possible.

**God's Date**

Every good thing bestowed and every perfect gift is from above, coming down from the Father of lights, with whom there is no variation or shifting shadow (James 1:17).*

Why is it that most people are not experiencing this perfect gift?
Because . . .

## LAW TWO

**2** MAN IS BASHFUL AND SEPARATED FROM THE WOMAN, THUS HE CAN'T KNOW AND EXPERIENCE THE WONDERFUL SATURDAY DATE.

Man is Bashful

I who am meek when face to face with you, but bold toward you when absent (II Cor. 10:1).

---

Man is Separated

And the Lord God fashioned into a woman the rib which He had taken from the man (Gen. 2).

Man was created to have fellowship with woman; but because of his own stubborn self-will, he chose to go his own independent way and fellowship with woman was broken.

MAN    WOMAN

A great chasm separates man from woman. Man is continually trying to reach woman and the wonderful Saturday Date through his own efforts: computer dating, blind dates, daydreaming, etc.

The Third Law gives us the only answer to the dilemma:

---

## LAW THREE

**3** DIRECT COMMUNICATION IS OUR GROUP'S ONLY PROVISION FOR MAN'S BASHFULNESS. THROUGH IT, YOU CAN KNOW AND EXPERIENCE THE WONDERFUL SATURDAY DATE.

It is the ONLY way

How then shall they call upon Him in whom they have not believed? And how shall they believe in Him whom they have not heard? And how shall they hear without a preacher? And how shall they preach unless they are sent? Just as it is written, "How beautiful are the feet of those who bring glad tidings of good things?" (Rom. 10:14-15).

---

MAN    WOMAN

Communication has bridged the chasm which separates man from woman by sending him the phone to speak in his place.

It is not enough just to know these three laws:

---

## LAW FOUR

**4** WE MUST INDIVIDUALLY ASK; THEN WE CAN KNOW AND EXPERIENCE THE WONDERFUL SATURDAY DATE.

We must ASK

But let him ask in faith without any doubting, for the one who doubts is like the surf of the sea, driven and tossed by the wind (James 1:6).

We ask by FAITH

And Jesus answered and said to them, "Truly I say to you, if you have faith and do not doubt, you shall not only do what was done to the fig tree, but even if you say to this mountain, 'Be taken up and cast into the sea,' it shall happen."

---

We ask by PERSONAL INVITATION

Ask, and it shall be given to you; seek, and you shall find; knock, and it shall be opened to you. For every one who asks receives and he who seeks finds and to him who knocks it shall be opened.

Asking for a date involves turning toward your sisters from self, trusting that you will get a date and that you will have a wonderful Saturday evening. It is not enough to give intellectual assent to these claims or to have an emotional experience.

These two circles represent two kinds of lives:

Which circle represents your life?
Which circle would you like to have represent your life?
The following explains how you can have a wonderful Saturday Date:

---

YOU CAN HAVE A WONDERFUL SATURDAY DATE RIGHT NOW THROUGH THE USE OF YOUR VOCAL CORDS.

(Vocal cords are used to talk to people.)

The woman knows the desire of your heart and is not so concerned with your words as she is with the attitude of your heart. Here is a suggested phone call:

*"Hello, Sue; this is Dick. I am calling to get your opinion on my merits as a date to go to the party Saturday. Is there any reason why you wouldn't want to say yes right now? Does this call express the desire of your heart? If so, you can have a wonderful Saturday Date by saying yes right now."*

---

How to know you will have a wonderful Saturday Date

Did you ask the woman to go out with you?
According to the promise in Matthew 7:7-8, where should the woman be in relation to you on Saturday night?
She said she would go out with you. Would she mislead you?

---

## (Contributed by Denny Finnegan, La Canada, CA)

## Mailer Prizes

Do you wonder if your mailer gets read thoroughly? Try including a contest which requires kids to report important facts from the newsletter to you.

For example, print on your mailer that the person who is the 15th caller to a certain number after 3:30 p.m. on Monday, October 18th (any time and any date), wins a pizza, an album, concert tickets, or any other prize.

Every caller must also answer several questions regarding upcoming activities announced in your newsletter. Many kids will read all the newsletter to get the answers and make the call. The better the prize, the better your mailer will be read! (Contributed by Todd Wagner, Hermiston, OR)

## The Mighty Mimeograph

Instead of dreaming about your church buying a new photocopier, try printing custom envelopes on your old mimeograph machine. By moving the paper side guides to fit the narrow width of the envelope, even the oldest and most despised machines can print interesting envelopes for your mailings.

Line up your design at the top of the stencil (most stencils have envelope guidelines indicated) and use a stylus or pen to draw a design. Print either on the back of the envelope or on the front, including a return address and phone number. Be sure to leave lots of room to write in a name and address.

IMMANUEL YOUTH FELLOWSHIP
657 W. 18TH STREET
LOS ANGELES, CA 90015

Sorry. We ran out of our regular envelopes. We had to get an ENVELOPE SUB

(Contributed by Don Warner, Los Angeles, CA)

# Mirror Mask

Another great attention-getter is to send a flyer that has to be read by looking at it in a mirror. On one side it can say:

THIS IS YOUR MESSAGE, should you choose to read it! There is a message for you on the back of this letter. The only way that you can decode this message is by looking through the two eyeball holes on the front, while peering into the mirror. The people of the Old Testament—the Hivites, the Maobites and the Mesquitobites used this method of decoding in ancient times—so it's Biblical (Hezekiah 4:7-8)!"

On the opposite side is your announcement. Cut holes where the "eyeballs" are, so that kids can hold it up to their faces and look through.

(Contributed by Richard A. Cooper, Memphis, TN)

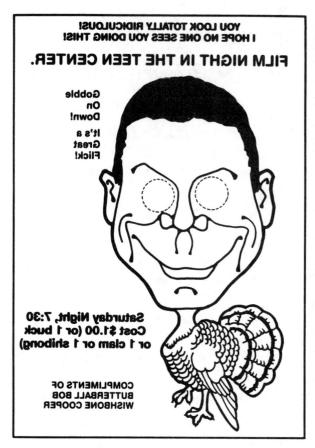

# "Missed You" Letters

Here is a batch of humorous letters to send to kids in your group when they have missed Sunday School or youth meetings. Be sure to keep track of who you send each letter to, so you don't send duplicates. Also, don't forget to write an occasional letter of appreciation to those who are always present. (Contributed by Greg Thomas, Watsonville, CA)

Dear fellow student of the hidden mysteries of God's eternally relevant and vitally dynamic message to mankind; in other words,

Dear College Student,

You probably didn't notice the mass exodus that took place last week -- mainly because you weren't there to notice that you and several others weren't there.

Well, knowing that you are basically a conscientious person, I'm sure you've been punishing yourself severely for the tremendous anguish I have been experiencing due to your absence. Knowing also that you are basically kind-hearted and unwilling to make a fuss, I suspect that you probably won't let me know the true reason for your absence. I have, therefore, provided the following list of excuses which sum up the five most likely reasons why a person would miss Sunday School. Simply check the appropriate box and hand it to me personally (folded, of course, so I won't know whose it is) this Sunday when you return to class.

__ 1. The rug clashed with your outfit last time you came and it was all you could do to keep from tearing your clothes off in order to avoid being such a spectacle.

__ 2. Every time you think about coming to class the last time, a little voice in your head says, "The Devil made me do it."

__ 3. Ever since we talked about angels several weeks ago, you've been scared stiff that God would give you your wings prematurely and let everybody know you are one.

__ 4. Someone else put a dollar in the offering too, and you knew you couldn't afford two dollars the next week in order to gain your sense of superiority back.

__ 5. You discovered that the blackboard was really green and you couldn't stand such hypocrisy in Church.

Whatever the reason, we missed having you in class.

See you next Sunday,

Greg
Greg

Dear Misser of the
Marvelous Mysteries,

In view of the fact (whether or not a
fact can be viewed is another matter
entirely and shouldn't be allowed to
confuse the issue. Of course, an issue
must have some intellignece in order to
become confused since any inanimate
object or abstract concept is certainly
not capable of thought and, therefore, it
couldn't become confused. You should
take great pleasure -- I wonder if it's
possible to "take" pleasure. Oh well, no
matter -- in knowing that you are not
inanimate, since I am quite sure that by
now you are thoroughly confused) that
your presence was missing (a situation
possibly only in conjunction with the
absence of your person or body inasmuch
as you are not a god and cannot have your
presence present at any place where your
person's presence or body's presence is
not presently present), I felt compelled
(or maybe it should be compulsed since
the emotion which spawned this letter
could more accurately be described as
compulsion rather than compelsion. And
please don't be alarmed that spawning
usually has to do with fish giving birth;
I have taken great liberties -- is that
possible? -- already in this letter) to
invite you to join us again this week.

See you,     P.S.  A prize awaits anyone who can
*Greg*          correctly determine the message of
Greg            this letter.

---

Dear Illustrious Imitator
of Important Information,

I was inspired to institute an intensive
investigation into an intriguing incident
of infinite importance as a result of your
insistence in being invisible in the
institute of instruction (i.e. Sunday
School).

Under such incredible inspiration I
initiated this interesting interruption
to your insidious and ill-advised
invisibility hoping to intervene and
incapacitate any increasing incidences
of invisibility and incite you to inter-
twine with us this week at the institute
of instruction.

I inestimably hope that this information
is not inconsequential in impressing
immediate interest to involve yourself
invariably in our impressive and incom-
parable institute.

Inspirationally Yours,

*Greg*
Greg

---

Dear Succultent S_pper
of the Savory Say_ngs,

_ have carefully co_posed a letter of
_nf_n_te del_ght wh_ch _ know w_ll thr_ll
and capt_vate you.

The object of th_s letter _s very s_ply
to deter__ne wh_ch letters of the alphabet
are __ss_ng fro_ th_s letter. Then you
_ust arrange these letters alphabet_cally
and say the_ three t__es _n qu_ck
success_on.

Th_s w_ll enable you to answer the
quest_on wh_ch _s the object of th_s
letter. That quest_on _s: "Who _s
__ss_ng fro_ Sunday School?" Say the
letters now for the answer.

Now that you have establ_shed personal
respons_b_l_ty for your act_ons, _ shall
expect you to repent fully and to jo_n us
aga_n th_s week.

See You,

*Greg*
Greg Thomas

P.S. For another _nterest_ng exerc_se,
try repeat_ng the follow_ng several t__es
_n qu_ck success_on and see _f you can
deter__ne the _ean_ng.

     OWAH TAGU S_AM

---

Dear Resplendent Reveler
in the Remarkable Revelation,

I recently reviewed the roster of
registrants who regularly receive the
remarkable revelations which recur without
rarity each week at Sunday School.

Reevaluating the results, I realized that
you resisted recognition last Sunday by
removing the only real resource for
recognition we retain: Yourself. To help
you resist a repetition of your recal-
citrant and reprehensible recourse (which
would realistically result in your
rapacious ruination), I rallied my
resources, rekindled my resolve, and wrote
this ridiculous reading to reassure you
that we missed you and really welcome your
resolve to reappear without reluctance
this week.

Rescusitatingly Yours,

*Greg*
Greg

## Plan Ahead

If your group takes an annual excursion to an amusement park, recreational area or camp, be sure to think about NEXT year's publicity on THIS year's trip. Take a camera and snap photos or slides of the group members on rides, eating, laughing, talking and having fun. Also take along a cassette recorder to tape their reactions, singing, giggling or other silliness.

Then, later in the year as the event comes up again, edit and produce a number of short "commercials" for the coming trip. Show these at several meetings or gatherings to remind everyone of the fun they had and to interest new members in signing up.

If the equipment is available, you could use video or film clips along with the audio tape. Additional photos could be used for posters and bulletin board displays. (Contributed by Dan Craig, Morrison, CO)

## Puzzle Piece Mailer

This little device is great for involving newcomers, making regulars feel special, and reaching out to inactives. The next time you have a special party or activity planned, buy a jigsaw puzzle and attach one piece to every invitation that you send. Explain how each person has a unique contribution to make to the group, and that this piece represents their unique gift.

Ask each person to bring their piece of the puzzle to the event, and find that particular place where their part fits.

Not only does this serve as an attention getter, it also encourages attendance. At the party itself, the puzzle becomes an ice-breaker as new people arrive with their piece and are immediately welcomed and involved in putting the puzzle together. (Contributed by Sylvan Knobloch, Charleston, IL)

## Puzzling Publicity

Try this idea for turning a drab publicity flyer into an intellectual experience. Print a regular flyer, using lots of wording and a cartoon or drawing. Then, take each flyer and cut it into puzzle pieces. Place the pieces in an envelope and mail them out, with an instruction sheet included. The kids have to put the pieces together in order to read the announcement.

It is best to cut each puzzle ONE at a time so that the pieces don't get all mixed up and to ensure that every envelope gets one complete announcement. (Contributed by Christopher Snow, Bakersfield, CA)

## Scrambled Letter

One way to make sure your young people read every line of your next flyer is to send them a "scrambled letter." First, type your letter and number the lines. Then, retype it with all of the lines scrambled. Include some instructions at the top and send it off.

---

**Why are you getting a letter in a sack? Well, read on. Each line is numbered to show you which line to read next. Find line number 1 and go from there.**

15  like us. Oh, and if you register early (by May 31), and attend all
 2  that we do things in very unconventional ways in Junior High Vacation
 5  ended up having fun. We do our own thing in our own room—even the
13  three-dimensional photo display for your room. It is real neat and
 8  and play volleyball, and <u>eat</u> (donuts, pizza and other yummies). Some-
 1  You see, we have chosen this unusual letter to try to convince you
10  decide what). Of course, we have lessons too. That is the real meat
16  five days of VBS, you'll be eligible to win a cassette tape player.
12  even keeps the church mice listening in. Our craft this year is a
14  you can personalize it if you want. Try us—we think that you'll
 4  have attended Junior High VBS before. Some of the real grumps even
 7  little kids. We even do our own music. Plus . . . we go on field trips
 3  Bible School. If you don't believe us, just ask some of the kids who
 9  times we bowl, play miniature golf, or go to a state park (you can help
11  of VBS but Mark is not your ordinary boring, preacher-type and he
 6  missionary comes down to us instead of us sitting up with all the

Come join us,

Mark Matthews
Connie Flick
Connie Hamilton

---

(Contributed by Connie Hamilton, Crawfordsville, IN)

---

## That's Incredible

Here's a mailer or handout idea that your kids will love. List these (or other) incredible facts along with information on upcoming events the next time you print up a flyer or reminder for your group. It could look something like this:

## All of the following Is Absolutely, Positively True!

1. Wearing suspenders is illegal in Nogales, Arizona.
2. Your statistical chance of being murdered is one in twenty thousand.
3. Forty percent of American adults cannot fill out a bank deposit slip correctly.
4. During his lifetime, the average American will eat 20,932 eggs and 4.1 tons of potatoes.
5. The automatic transmission fluid in almost every car is whale oil.
6. The average adult has enough iron in his body to make a two-inch nail.
7. A Volkswagen has been compressed into a two-foot cube to serve as a coffee table for a Mahtomedi, Minnesota couple.
8. Rats are fastidiously clean. "You dirty rat" slanders this furry pest. In addition, rats are not mentioned in the Bible.
9. In Norton, Virginia, it's illegal to tickle a girl.
10. "TNT"* WILL BE AT LAUREN BUTLER'S HOUSE THIS WEEK, BEGINNING AT 7:01 SHARP. HERE'S A MAP THAT'S **FACTUALLY** CORRECT:

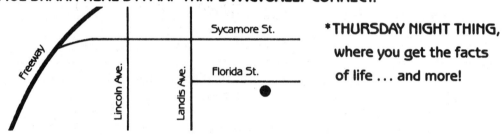

*THURSDAY NIGHT THING, where you get the facts of life ... and more!

(Contributed by Len Woods, Dallas, TX)

# Youth Arrest

Here's a way to familiarize the adults and the uninvolved youth in your church with the youth group.

Have several of your young people or adult leaders dress up like police officers. Arrange with the local law enforcement agencies or a costume rental company to get enough uniforms so that each entrance to the church can be manned by two "officers." You might want to hook up a traffic light in front of the church entrance or park a motorcycle by the door.

As every teenager enters the door, tell them that they are under arrest for being in violation of being a high school student. Take them aside and give them a "summons" to appear before "Youth Court" the night of your youth meeting. When families without young people enter, briefly explain what you are doing and tell them about your youth group.

This is what the "summons" can say:

# CERTIFICATE OF SUMMONS

You, _____ , are hereby and forthwith placed under arrest for being in _____ grade. Your arrest is made possible because of the long arm of the law handed down in the decision of **The Supreme Judge** in His very historic case in John, Chapter 3, Verse 16.

You are hereby and forthwith summoned to appear in court before de youth minister (Judge Wash) on September 21, 1983 in the basement of the Nativity School Courthouse. People's Court will start at **7:00 p.m. SHARP,** where you shall be given a 3-minute trial. (Since de judge is known as "hang 'em high Washburn," your trial will be very short!) You will be sentenced to eat pizza and laugh a lot . . . but . . . not before working on Wash's chain gang for about an hour in a trade-up scavenger hunt.

If you wish to plead your case, you are free to bring a teenage lawyer friend whom did not appear at church today.

Signed,

*Dave*

Dave Washburn
Senior Love Officer

and . . . Junior Love Officers:

(kids' signatures)

(Contributed by David Washburn, Brockport, NY)

# CHAPTER TEN

# FUND RAISING

## Candy Sales

If your group is thinking of selling candy as a fund-raising project, check with a local candy wholesaler as a supplier. Often a local dealer can save you much more money than a fund-raising company, and still obtain "fund-raiser" sizes for you to sell. Just look in the yellow pages under "Candy Wholesalers." (Contributed by Richard Everett, North Haven, CT)

## Doggie Dip

For an unusual fund raiser that would work with any size youth group, try having a "doggie dip." Advertise that your youth will wash dogs (pets) on a certain Saturday for a small fee. Most dog owners hate to wash their dogs so the response will undoubtedly be tremendous.

Get together lots of metal or plastic tubs, some dog shampoo, towels and hoses—and be ready for everything from bloodhounds to beagles. (Contributed by Mike and Donna Youmus, Harleysville, PA)

"Come on, Roy, getting a bath's not all that bad."

# DOGGIE DIPPING:
## Cool way to earn fast money

# Fairgrounds Clean-up

Here's a profitable and dependable fund raiser that can become an annual project for your youth group. Contract with your local fairgrounds, stadium, or parade organizer to do clean-up after a major event. The job usually takes about a day and a half and can earn hundreds of dollars. With good organization and teamwork this kind of job doesn't have to be overwhelming, and good work will pay off in getting next year's contract. (Contributed by Robert Crosby, Rochester, NY)

# Lawn-A-Thon

This is a unique way to raise money for your group. Line up as many kids as you can with lawn mowers and transportation for each of them. Advertise with flyers and posters that on a certain Saturday, your group will mow lawns for free! Get as many people as you can to sign up to have their lawn mowed

Now, for the money-making part. Pass out pledge sheets to all of your youth and have them get people to pledge 10¢, 20¢ or whatever for each lawn that your group mows from 6:00 am to 6:00 pm that day. This not only raises money for your group, but also provides a real service to people in your community. (Contributed by Rick Wheeler, Lubbock, TX)

# Memoriz-athon

Here's a fund-raising "athon" that has spiritual benefits for your group as well as financial ones. Have a Bible Verse Memoriz-athon where your youth get pledges for every Bible verse that they learn. It's a contest that many people in your church will be eager to support.

You might want to establish some guidelines to avoid kids "learning" verses that are already well-known. Pick out certain portions of Scripture that everyone must memorize, and place a maximum limit on the number of verses. When it comes time for payment, all pledgers have the right to ask the kids to quote the verses they have learned. (Contributed by John Stumbo, Monticello, MN)

## Potluck Auction

One good way to raise money for your group is to sponsor a potluck dinner and invite your entire congregation to attend. Half of the alphabet can bring a main dish, the other half a salad. Have your youth provide the dessert, coffee and punch. They should also be responsible for serving and clean-up.

Ask each family to bring along a "gift" to be auctioned off—special cakes or pies, other baked goods, handcrafted items or household goods of some value. Place these items on a table and invite everyone to browse during the dinner hour and view the items for auction.

When the tables are cleared, begin to auction off each item, saving the most expensive for last. If there is someone in your church with auctioneer experience, try to take advantage of that. Otherwise, find a person who can "ham it up" and generate lots of enthusiasm for every item. (Contributed by Linda Behrendt, Orange, CA)

## Record Bake Sale

Here's a fund-raising idea that can be a big money-maker for your group, and lots of fun for your church. Have your group make cakes and baked goods for an auction or sale and calculate the cost. Next, gather up some donated record albums. These should be in good condition and can be any kind of music. Wrap the albums in foil, so their identity is hidden. Place a cake on each album and price each one, or auction them off to the highest bidder.
(WARNING: Do NOT put a HOT cake on an album.) You'll earn enough to make a profit plus everyone will enjoy their cake and their "surprise" record. You might

also want to wrap up cassette tapes with candy to sell in the same way. (Contributed by Jim Burton, Riverdale, GA)